From Gaul to De Gaulle

American University Studies

Series IX
History

Vol. 43

PETER LANG
New York • San Francisco • Bern • Baltimore
Frankfurt am Main • Berlin • Wien • Paris

Monique Wagner

From Gaul to De Gaulle

An Outline of French Civilization

PETER LANG
New York • San Francisco • Bern • Baltimore
Frankfurt am Main • Berlin • Wien • Paris

Library of Congress Cataloging-in-Publication Data

Wagner, Monique.
   From Gaul to De Gaulle : an outline of French civilization /
Monique Wagner.
      p. cm. — (American university studies. Series IX, History ; vol. 43)
   1. France—Civilization—Chronology.   I. Title.   II. Series.
DC33.W34   1989, 1993   944'.002'02—dc19   88-25122
ISBN 0-8204-2277-0(pbk)   CIP
ISSN 0740-0462

Die Deutsche Bibliothek-CIP-Einheitsaufnahme

Wagner, Monique:
From Gaul to De Gaulle : an outline of French civilization / Monique
Wagner.—New York; Berlin; Bern; Frankfurt/M.; Paris; Wien: Lang,
1989, 1993
   (American university studies : Ser. 9, History ; Vol. 43)
   ISBN 0-8204-2277-0(pbk)
NE: American university studies/09

The paper in this book meets the guidelines for permanence and
durability of the Committee on Production Guidelines for
Book Longevity of the Council on Library Resources.

Printed in the United States of America.

To Anne-Marie

who knows and loves France

drawings by Robert Hyde

Civilization is the graceful relation of all varieties
of experience to a central humane system of thought.

Robert Graves

La justification de l'art, c'est de révéler aux hommes
la grandeur qu'ils ignorent en eux.

Malraux

Errata

p. xiii, #1 & p. 64: should read "St. Michel d'Aiguilhe"

p. 64, line 11: "other" in lieu of "others"

p. 80, line 20: add to end of line "officially named le-Bien-Aimé"

p. 86, line 4: "in" should read "is"

p. 186, line 3: add "of" after "because"

p. 194: last date should read "1923-1973"

p. 275, line 10: "great-grandson" should replace "grandson"

p. 308, line 37 & 38: "great-grandson" should replace "grandson"

p. 322: add Impressionism, 125, 174, 184, 186-190, 311

Contents

Part One
GEOGRAPHY AND DEMOGRAPHY

Part Two
FRANCE THROUGH THE AGES

CHAPTER 9. THE TWENTIETH CENTURY

Part Three
FRANCE TODAY

List of Illustrations

If not otherwise acknowledged, the illustrations listed below have been graciously supplied by the French Government Tourist Office and Services de Presse et d'Information.

xiv

Foreword

This book was conceived in order to fill an important and long-standing gap, which is difficult to understand in view of the spectacular increase in Foreign Culture course offerings at American universities and the ever-growing nationwide interest in France, the French, their country and their heritage. There has never been, until now, a single publication in English dealing with French culture and the great French contribution to world civilization.

Professor Laurence Wylie wrote in Georges Santoni's *Société et Culture de la France Contemporaine* (SUNY Press, Albany, N.Y., 1981): "My conviction is that, since up to the present generation the French have so emphasized the learning of their history and geography, it is impossible to understand French behavior without learning the rudiments of these subjects, without knowing for instance the basic names, dates, geographical areas...The two problems involved....are....to find a history and geography text in English that furnishes the basic information in palpable form...." (p. 6).

This publication attempts to present the essentials of both geography and history within the much wider scope of French civilization as a whole, while discussing the interaction of historic, social, cultural and literary developments. In spite of the pitfalls of generalization and oversimplification, the material is presented in chronological order, while defining the most striking characteristics of each period. Readers who would have to look for the data they need in separate, specialized source materials, can find them in this comprehensive, yet concise overview. Clearly, the very nature of the work made it impossible to deal with the history of French civilization in a complete or exhaustive fashion and frequently involved a difficult selection.

An effort has been made to strike the proper balance between the study of history and social structures on the one hand, and the consideration of ideas and artistic and literary trends on the other, and to provide information that would be both vital and interesting to readers of different degrees of sophistication.

This work is thus directed at a variety of readers, such as students of courses relating to French civilization, history, literature and arts, and all students and teachers of the French language. It is well-suited to become a "Companion to French Studies" on all levels (D.G. Charlton's acclaimed *France, Companion to French Studies*, Methuen & Co. Ltd., 1979, is almost 700 pages long and starts only with the Renaissance). It could also play a role in more general curricula where the focus is on Western humanities, history and art. It is of interest to all francophiles and to people wishing to increase their knowledge of France, be it for their personal enrichment or because they intend travel to that country with a higher degree of understanding of the historic and artistic sites they will be viewing. It can be useful to members of various organizations, such as the Alliances Françaises, and to business representatives seeking to establish or expand commercial ties with France and wishing to deal intelligently with their French counterparts. The book offers practical guidelines to tourists and constitutes a basic introduction to France as a country.

Each chapter subdivision is followed by a list of things to see, which illustrate the text itself, while a list of "Things to Remember" at the close of the book identifies the most important figures and events and is intended to simplify the students' and the instructors' task. A brief chronology spells out some of the milestones of French history, and numerous maps, sketches, drawings and illustrations provide a visual dimension to the material discussed. The text is enriched with an Appendix—it consists of "further reading" on selected subjects and of several excerpts from French literature, illustrative of a given period.

Since the contents of Parts I and III are clearly delineated, the Index is limited to proper names and major artistic and literary movements discussed in Part II.

While the work's title is *From Gaul to De Gaulle*, the discussion does not end with the death of the General who gave France the 1958 Constitution by which it still abides, but follows developments up to the late 1980s.

I wish to express my sincere gratitude to Wayne State University's Professor Richard Vernier and Dean Martin Herman of the College of Liberal Arts, and Mr. Daniel Graf, Director of the Office of Research and Sponsored Programs, for their assistance which made the execution of this project possible; to Dean Louise Jefferson for her invaluable advice on pages concerning 20th century literature; and to my colleagues in the Department of Romance and Germanic Languages and Literatures for their support and encouragement.

Monique Wagner

Part I

GEOGRAPHY AND DEMOGRAPHY

THE CHANNEL
(LA MANCHE)

Ardennes

Seine

Vosges

Massif
Armoricain

Rhin

Loire

Jura

ATLANTIC
OCEAN

Massif
Central

Alpes

Rhône

Dordogne

Garonne

Pyrénées

MEDITERRANEAN
SEA

Broken to every known mischance; lighted over all
By the lightsome joy of life, the buckler of the Gaul
Furious in luxury, merciless in toil
Terrible with strength that draws from her tireless soil
Strictest judge of her own worth, gentlest of man's mind
First to follow truth and last to leave old truth behind
FRANCE beloved of every soul that loves its fellowkind!

RUDYARD KIPLING
"Ode to FRANCE"

4

THE PROVINCES

The Land and the People

The French have always called their country "la belle France" and "la douce France"—this last expression dates back to the oldest, 11th century French epic, *The Song of Roland*. And if France enjoys a privileged place also in the hearts and minds of enlightened, refined and inquisitive people in other nations, this is due not only to its unique contribution to world civilization, but also to the unparalleled beauty and charm of the countryside itself. Diversity is its chief characteristic, in spite of the unifying cultural factors of many centuries of history. It can be said that France as a country—and as a people—embodies the artistic and literary ideal of French classicism: "variety within unity."

This harmonious unity is also present in the shape and proportions of the so-called French "hexagon", which covers an area of 551,000 square kilometers (1/18th of Europe, slightly smaller in size than the state of Texas). It has a population of roughly 55 million people, about 2,700 kms of coastline and 2,800 kms of land frontiers. This is why, as André Siegfried so aptly put it in an often quoted essay (*The Soul of the Peoples*), France is at the same time western—its Atlantic front being open to influences from overseas and the liberal Anglo-Saxon influences—continental, since she is indissolubly linked by flesh and blood to Europe, and Mediterranean, in direct contact with Africa, Asia and East, "this fabulous and exotic world" and "the oldest and most important roots of the history of mankind."

France is blessed with natural frontiers, seas and mountains on all sides, except in the north-east. The North Sea (Mer du Nord), the English Channel (la Manche), the Atlantic ocean and the Mediterranean constitute excellent defense lines. They are also, however, as mentioned above, openings which expose France to influences from abroad and encourage exploration and trade. The largest and most important cities and urban agglomerations are, as can be expected, sea and river ports (Paris, Marseille, Lyon, Toulouse, Nice, Bordeaux, Nantes, Strasbourg, St. Etienne, Le Havre, Toulon. Lille is not a port, but a large industrial center.) The most important mountain ranges are: on the border with Spain the steep, forbidding and inhospitable Pyrenées; in the east, between France and Switzerland, from south to north, the formidable and impressive Alps which boast the highest peak in Europe, the Mont-Blanc (15,782 feet), then the crescent-shaped Jura and finally the old, round shaped Vosges; in the heart of Brittany, another hercinian range leveled by erosion, the Massif Armoricain; in the north-east the plateau-like Ardennes; and in the very heart of France, the old volcanic Massif Central (3,000 feet above sea-level), an important "natural fortress" which separates and helps define the adjacent river basins.

France is fortunate in having four major river systems which irrigate the land and constitute excellent channels of exchange and communication: the Rhône with its characteristic delta (it has had a predominant historical role, since it helped bring the Mediterranean culture to the central and northern areas); the Garonne, which flows through the Bassin Aquitain and empties into the Atlantic by way of a spectacular mouth called la Gironde; the longest of all (about 1,000 kms), picturesque but extremely irregular and least navigable Loire river which connects through its fertile valley the Massif Central with the Bassin Parisien and the Atlantic ocean; and the best known, best loved and most useful to navigation, the Seine, which springs out of Burgundy, flows through Paris and crosses the rich countryside of Normandy before emptying into the English Channel.

The French climate, on the whole mild and temperate, is a summary of the climate of all of Europe and is subject at the same time to oceanic, continental and Mediterranean influences, whence its diversity. The oceanic climate (mild winters, abundant rainfall, high humidity) affects much of the country, particularly the northern and western coastal zones. It gradually changes as one moves inland into a mountain climate, which is characterized by long and harsh winters, a short summer season, and rain (as well as snowfall) throughout the year. The Mediterranean climate—mild winters, hot and dry summers, with torrential rains in the fall and spring—affects, as can be expected, the southern part of the country.

As for the French people, they are as diverse as their climate and landscape. France has for centuries been a melting pot of races, peoples, traditions and civilizations: the aboriginal groups (Ligurians and Iberians), the Celts, generally recognized by the French as their forefathers, the Greeks and Romans from the south, the Germanic tribes from the continent, and finally the Normans from Scandinavia. Roughly, three main ethnic types can be distinguished: the tall, nordic, blond, blue-eyed and "long headed" ("dolichocéphale"); the Mediterranean, dark-eyed, olive skinned, short and long headed; and the Alpine, grey-eyed, chestnut-haired, medium-sized, "round-headed" ("brachycéphale"). The unique character of French psychology comes, again according to Siegfried, from this very diversity "forged by the passing of centuries into a new, contradictory unity, oriented at the same time toward the east and the west, the past and the future, tradition and progress." This psychological diversity has given birth to a number of clichés, such as the belief that the French have inherited their individualism from the Celts, their love of law and order from the Romans, their constructive genius from the Germans and their initiative and taste for adventure from the Normans.

The French like to describe themselves both as realistic and idealistic, generous and parsimonious, adventurous and cautious, sensitive and sensible, imaginative and logical—clear-thinking— "Cartesian."

Historic "Provinces," Departments and "Régions"

The different French regions and their landscapes reflect the same variety and contrast; each has its own well-defined personality, although the contrasts are not violent. Although the former historic "provinces" were replaced during the Revolution of 1789 by "départements", recently grouped into "régions" (see maps), they continue to offer distinct and fascinating characteristics. In the rapid overview which follows, the most important and interesting ones are marked with an asterisk:

- **The France du Nord** (former provinces of Flandre and Artois). A highly industrialized plain: mining, textiles; important city: Lille.

- **The Picardie** (situated in the Ardennes). Rich in agriculture and horticulture. Cities: Amiens and Beauvais (famous Gothic cathedrals).

- * **The Champagne.** Known all over the world for its sparkling wine invented by Dom Pérignon. Important trade crossroads (famous fairs during the Middle Ages). Cities: Troyes and Reims (famous Gothic cathedral).

- * **The Lorraine** (birthplace of Joan of Arc). Historic battlefield between France and Germany (World War I: Verdun). Cities: Metz, Nancy (famous 18th century Place Stanislas).

- * **The Alsace** (Vosges, Rhine river). Bone of contention between France and Germany. Forests, wood industry, regional gastronomy, spas. Old picturesque towns with typical provincial architecture. Capital: Strasbourg (famous Gothic cathedral).

- * **The Bourgogne** (Burgundy: annexed by France in the 15th century). Important crossroads. Prehistory. Cradle of Christianity. Famous Romanesque abbeys (Cluny, Vézelay, Autun). Reputed for wines and food (beef, poultry, snails). Historic city of Dijon.

- **The Franche-Comté** (in the Jura). Forests, industry (Peugeot). City: Besançon.

- * **The Normandie** (Normandy). Historic province of prime importance: Norman invasions, William the Conqueror (Bayeux tapestry), World War II (Omaha Beach). Most famous abbey of all: the Mont Saint-Michel. Cities: Caen, Rouen

(Gothic cathedral), port of Le Havre. Rich in natural resources: agriculture, cattle, dairy products (butter, cheese),
apples, "cidre".

- * **The Bretagne** (Brittany: became part of France in the 16th
century). "Land of sea": fishing, ports, merchant marine, navy.
Prehistory (menhirs, dolmens). Celtic language still spoken.
Capital: Rennes.

- **The Pays de la Loire and Centre** (Anjou, Berry, Touraine,
Sologne). Agriculture, wine industry. The Loire Valley, famous
for its beauty and architecture (châteaux), will be discussed in
Part II. Cities: Tours, Orléans.

- **The Centre-Ouest**: Poitou (historical province: city Poitiers), Vendée (beaches), and the Charentes (cognac).

- **The Massif-Central** (Limousin, Auvergne). High isolated
plateau, some farming, cattle; spas. Romanesque churches in
Le Puy. Industry around Clermont-Ferrand and St. Etienne
(Michelin tires).

- * **The Aquitaine** (Périgord, part of former Guyenne and
Gascogne, Landes, Pays Basque, Béarn). River: Garonne;
port: Bordeaux. Wood, wine industry, commerce, gastronomy
(truffles, foie gras), beaches. Extremely important for prehistory.

- **The Midi-Pyrénées** (part of former Gascogne and Guyenne,
Foix, Roussillon). Historically important region, trade routes
(Garonne river), pilgrimage route during the Middle Ages. Cattle, spas in mountainous parts of region. Cities: Toulouse
(trade, industry, Romanesque church of St. Sernin) and Albi
(center of Albigensian heresy, Gothic cathedral).

- * **The Languedoc.** The lowlands of this province have extensive vineyards. Spas. Beaches. Cities: Montpellier (famous

university dating back to the Middle-Ages) and fortified medieval city of Carcassonne.

- **The Rhône-Alpes.** Diversity of landscape and resources with numerous traces of Roman civilization. Central city of Lyon (second largest in France), former capital of Roman and Christian Gaul. Important industrial and intellectual center. Commerce. In the Alps, milk products and ski resorts.

- *** The Provence and Côte d'Azur.** Warm, sunny province. Historically most important of all. Former Roman "Provincia". Beautiful landscapes. Beaches. The Camargue in the Rhône delta: picturesque habitat of wildlife, horses and bulls. Variety of natural resources: fruit and flowers (perfume), vineyards (Rhône Valley). Beloved by painters such as Cézanne, Van Gogh, Renoir, Matisse, Chagall. Cities: Marseille, Nice, Toulon, Cannes, Menton, Avignon, Aix-en-Provence (university).

- **The Corse** (Corsica). Acquired by France in 1768. Land of "maquis". Agriculture (fruit), beaches, tourism industry.

- *** The Ile de France**, "cradle" and "heart" of France: former domain and territorial basis of French kings. Rich in history and art (birthplace of the Gothic). Cathedrals of Chartres, basilica of St. Denis, Châteaux of Vincennes, Versailles, Chantilly, Fontainebleau, Pierrefonds, Vaux-le-Vicomte. The capital Paris will be discussed in Part III.

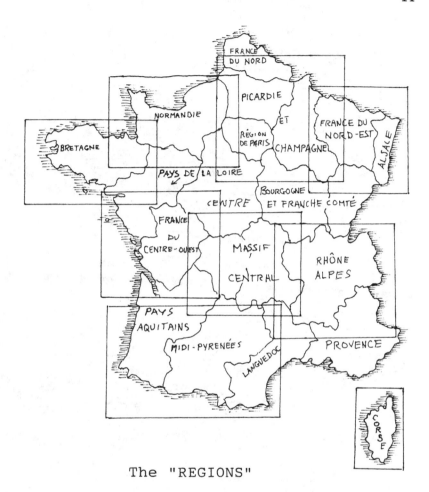

The "REGIONS"

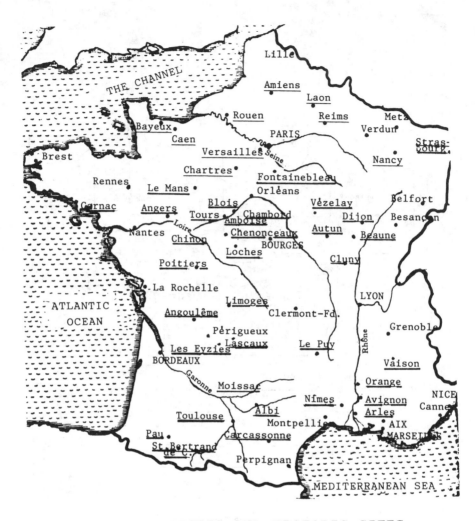

FRANCE: ARTISTIC AND HISTORIC SITES

Part II

FRANCE THROUGH
THE AGES

Chapter 1

THE BEGINNINGS

Prehistory

Men of all times must have realized that France, with its temperate climate and abundant resources, was a good place to live, for prehistoric dwellers have left their traces throughout the hexagon. A number of archaeological epochs and several "types of man" bear the name of French sites where remnants of early life have been found.[1]

Recently discovered foot imprints of the *homo erectus* ("the upright man") and an assortment of tools in Terra Amata, Nice, have led to a reconstruction in that location of a 400,000 year old human settlement of nomadic elephant hunters, the most ancient ever to be found in Europe.[2] Traces of the *homo sapiens* of the Paleolithic and Neolithic periods (Old and New Stone Ages, from Greek lithos-stone) abound in various regions of France. The southwest is particularly rich in caves which bear witness to early civilizations, such as the Cro-Magnon (20-30,000 years B.C.), the "Grotte de la Madeleine" (about 10,000 years B.C.) and the numerous grottos in

---

[1] E.g., the Abbevillian and Magdalenian epochs, the Acheulean and Cro-Magnon men.

[2] The very latest diggings in the Roussillon (Eastern Pyrénées) have brought about the significant discovery of the Tautavel man who lived 450,000 years ago.

the Dordogne Valley. Caves around Les Eyzies[3] and the most famous
of all Lascaux, have yielded not only, like other locations, artifacts,
rough carvings in bone, stone, amber and ivory as well as harpoons,
various other weapons and tools, but also mural paintings of incredible beauty, at the same time realistic and abstract. Most of them
represent animals (bulls, stags, horses, reindeers, bisons) with the
striking characteristics of each species. The primitive artists had,
with a keen sense of observation, a great feeling for composition and
color, mainly brown, black, ochre and a bright yellow, such as was
used for the "Chinese horse". The meaning of these mural paintings
is a mystery which may never be resolved. Did man, who lived by
hunting, use a kind of voodoo ritual to help him capture the beasts
which provided meat (some of them are pictured pierced with ar-
rows), or were these caves meeting places for primeval religious rites,
such as rituals of fecundity?[4]

Several thousand years later men of the Megalithic Age left behind them, mainly in Brittany, huge monolithic stones, "megaliths",[5]
some vertical ("menhirs"), and others forming horizontal "tables"
("dolmens")[6] curiously arranged in "alignements" or "cromlechs",[7]
similar to those found in Stonehenge in England. These imposing vestiges of an early organized human group can be considered as man's
first attempt at architecture, though their meaning is also unknown.
It appears likely that they, as well, had religious connotations. The
dolmens seem to have been burial sites, while the menhirs may have
marked boundaries of grounds used for worship or been erected as

---

[3] Les Eyzies houses a museum rich in prehistoric artifacts such as the "sleeping
bison" carved in ivory. Perhaps the most interesting ivory sculpture found in the
southwest of France is the miniature head of a woman with an intricate coiffure,
called "La Vénus de Brassempouy." It is now displayed at the museum of St.
Germain-en-Laye near Paris.

[4] While the represenation of man is infrequent, the projection of human hands
on the walls may very well be symbolic of his presence in the world and his wish
to possess and dominate it.

[5] Greek "megas" = big.

[6] In Celtic: men = stone, hir = large, dol (taol) = table.

[7] Where the stones are arranged in a circle around a mound.

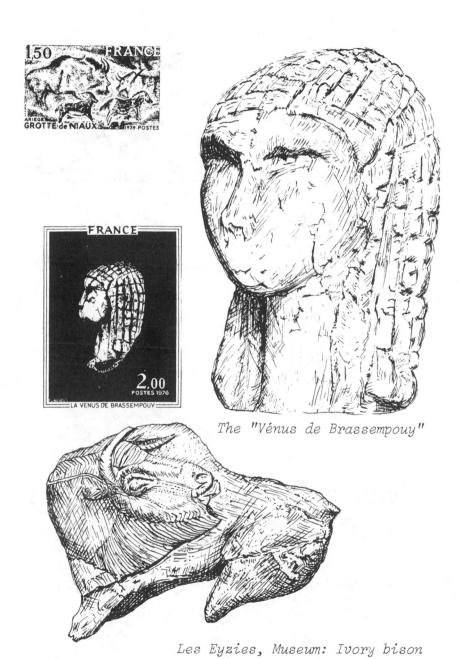

The "Vénus de Brassempouy"

Les Eyzies, Museum: Ivory bison

Les Eyzies : Font-de-Gaume grotto

A dolmen   *A menhir*

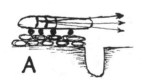

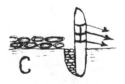

The way a menhir was put in place

"fecundity stones," capable of attracting and accumulating the beneficial qualities of both telluric and cosmic currents.

WHAT TO SEE

- Nice: Terra Amata
    The Lazaret Grotto
- The Dordogne Valley: Lascaux
    Les Eyzies: surrounding caves, especially Font-de-Gaume
        "Grotte de la Madeleine"
        Musée de la préhistoire
    Périgueux: museum
- Pyrénées: Caverne de Tuc d'Audoubert-clay bisons
    Grotte de Niaux
- Brittany: Carnac: Museum, "alignements"
    Locqmariaquer
    Various menhirs and dolmens
    Quimper: Musée d'histoire, d'archéologie et d'etnographie
- Paris: Musée de l'homme
- Near Paris: Museums of St. Germain-en-Laye, of Dourdan,
    Meaux and Provins

The Celts • Greek Colonization • Caesar's Conquest of Gaul

During the Bronze Age, about 2000 years B.C., various peoples settled in France, among others the Iberians and Ligurians. By the first millenium before Christ (time of the Iron Age), Celtic tribes occupied most of the territory of present-day France, and mingled with its former inhabitants. About 600 B.C., Phocean Greeks founded the port of Marseille or Massilia (before them Phoenician navigators had already ventured into this part of France), and penetrated deep into the land, up the Valley of the Rhône. Traces of Greek colonization

Celtic Gaul

REPUBLIQUE FRANÇAISE

4,00

EPHEBE D'AGDE POSTES 1982

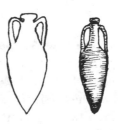

Greek amphorae

are scattered not only along the Mediterranean coast from Cap Ferrat in France to the Spanish port of Alicante (notably in Nice, Antibes, the Iles d'Hyères),[8] but also in such cities as Arles, where the Greeks had permanent trading posts. The Greeks were active merchants and established an important commerce with the Celts as far as the Seine river. Recent diggings in Vix have unearthed the tomb of a Celtic princess from the sixth century B.C. containing among various large and small objects (such as a war-chariot and artistic jewelry of gold and amber) a beautifully crafted bronze vase of Greek workmanship, the largest (1 m 74) ever to be found anywhere.[9]

It is known that the Greeks furnished wine to the Celts, among others to those who had settled in the region of today's Burgundy and were mining iron and copper. They used difficult to handle amphorae for the shipping of the spirits which later became the beloved drink of the French. The Celts replaced them with wooden barrels not only for the shipping, but the storage of wine as well. They eventually also tired of importing the precious liquid and started their own vineyards long before the Roman conquest. Some prestigious Burgundy vineyards boast of being well over 2000 years old!

The Celts—Gauls as the Romans called them—were not a unified people. The numerous Gallic tribes, among which the Parisii, the Belgae, the Sequanes (Sequana-Seine) and the Arverns (in the Auvergne region), were mostly at war with one another. They shared, however, the same religion, traditions, customs, way of life and clothing. In the eyes of the Greeks and Romans they were barbarians, and their numerous incursions into adjacent countries as well as faraway lands, such as Greece and Turkey, were dreaded; they had a well established reputation of being savage, destructive and avid of riches (see Appendix).

At one time in their history, however, the Gauls put aside their tribal differences and united in the face of the invasion by Julius

---

[8] Nice comes from the Greek "Nike" or victory, Antibes from "Antipolis" or city across. The town of Agde comes from "Agathois" (good).

[9] The "Vase de Vix" is contemporary with the reign of Croesus. It is displayed at the museum of Chatillon-sur-Seine in Burgundy.

Caesar's army. By 120 B.C., Rome had already established a Roman province (Latin: "provincia") in the southern part of Gaul; it later became the Provence. In 52 B.C. Caesar undertook his famous campaign to subdue the entire Gallic territory and his *Commentaries* on the war he waged give us precious information about the people he was to conquer (the Gauls did not leave any written records). A young Arvern chief, Vercingétorix, who was later to become France's first national hero, rallied different hitherto hostile tribes under his command and put up a fierce and valiant resistance. While pursuing a sort of guerilla warfare, he inflicted upon Caesar several smarting defeats. But he was finally forced to surrender at the siege of Alésia (Alise-Ste-Reine in Burgundy) in the heroic way familiar to every French school-child; sadly enough Caesar did not live up to the gallant behaviour of his foe and had him strangled in prison some time after the traditional triumphal procession held in Rome.

WHAT TO SEE

- Autoroute A6 (in Burgundy): the "Archéodrome"
- Alise-Ste Reine (in Burgundy):
    battlefield, museum and ruins of Roman city
- Chatillon s/Seine: museum
- Paris: Bibliothèque Nationale: coin of Vercingétorix
- St. Germain-en-Laye: museum

The Roman Colonization and Heritage

The Roman conquest was ultimately beneficial to Gaul, which underwent a rapid romanization. The new occupants gave its inhabitants security, stable frontiers, peace—the famous Pax Romana—and an administrative unity, centered in Lyons, as well as a perfected legal system, excellent roads, large cities with brick, stone and marble

buildings, a flourishing commerce, a new way of farming and a superior lifestyle. The Romans were great builders and innumerable
vestiges of their civilization can be admired to this day throughout France: villas or Roman-style farms and houses, baths (such as
the one on Boulevard St. Michel in the Latin Quarter close to the
Sorbonne), temples (in Nîmes, Arles, Vienne), arenas and theatres
(Nîmes, Arles, Vienne, Orange), and remnants of roads and aqueducts, such as the unparalleled "Pont du Gard" which has withstood
the test of time; it is still used as a tri-level road. These are often of
great architectural and historical interest.[10] For example the Arch of
Triumph in Orange is older than any existing in Italy and the statue
of Augustus in that city's theater is the only one still to be found
on its original pedestal. Much of the network of France's "routes
nationales" follows the track of the old Roman roads.

The Romans gave the Gauls their customs, their garb, and their
religion; some of their gods could be easily identified with the Celtic
deities and the Romans built new temples on the sites of old Gallic
shrines, a practice which was later also adopted by the Christian
Church.[11]

However, the most lasting and significant of all the Roman bequests to the Gauls was the language: the spoken Latin brought by
administrators, colonists and soldiers was gradually adopted by the
entire population. By 300 A.D. a tongue called "vulgar Latin" spread
throughout Gaul. The old Celtic had been virtually eradicated with
the exception of some words mostly pertaining to rural life, farming tools, plants and trees, which have survived to our day.[12] From
this "vulgar Latin" stems French, which belongs to the vast family
of "Romance languages" side by side with Spanish, Italian, Roma-
nian, Portuguese, Provençal, Catalan, and several other dialects still
spoken in some parts of Europe. The western European calendar al-

---

[10] It is frequently imperative for students of Roman art and history to view these
monuments in France: some of them are the best preserved and most carefully
maintained in the world.

[11] E.g., Notre Dame in Paris and the Cathedral of Chartres.

[12] They constitute the *substratum* of modern French.

ALIGNEMENTS DE CARNAC 1.00

POSTES

RÉPUBLIQUE FRANÇAISE

Vercingétorix

Eze, La Turbie:
"Monument romain"

Pont du Gard

RÉPUBLIQUE FRANÇAISE

POSTES

SAINT-REMY-LES-ANTIQUES

so basically dates back to the Gallo-Roman times; the names of virtually all days and a number of months are reminiscent of Roman gods and emperors.[13]

Christianity also came from Rome, although some missionaries from Greece and the Middle-East had made their way to southern France as early as the 1st century A.D.[14] The number of Christian communities steadily increased in number. Many of them suffered cruel persecutions. The one which took place in Lyon in 170 A.D. resulted in the martyrdom of one of France's favorite saints, St. Blandine. In the 3rd century A.D., while there were as many as seven bishoprics in France, persecutions of Christians were still widespread. St. Denis, who was beheaded on the hill of Montmartre ("Mont des martyrs", where the Roman god Mercury was worshipped) is said to have picked up his head and carried it to a small town along the edge of the Roman way, where he was buried. There, in the 5th century (475 A.D.), at the instance of St. Geneviève, a first oratory was built in honor of St. Denis who had become the patron saint of France. In the 7th century a sizeable church was erected by "Good King Dagobert" as a gesture of gratitude to St. Denis and a community of Benedictine monks was established at the same site. It soon became a shrine of great renown, which attracted throngs of pilgrims. The French monarchs chose the abbey of St. Denis as their necropolis (burial place). The beautiful Gothic basilica (see below) hosts the tombs[15] of generations of kings and is a "must" for any serious visitor of the Paris area.

---

[13] E.g., mars - March, août - August, juillet - July (Julius); mardi (Tuesday) - day of Mars, mercredi (Wednesday) - day of Mercury, jeudi (Thursday) - day of "Jove", vendredi (Friday) - day of Venus. Lundi (Monday) is, naturally the "lunar" day, or day of the moon (the calendar underwent some changes in the 16th century). The Roman colonization also left its mark on the names of great numbers of cities, such as Lyon (Lugdunum), Autun (Augustudunum), Aix (Aquas).

[14] Among others, St. Mary-Magdalen who is said to have disembarked in the Camargue and whose tomb can be visited in St. Maximin (Provence).

[15] These are actually cenotaphs, or empty tombs, erected in honor of the deceased. The kings' bodies were buried in the crypt and during the French Revolution in 1789, unearthed by the furious mob and thrown into quick-lime.

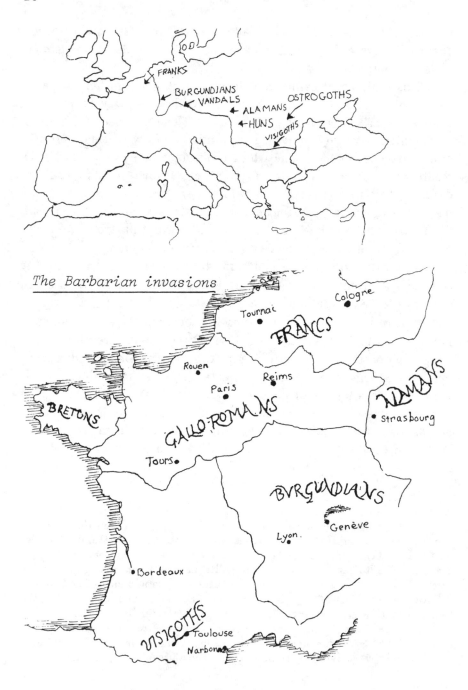

The Barbarian invasions

In 312 A.D. the Roman Emperor Constantine, founder of Constantinople, defeated the "other emperor" Maxentius. Before the battle a cross in the sky with the words "In hoc signo vinces"—in this sign you will conquer—appeared to Constantine. He eventually converted to Christianity, which became the official religion of the Roman empire. By the 5th century, St. Martin of Tours had evangelized even the Gallic country dwellers,[16] and the Christian church was solidly established in Gaul. The stability of the Church enabled it to provide continuity to a "world in full decadence" and to salvage many elements of the disappearing Roman civilization, now threatened by the destructive incursions from the east.

WHAT TO SEE

From north to south:
- Paris: the Roman baths on Boulevard St. Michel
  the "Lutèce arenas" (*Lutetia* was the Latin name of Paris)
  the Louvre
- Autun (Burgundy): ruins of Roman theatre
- Near Paris: the basilica of St. Denis
- Besançon: Roman arch
- Lyon: numerous vestiges of Roman architecture
- Vaison-la-Romaine: Roman villas
- Vienne near Lyon: Pyramid, Roman theater and temple
- Orange: Roman theatre, Arch of Triumph
- St. Rémy-en-Provence: ruins of Glanum
- Nîmes: "Arènes"
  "Maison carrée" (temple)
  Nearby: aqueduct of Pont-du-Gard
- Arles: "Arènes"
  Roman theatre

---

[16]The word "pagan" comes from "paganus", inhabitant of a "pagus" or peasant. In French this Latin word is the root at the same time of "païen" (pagan), "paganisme" and "paysan" (peasant).

Alyscamps cemetery

"Musée Lapidaire"

- Fréjus: Roman ruins
- Eze (La Turbie): "Monument romain"

The Barbarian Invasions and the Birth of France • The Merovingian Dynasty

Although the Roman Empire did not completely collapse until 476 A.D., various Germanic tribes had already sacked most of Gaul's territory at the beginning of the century. Even earlier, more and more menacing incursions were occurring at an increasingly accelerated pace, but had been hitherto successfully repelled by the Gallo-Romans.

Many of the Teutonic barbarians who crossed into Italy, Gaul and Spain at the end of the fifth century left terror in man's memory and vocabulary, as their passage invariably meant carnage, ashes and ruins. From these different Germanic tribes, such as the Alamans,[17] Goths, Visigoths, Vandals, Burgundians and Franks, only the latter two did not acquire a sinister reputation. The Salian Franks were the ones to eventually establish their supremacy, give their name to France,[18] and found the first French kingdom.

The Franks under their chief Maeroveus (Mérovée) helped the Romans repel the formidable invasion of Attila's Huns who had crossed the Rhine and were threatening Paris. At that time, a pious maiden, Geneviève, predicted that the city would be spared by prayer. She later became the patron saint of Paris: the hill "Mont-Geneviève" in the heart of the student quarter (the "Quartier Latin") was named for her and her tomb can still be viewed in the historic church of St. Etienne-du-Mont.[19] Visitors to Paris may admire the famous mural

---

[17] Who gave their name to Germany in several Romance languages.

[18] "Franc" in modern France means both honest and free.

[19] It also contains the earthly remains of Pascal and Racine. Scholars from

painting of Sainte Geneviève, done by Puvis de Chavannes at the nearby Panthéon.

Attila's hordes, definitively reduced at the battle of the Catalaunic Fields (near Troyes, 451 A.D.) withdrew from Gaul. The grandson of Merovaeus and son of Childeric, Clojo, known as Clovis,[20] subdued both the Visigoths and the Burgundians, and was the founder of the first French dynasty, the Merovingians. Married to a Burgundian Christian princess, Clotilde, who was later canonized, he converted to the new faith in fulfillment of a vow he had made before his victorious battle against the Alamans.[21] He was both baptized and solemnly anointed on Christmas day, 496 A.D., by St. Rémi in the city of Reims, which was to be later endowed with a superb cathedral: it became the traditional crowning place of French kings and queens (36 heads were anointed there, the last one in 1825). Clovis' reign was officially recognized by the Emperor in Constantinople. He eventually settled in Paris, and chose it as the capital of the new Frankish kingdom.

The Merovingians who succeeded Clovis, however, were incompetent rulers who merited their nickname of "fainéants" or "do-nothing kings". They engaged in the disastrous Germanic practice of dividing the father's patrimony among all the sons, thus engendering family rivalries, fratricidal plots and warfare. Virtually none of the Merovingians left reputable memories, with the possible exception of the legendary King Dagobert who was pious and quite sophisticated, fond of beautiful clothes and fine jewelry. He surrounded himself with luxurious appointments and encouraged art and architecture.

While the Merovingian kings kept the Germanic hierarchy, cus-

---

all over the world are familiar with the well endowed nearby Bibliothèque Ste. Geneviève located in the Latin Quarter.

[20] "Clovis" eventually became "Louis" and seventeen French kings were to reign under this name. There was a Louis XVIII but no Louis XVIIth. The name had been reserved for the young son of Louis XVIth who most likely died during the French Revolution.

[21] Another legend speaks of Queen Clotilde's various attempts at converting her husband, who made the vow to become a Christian if his third son would survive (two had died in infancy).

St.Denis

Clovis' baptism
in Reims

Reims: Cathedral

toms and "man to man" allegiances, they adopted the Romance language. Only some small traces of Germanic idioms still remain in modern French (words pertaining mostly to institutions, warfare and weapons, e.g., fief, haubert, guerre, garde, etc.).[22]

During the 8th century, another formidable invasion threatened the Frankish kingdom, this time from the south. The Moors (Saracens) from North Africa, who had conquered Spain, were now rapidly advancing toward the heart of France after having taken such key cities as Narbonne, Bordeaux, Nîmes and Autun. Between Tours and Poitiers, a "mayor of the palace", Charles-Martel ("the Hammer"), who, like others before him, actually ruled in lieu of the decadent Merovingian king, confronted the Saracen armies and inflicted upon them a crushing defeat (732 A.D.). Charles-Martel thus preserved not only France, but the entire Christian world from Moorish domination.[23]

WHAT TO SEE

- Paris: Musée du Louvre, jewelry and various objects belonging to Merovingian kings
- Epernay, Belfort: museums
- Poitiers: "Baptistère St. Jean"
- Reims: Cathedral, Palais du Tau museum

---

[22] They constitute what is called the *superstratum*.

[23] The Moors were not definitively expelled from Europe by the Spaniards until 1492, the year of Columbus' discovery of America.

The Carolingians • Charlemagne and the Carolingian Renaissance

Some twenty years later, Charles Martel's son, Pepin-the-Short (Pépin-le-Bref) became king of France and was solemnly anointed by the pope in 754. He founded the second French dynasty, the Carolingians. It was Pepin's son, Charlemagne (Charles-the-Great) who brought the French kingdom's power to its apogee. He was crowned Holy Roman Emperor by the pope in Rome in 800 A.D.[24]

Charlemagne ruled over vast territories which he continually extended. He was a truly tireless warrior, constantly fighting all foes of Christianity, the Saxons in the north, the Lombards in Italy, the nomadic Avars in Central Europe and the Saracens in Spain. The defeat of his rear-guard at the Cap of Roncesvalles (Roncevaux) in the Pyrénées mountains inspired the most famous medieval epic of all, the *Song of Roland* (see below).

Equally, if not more important than his campaign, was Charlemagne's legacy of peace, order and culture, known as the Carolingian Renaissance. Though he himself could neither read nor write—he took painstaking troubles to sign his name—he surrounded himself with artists, craftsmen and scholars (one of them, Eginhard, left an excellent biography of the Emperor). Seconded by his wise counselor Alcuin,[25] he became a sort of Maecenas and ordered that existing classical texts be copied by monks in various monasteries. We owe to his reign the "modern" script which eventually replaced the awkward Roman letters: it was called "minuscule caroline" or "de Corbie" from the name of the abbey where it was used for the first time. Charlemagne ruled his huge empire with the help of "comtes" or counts[26] who were chiefs of territories, but he regularly checked on

---

[24] Almost exactly 1000 years before Napoleon's crowning at Notre-Dame in Paris in 1804.

[25] Charlemagne was considered for centuries as "the patron" of schools. Until recently, the feast of "la Ste. Charlemagne" was solemnly celebrated in January by all French school children.

[26] From Latin: comitem = companion. The American "counties" stem from

them by dispatching personal messengers *missi dominici* throughout the kingdom. These were also in charge of administering justice.

Charlemagne, known as a great champion of Christianity, was extremely religious, though at times capable of ruthlessness and cruelty worthy of his forefathers. The "Emperor with the flowery beard" became a legend: he was allegedly helped in his feats by a prestigious relic enclosed in the handle of his sword, the "Joyeuse", namely a fragment of the lance used during the crucifixion. He encouraged the building of churches and his own octogonal chapel still exists in Aix-la-Chapelle, today's German city of Aachen. Charlemagne's son, Louis-the-Pious or "Débonnaire", was as religious as his father, but had none of his stamina or administrative genius. He reverted to the old Germanic custom of dividing the kingdom among his sons. This resulted in the end of the Empire and caused warfare between his offspring. The oldest son Lothaire, who had inherited the title and the "central" territories was dissatisfied with his share, and soon found himself at odds with his younger brothers, Charles-the-Bald (Charles-le-Chauve) and Louis-the-German. The latter two formed alliance against Lothaire and swore allegiance to each other according to a bilingual text called the "Strasbourg Oaths" (842 A.D.). While Charles pronounced the oath in Germanic ("tudesque") so as to be understood by his brother's army, Louis read it off in the Romance vernacular spoken by Charles' soldiers. This is an extremely important document, the first one ever written in the language which later became French. A treaty eventually signed by the three brothers at Verdun definitively split Charlemagne's empire into three parts which gave rise in the west to France and in the east to Germany; between them, Lothaire's share (he gave his name to Lotharingia or Lorraine) was to become a territory contested by these two nations during centuries to come.

Charles-the-Bald never achieved the greatness of his grandfather, though he did strive to regain some of the eastern territories that had been lost. He and his descendants had now to face the threat of

---

that word.

new invaders: the Hungarians, dreaded for their cruelty,[27] and the formidable Vikings arriving by way of sea from Scandinavian lands.

WHAT TO SEE

- Paris: Louvre and Bibliothèque Nationale,
    objects belonging to Carolingian Kings
- Aachen: (Aix-la-Chapelle), Germany: Charlemagne's chapel
- Reims: Palais du Tau Museum

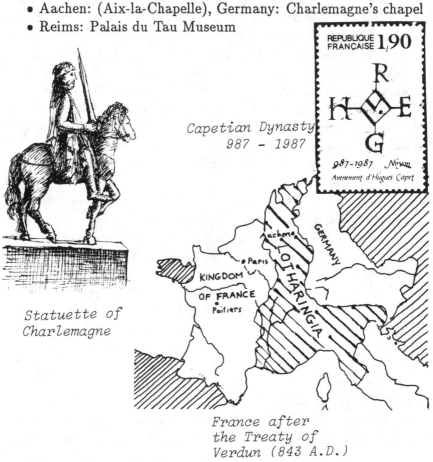

Capetian Dynasty
987 - 1987

Statuette of
Charlemagne

France after
the Treaty of
Verdun (843 A.D.)

---

[27] The word "ogre" is derived from "Hungarian". The Hungarians were eventually repelled.

Chapter 2

THE MIDDLE AGES: FRANCE FROM THE TENTH TO THE THIRTEENTH CENTURY

The Norman Invasions • The Capetian Dynasty • William the Conqueror • Aliénor of Aquitaine and the Plantagenets

Fearless and ruthless Norse pirates who were making ever deeper incursions into the French territory, while pillaging and massacring on their path, had at several different times reached Paris and set fire to the city. Unable to repel them, Charles-the-Simple was forced to treat: he gave to the Norman chief Rollo his daughter Gisèle in marriage and the vast territory later to be known as the province of Normandy in "fief".[1] Rollo in turn accepted Christianity and

---

[1] A fief in the feudal system was a heritable land held from a lord in return for

became, though reluctantly,[2] a vassal of the French king.

When, upon the death of the last Carolingian, Hugues Capet was elected to the throne of France (987 A.D.), thus marking the advent of the Capetian dynasty,[3] the Norsemen were solidly established in Normandy and had adopted the French language and way of life. They had not lost, however, their taste for conquest and adventure. One of the powerful Norman dukes, Robert (he was according to legend nicknamed "The Devil" because of his cruelty and violent character) fell in love with the daughter of a tanner, Arlette (the ruins of the castle from which he first caught a glimpse of her doing her laundry in the stream below can still be seen in Falaise), and the illegitimate son born from the romance that ensued, William-the-Bastard, later became famous as William-the-Conqueror. Robert arranged Arlette's marriage with a feudal lord, kept the child at his court and one day, overcome by repentance, set out on a pilgrimage to the Holy Land to atone for the sins of his youth. He never returned and it took the young William many years and much astuteness and courage to finally triumph over the attempts of his father's vassals to supress him. Once his power was firmly established in Normandy, William decided to claim the throne of England at the time King Edward, his kin, died without posterity. He set out to conquer England by crossing the Channel with his troops and subdued his duplicitous enemy Harold[4] at the famous battle of Hastings (1066), which

---

service.

[2] Unwilling to pay homage, which involved the kissing of the suzerain's foot, he delegated to the ceremony a replacement, while instructing him not to bow too low. The Viking followed the instruction so closely, that instead of stooping down, he propped up the king's foot and caused him to tumble backwards.

[3] This last and third dynasty was to rule France for as long as the French monarchy lasted, i.e., for roughly the next 900 years. At his trial during the French Revolution, Louis XVI was referred to as "Louis Capet". Hugues was so nicknamed because he had been the abbot at St. Martin-de-Tours, where the cape of the great saint was kept. In 1987, various celebrations marked the millenium of the dynasty and the so-called "Mécénat Capétien" or Capetian patronage of the arts and letters.

[4] Harold had pledged his support for William, but proclaimed himself king at the death of Edward.

changed the course of history. He was then anointed King of England at Westminister Abbey.

The story of this memorable expedition was immortalized in what is known to the English-speaking world as the "Bayeux tapestry"— the French call it "la tapisserie de la reine Mathilde". It is displayed to this day in a tiny museum in Bayeux. This 77-yard-long strip of embroidered cloth, in a perfect state of conservation, is hailed as the first French "bande dessinée", or "comic strip", as it occasionally adds a written commentary to the pictorial narrative of events. It was woven on the orders of queen Mathilda, William's cousin whom he married, in spite of "consanguinity" which was universally condemned by the Church. In a gesture of repentance, William and his wife had two beautiful Romanesque churches built in Caen, the "Abbaye-aux-Hommes and the "Abbaye-aux-Dames," where they were later buried in separate tombs.

William's conquest had far-reaching cultural and political consequences for both France and England. During the next two centuries the Normans were the elite of England, considered themselves superior to the Anglo-Saxons, and adopted French as the official language of the court. French was to leave a durable imprint on the English which eventually replaced it (today, some 60% of all English words are of Romance origin). The English court turned into a lively foyer for the dissemination of French art and literature (see below). And, even though William became king of England, he was still Duke of Normandy, and as such, a vassal of the French king. He was by far the most powerful of all the lords whose fiefs surrounded the relatively small territories of the Crown.

The French monarch himself was increasingly becoming less the real ruler of the lands under his domination, which extended as far as Barcelona, than merely a first among many other lords who owed him allegiance but were far richer than he. Even though Hughes Capet and his descendants enforced the rule of "primogeniture", whereby the eldest son alone inherited the Crown—the title and the land—he effectively controlled what barely corresponds to the Ile-de-France and some adjoining territories.[5] The entire history of the medieval Capetians revolved around one chief preoccupation: to consolidate the strength of the Crown and assert not only its feudal "superiority" but also effective sovereignty over the entire kingdom. In order to achieve this end, they often had to resort to astute manoeuvering, intrigue, marriage, inheritance, the annexation and acquisition of neighboring lands and even warfare with different vassals.

Acts of hostility erupted almost immediately between William and the French king, but the presence on French territory of the English "liege" threatened to turn into real disaster several times in the course of centuries. The first acute crisis arose because of Aliénor of Aquitaine, one of the most remarkable and colorful figures in all French history, whose life reads like fiction.[6] As daughter of Guillaume (William) III, Count of Poitiers and Duke of Aquitaine, Aliénor was to inherit the largest portion of lands in the French Kingdom, comprising not only the vast Aquitaine itself, but also the Limousin, the Gascogne, the Poitou, the Saintonge and the Périgord (as well as the right of suzerainty over the Auvergne and the Comté de Toulouse). The fifteen-year-old heiress was about to marry the French king Louis VII in 1137, when she learned that her father had died during a pilgrimage to Santiago de Compostela. She arranged her own wedding and, as queen of France, took part in the 2nd Crusade side by side with her husband. While in the Holy Land, she fell in love with another crusading lord, her kin from Poitou. She had given the King no male heirs (their two daughters, Marie and Aélis, married the Counts of Champagne and of Blois), and eventually Louis was able to repudiate her after their return to France. However, two months after the annulment was pronounced, Aliénor, who had taken back all of her provinces, married the dashing Comte d'Anjou, Henri Plantagenêt, who was some ten years her junior and who shortly after the wedding was anointed as England's King Henry

---

[5]Such as Brie, Beauce, Bauvaisis, Valois. He possessed, however, moral superiority, since he was the "anointed" and thus ruler not only by the choice of men, but by the grace of God.

[6]She has inspired scores of authors, playwrights and film makers.

II.[7] Henry became at that time the master of huge territories on both sides of the Channel, which were referred to as the "Angevin Empire," extending from England to the Pyrénées.

Aliénor and Henry had ten children, and two of their sons were to reign over England: Richard-the-Lionhearted and John Lackland, so nicknamed because of the territories he lost to the French king (see below).[8] Aliénor's pivotal role both in matters of political history and of letters cannot be overstressed: as the daughter of an accomplished "troubadour" who sang beautiful lyric poems he himself composed, she brought the tradition of courtly love and the spirit of southern literature not only to the court of France,[9] but also to that of England. When Aliénor died in 1204, she was buried in the Plantagenet necropolis, the Abbey of Fontevrault, side by side with her husband Henry II and her son Richard-the-Lionhearted who was killed while fighting against Louis VII's son, Philippe-Auguste. It took the French kings two and a half centuries more of astute plotting and warfare to win back all the French territories belonging to their English vassals from across the Channel.

---

[7] Henry II was also immortalized in a number of literary works, often centering on his conflict with the Archbishop of Canterbury, Thomas Becket (Saint), whom he had "murdered in the cathedral" (such as the film *The Devil's Crown* featuring Richard Burton and Peter O'Toole). His life with Aliénor and his power-thirsty sons was the subject of a famous play and film, *The Lion in Winter.*

[8] This union was not happy, either, and towards the end of her life Aliénor returned to her native Aquitaine and personally took care of the administration of her lands. As her son Richard was being held prisoner in Austria on his way back from the 3rd Crusade (see below), she insisted on delivering the required ransom in person and travelled on horseback to the other end of Europe at the age of 72.

[9] Also, thanks to the protection of Aliénor's daughter, Marie de Champagne, Chrétien de Troyes was able to bring to its apogee the genre of "roman courtois" or "courtly romance" (see below).

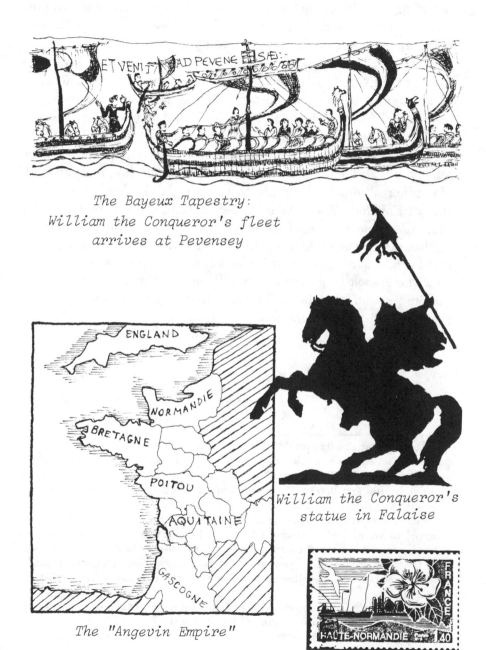

The Bayeux Tapestry:
William the Conqueror's fleet
arrives at Pevensey

William the Conqueror's
statue in Falaise

The "Angevin Empire"

WHAT TO SEE

- In the Loire Valley: Abbey of Fontevrault, tombs of Aliénor,
     Henry II, Richard-the-Lionhearted, and John Lackland's
     wife.
- In Normandy: Bayeux:
     The Bayeux tapestry (see also in the National Geographic
         magazine of August, 1966, an excellent article
         on the Bayeux tapestry).
     The Bayeux cathedral's south portal of the transept, por-
         traying the life of Thomas Becket.
     Caen: The castle of William the Conqueror
     The Abbaye-aux-Hommes
     The Abbaye-aux-Dames
     Falaise: The statue of William the Conqueror
- In Poitou: The castle of the Norman Dukes
     The Poitiers palace of the Ducs d'Aquitaine
- Near Paris: Dourdan, château of Philippe-Auguste

North and South

In the Middle Ages significant differences existed between the
"North" and the "South" of France, which was at the time cultur-
ally divided in two: the lands of the "langue d'oïl"[10] in the upper
part of the "hexagon", and the land of the "langue d'oc" in the
South, which had kept many of the Gallo-Roman traditions intact
and whose literature was written in Provençal. While common law
was in force in the North, the South was abiding by the Roman law
as had been codified by the emperor Justinian. The city of Toulouse,

---

[10] They were so called because of the way the population said "yes". The Latin
"hoc illud" became "oïl" and then "oui" in modern French. The affirmative
particle in the South was just "oc".

famous for its legal studies, was a flourishing center of arts and letters and had acquired a great renown on account of the poetry of the troubadours, widespread in the Aquitaine region. Whereas the fact that Paris and the Ile-de-France were domains of the anointed kings assured a spiritual supremacy to the North, the southern lords had more brilliant courts and were infinitely more refined and cultured than their northern counterparts. The latter, incited by envy, were only waiting for the appropriate moment to invade the southern lands. In 1208, under the pretext that the Count of Toulouse was protecting the Cathar heresy[11] and with the blessing of the pope, the Albigensian[12] crusade was launched against the South and for the following fifteen years the northern barons pillaged and devastated with fire and sword the entire region, until the Cathar heresy was stamped out. In 1229, the Count of Toulouse conceded his fief to the French Crown, while giving his only daughter in marriage to the king's brother. The domain of the French kings now extended to the Mediterranean sea and the newly acquired territories became a province still known today as "Languedoc".

The South never recovered from this vicious domestic war, nor has it forgotten or forgiven it: it is constantly brought back to twentieth-century minds by separatists, who are trying to rekindle the struggle for a free "Occitanie".

Society in the Middle-Ages: The Feudal System

The social structure in the Middle-Ages was based on respective needs: the need for protection and the need for labor, and is characterized by a man-to-man allegiance. The French society was roughly composed of three distinct classes, which evolved into the

---

[11] Cathar means "pure".

[12] From the city of Albi, one of the centers of the heresy.

so-called three "Estates-General" (Etats-Généraux), a designation that was kept until the French Revolution of 1789: the Nobility or warring class, the Clergy, in charge of spiritual life and welfare, and the Third-Estate (Tiers-Etat) or Commons, the mass of people who were the working class.

a) The Nobility

The lay power, which was not entirely independent of that of the Church, was in the hands of an elite of noblemen, governed by strict laws of hierarchy. At the bottom was the minor gentry, men of arms, owners of châteaux and of small pieces of land, who protected the peasants and lived off their work. They owed allegiance to barons, owners of vaster lands, who in turn were "liege-men"[13] of still more powerful lords. Many of these held their fiefs directly from the king, and thus were his vassals. Every noble was bound to his lord (suzerain) by homage (homme = man) and an oath of fidelity and owed him both "consilium" (counsel) and "auxilium" (aid), i.e., military assistance especially in time of war as well as financial aid on special occasions, such as the marriage of his daughters, the "adoubement" (dubbing) of his sons or imprisonment requiring ransom.

A young noble who had reached the age of bearing arms became a full-fledged knight after the "adoubement," an important ceremony endowed with a strongly religious character. Clad in colors of white (for purity), black (for death) and red (for the blood he was going to shed in the defense of his faith, his lord and land), the candidate spent a night praying in the chapel of the castle, before he was given the next morning a sword, some advice on knightly behaviour (such as "sois preux": be virtuous, daring, true to friends and your own words, always honorable and a devoted servant of the Church), as well as the traditional "accolade".[14]

In the 12th and 13th centuries, at the time of the development of the cult of the Virgin Mary, an increasing importance was given

---

[13] From the Germanic "let" = free.
[14] This was a symbolic blow across the neck with the flat of the sword.

to the spiritual qualities and moral values of knighthood: defense of the weak, respect for women and aid to widows and orphans. From these days stem the code of honor and "courtoisie" which have by tradition survived to our own times in the noble classes. A felonious vassal, who did not keep his oath of fidelity, and a felonious knight, who failed to meet the obligations imposed upon him, were "félons" scorned by their peers and social outcasts.

The nobleman's chief occupation and often chief distraction was continuous warfare with his neighbors and with other lords in the country or in far-away lands. Distant expeditions were greeted as a welcome opportunity for adventure, great feats, glory and, at times, booty. A knight's closest companions were his horse and his arms, in particular his sword, which he cherished above all.[15]

Members of the noble classes lived in stone châteaux, built like fortresses for protection and perched on the highest possible hill which offered a natural defense and from which the oncoming enemy could easily be spotted. The château was surrounded by a moat and the access was a draw-bridge, as seen on the figure below.

Life in these somber dwellings (the windows, vulnerable in case of attack, had the tiniest possible openings) was rather hard and uncomfortable. It was *cold*. Even when castles became luxurious residences, the problem of heating lasted well into the 18th century: Louis XV used to throw logs into his own fireplace to keep himself warm. The interiors were, however, not as bleak as is often represented in films, since the walls were usually adorned with mural paintings, Cordovan leather or tapestries. Entertainment consisted chiefly of hunting, which was a real passion of the noble class as well as of a number of French kings including the unfortunate Louis XVI.[16] Feasts and long winter evenings were highlighted by the performances of acrobats, the displaying of dwarfs and freaks and the

---

[15] Roland's last gesture, before he dies of wounds received at Roncevaux, is to break his beloved "Durandal" in order not to permit it to fall into enemy hands (see below). Charlemagne's sword was called the "Joyeuse" and King Arthur's "Excalibur".

[16] He went hunting even on the most crucial and dramatic days of the 1789 Revolution.

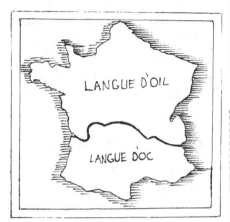

CHATEAU-FORT
1. Moat 2.Drawbridge 3. Machicolation
4.Apartments 5.Watch tower 6."Donjon" (keep)
7. Crenellation 8. Sentry walk

reciting by traveling minstrels of poems written by "trouvères" in the north and "troubadours" in the south.[17] On festival days, tournaments ("tournois") or jousts were held in the presence of ladies and numerous onlookers. These encounters between two knights who charged armed with a lance and tried to unhorse each other were a bloody and dangerous game. Later on it became customary for the knight to fight under the colors "of his lady" or beloved, who was traditionally other than his wedded wife.[18]

b) The Commons. Peasants and Burghers. Cities: Paris

Of the class known as the "Tiers-Etat"—Third Estate or Commons—which constituted over 95% of the entire population, by far the most numerous were the peasants who tilled the soil: either "vilains",[19] who were theoretically free, or serfs, who like slaves were actually "owned" by their lord. The lot of both of these peasant classes was miserable: they were taxable in kind and tender and liable to forced labor (building and repairs of the castle, of bridges, roads, etc.) at the master's pleasure. If crops failed, the peasants sometimes died of starvation and their diet consisted mostly of rye, oats and vegetables. Meat was a rarity—mainly pork whenever available.

Sadly enough the worst of all calamities besides the occasional famines was the incessant warfare between the lords, who regularly devastated the arable lands of their foes and gleefully set fire to their peasants' crops.

The "trève de Dieu"[20] imposed by the Church brought some relief from that misery, and the life of the peasants became more bearable in the 12th century.

---

[17] "Trobar"—"trouver" in modern French means to find or invent.

[18] In the 15th and 16th centuries tournaments became colorful and harmless pageants. Henri II, however, did lose his life as a consequence of his joust against Lord Montgomery: a splinter from the lance had lodged in his eye. He was wearing at the tournament the colors of his mistress, Diane de Poitiers.

[19] "Vilain" means ugly in French; the word mirrors the prevailing attitude toward them in the Middle Ages.

[20] See below.

City dwellers or "bourgeois" (burghers), chiefly tradesmen and craftsmen, such as furriers, tanners, butchers, etc., often formed guilds or "corporations", which grouped both manufacturers and merchants. Working hours lasted from sunrise to sunset and activities were clocked by daylight and church bells. Members of the same trade were also united in "brotherhoods" placed under the patronage of a saint (each owned their own chapel). The aim of the guilds was twofold: to help the less fortunate ones and to join in entertainment. In the early Middle Ages there was even more visible misery in the cities than in the country. Their narrow streets without sewers (cities notoriously suffered from a catastrophic lack of hygiene) were lined with beggars as well as maimed and sick people. While epidemics such as the black plague were playing havoc with the life expectancy of the inhabitants, there was a more dreaded disease yet. To each age its own scourge and in the Middle Ages it was leprosy, which was considered in those days as highly contagious. Those who had contracted it were forced to live in leprosariums and warn passersby in the streets of their presence by carrying a hand rattle.

As time passed, cities acquired more and more wealth and independence. They often took advantage of a feudal lord's prolonged absence or his need for money brought about by his departure for far-away expeditions, such as the Crusades, to gain various privileges. The king was usually on the side of the cities—and against his vassals; some of them became "communes" with the right of self-government which was often given to newly founded cities ("villes-neuves").[21] Others, "villes-franches", were exempted of a certain number of taxes and charges. As these cities steadily grew in size and population, they took an increasingly important political role.

Paris,[22] which in 1957 celebrated its 2000th anniversary (it was called Lutetia by the Romans), naturally held a very special meaning for the French, since the first French king had chosen it as his cap-

---

[21] This indication of "status" often became a name; there are hundreds of "Ville-franches" and "Villeneuves" scattered throughout France.

[22] The name Paris, and that of the Celtic tribe Parisii which inhabited the Ile de la Cité, comes from the Celtic word "par" or boat.

Château de Montségur

Carcassonne

ital. Louis' VIIth son, Philippe-Auguste, was particularly attached to the royal city, surrounded it with a wall three feet thick, built the Louvre[23] and gave a charter to the University of Paris, which helped it become the most renowned learning center of all medieval Europe (see below). He founded the Cathedral of Notre-Dame and established a permanent central marketplace which for centuries was known as "les Halles":[24] it was already in the 12th century an extremely active trading center. Paris at that time was divided into three parts: the Cité on the Ile de la Cité; the Ville, on the right bank of the Seine; and the Latin Quarter on its left bank.

WHAT TO SEE

- In the southwest (near Foix): ruins of Château de Montségur, a Cathar stronghold.
- Innumerable medieval châteaux and ruins of châteaux-forts, such as Château-Gaillard, Chinon, Loches, Les Baux, etc. (Pierrefonds is a 19th century reconstruction of Viollet-le-Duc).
- Bas-reliefs of Romanesque and Gothic churches throughout the country, e.g. at Reims.
- Various city ramparts (ex.: Aigues-Mortes, Angers, Beaune, Carcassonne).
- Various cities which have kept their medieval appearance such as Provins (Ile-de-France), Cordes (S.W.) and Pérouges (S.E.).

---

[23] The origin of this name is unknown. It may be traced back to either an old French word for lepers or to packs of dogs trained for wolf hunting and called "louvèterie". Both lepers and dogs were supposedly kept in the dungeon of the château. Philippe-Auguste resided on the Ile de la Cité in a château facing Notre-Dame, where you can see today the Palais de Justice, the Sainte-Chapelle and the Conciergerie.

[24] It was moved to an area near Paris only recently. In its former location now stands the controversial Centre Pompidou or Beaubourg Cultural Center which is to many Parisians, in spite of its usefulness, the ugliest structure in their beloved city.

c) The Clergy and Religious Life

During the 10th century, after a series of reforms, the Church gathered new strength and became a powerful unifying factor in the Western world. It enjoyed universal authority and exerted an uncontestable influence on all realms of life.

The clergy was either secular—living in the world (such as bishops acting in cities as feudal lords with their own tribunals and vassals)—or regular, living in abbeys and whose life was subjected to a monastic rule.

The Benedictines were the first order to spread in France[25] and their rule was adopted by the most important monastery in the Middle Ages, Cluny, founded in 910 A.D. thanks to a donation of the Duke of Aquitaine. Its abbot was directly responsible to the pope, and no secular ruler had more power than he: through the 2000 branches of the convent, scattered throughout Europe, in England, Poland, Italy, Spain and other countries, he made his influence felt all over the Christian world. The "abbatiale" or convent-church in its third and final form, Cluny III, was the largest of all churches until the erection of St. Peter's basilica in Rome in the 16th century.[26] Three popes and some fifty cardinals and prelates were former Cluniac monks. Peace and charity were the primary goals of monasteries. Cluny's abbots exercised their conciliatory powers in all directions. They forced feuding lords to suspend hostilities from Wednesday through Sunday and on days and evenings of religious holidays by imposing the "paix de Dieu" and the "trêve de Dieu" ("peace of God" and "truce of God"). This was, as mentioned before, an important step toward the improvement of the peasants' lot.[27]

---

[25] Many of the Benedictine abbeys which sprang up on the routes to famous pilgrimages, particularly those leading to Santiago de Compostela, such as Mt. St. Michel, Caen, Autun, Vézelay, Conques and Toulouse, enjoyed an extraordinary renown.

[26] It had to be of a huge size to accommodate thousands of visitors and throngs of pilgrims, who were sheltered and fed. There was in the Middle Ages such a thing as a free hostel: all abbeys furnished lodging and food to travelers, especially if they were pilgrims en route to a shrine.

[27] In times where compassion was far from being a widespread feeling, the monks

Above all, Cluny was a great center of art, learning and knowledge. It was instrumental in the spreading of Romanesque architecture and art[28] and the copying and preservation of texts in the monastery's library. Cluny's wisdom also saved the most renowned of all medieval philosophers and teachers, Abélard, whose work was condemned by St. Bernard. Abélard was allowed to retire and to end his days within the walls of the abbey (see below).

The Benedictine rule was austere: the monks were bound to vows of chastity, poverty and obedience. They rose before daybreak and spent their entire time on work, prayer, and religious services. These were accompanied by Gregorian chants, or "plain chant". Instruments were not allowed in churches until several centuries later.[29] The Cluniac monks brought beautiful music and a beautiful liturgy to their splendid churches, adorned with paintings, mosaics and sculptures. They believed that earthly beauty is but a weak replica of the beauty in the other world. To them nothing seemed fine enough to glorify God. The practical side of life was, however, not neglected either. Cluny gradually amassed a great deal of wealth, thanks to innumerable bequests made by rich nobles and burghers who were concerned with the salvation of their souls. The saying "Où vent vente, Cluny reçoit rente" (wherever the wind blows, Cluny receives riches) held more than a grain of truth. The Abbey owned an elegant residence in Paris, which is today the well known Musée de Cluny, across from the Sorbonne.

There are many different ways of worshipping God, and St. Bernard de Clairvaux, one of the most outstanding figures of the Mid-

offered refuge to the persecuted and cared for the sick in hospitals called at the time Hotels-Dieu (this designation has survived to this day in Canada). Also, for a number of centuries the Capuchin monks were the only existing firemen who could be called upon to help extinguish the innumerable fires stemming from defective fireplaces, which swiftly engulfed the crowded adjoining buildings.

[28] Cluny was the first to use the "ogive" or broken arch in its Romanesque abbey.

[29] From the middle of the 12th to the end of the 13th century the musicians of Notre-Dame de Paris set the rules of polyphony; the great master was Pérotin-le-Grand. Today, the Abbaye de Solesmes has revived Gregorian music.

Cistercian Abbey of Fontenay

Benedictine Abbey of Solesmes

Romanesque Abbey of Moissac

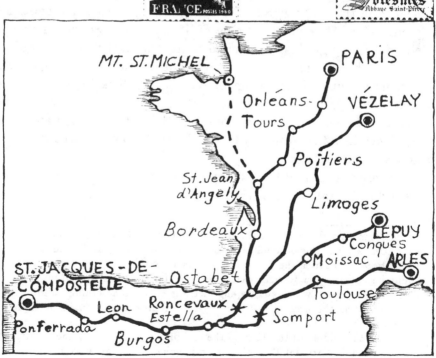

Medieval pilgrimage routes

dle Ages, did not approve of what he saw at Cluny. He chastised the Abbey's richness, refinement, feeling for aesthetics and quest for knowledge. He considered works of art as vain idols and applied the Benedictine rule in its original austerity at the abbey he founded in Cîteaux. There friars drank only water (no more good Burgundy wines!), ate bread and vegetables and wore the coarsest habits, fit for the hard manual work and the tilling of soil, which outside of prayer were their only occupations. Cistercian abbeys also multiplied and many can still be admired in the stern purity of their lines, devoid of any "useless" frills or ornaments capable of diverting man's thoughts away from God.

Benedictines and Cistercians lived in seclusion. The growth of cities and the urgent need for monks who could instruct the people and assist them in everyday life gave rise to new orders, which would mingle with the population. Such were the Dominicans, founded by a Spaniard, St. Dominic (their convent in Paris located on "rue St. Jacques" earned them the popular name of "Jacobins") and the Franciscans, founded by St. Francis of Assisi, whose original abbey in Paris was the famous church of St. Germain-des-Prés.

Religion played an extremely important role in the lives of people in the Middle Ages. They sincerely repented for their violent sins committed in those violent times. One of the best ways to achieve salvation was to undertake a far away, exhausting and perilous pilgrimage. Fervent faith was often the driving force behind the deeds of medieval men who were not afraid of death and knew how to die. Death was a natural thing with which they were at ease. They also believed that by giving their lives for a good cause they would earn celestial rewards in heaven. It is with this spirit of incredible religious fervor that hundreds of thousands of Christians responded to the call of a former Cluniac monk, Pope Urban II, and launched one of the most fantastic military ventures of all times: the Crusades.

WHAT TO SEE

- Near Le Mans: the Abbey of Solesmes
- Provence: Cistercian abbeys: Le Thoronet and the abbey of Sénanque
- Normandy: Mt. St. Michel
- Burgundy: Ruins of Cluny, Cistercian abbey of Fontenay
- Paris: St. Germain-des-Prés, Museum at Hôtel de Cluny
- North of Paris: Cistercian abbey of Royaumont

The Crusades

The direct cause of the Crusades, of which there were eight altogether, was the collective effort of European Christians to regain access to the Holy Sepulchre, the single most important shrine in the distant Holy Land, and to win it away from the infidels. When Peter-the-Hermit's gruesome accounts of atrocities and persecutions inflicted upon pilgrims and Syrian Christians by the new occupants of that part of Asia Minor, the Seldjuk Turks, reached the West, pope Urban II delivered an inflammatory speech at Clermont-Ferrand and the first Crusade was launched in the midst of unparalleled enthusiasm. Whereas the 100,000 strong mob of commoners—old men, women and children, priests and monks—led by Peter-the-Hermit and Walter the Penniless (Gauthier-sans-Avoir) was wiped out before it reached its destination, the threefold French army of feudal lords and knights arrived in the Holy Land after sustaining terrible losses, and eventually captured first Antioch and then Jerusalem (1099). These victories paved the way for the founding of the Latin, or Frankish kingdom of Jerusalem, which was to last less than two hundred years. In order to provide protection from relentless Moslem attacks, medieval fortresses were erected on the occupied territories and two new orders of soldier-monks were created, the Hospitalers and the Templars. These were supposed to insure the safety of land and maritime routes and to act as permanent agents for the kingdom. Seven more Crusades followed. Louis VII and his wife Aliénor took part in the second Crusade, inspired by the preaching of St. Bernard at Vézelay. Philippe-Auguste and Richard-the-Lionhearted embarked together for the third one.

The fourth Crusade ended unhappily in the pillaging of the opulent Christian city of Byzantium (Constantinople) which unfolded before the marvelling eyes of crude Western knights like a dream of a thousand and one nights.

As time went on, the Christians lost ground and in the first half of the 12th century Jerusalem fell back into Moslem hands.

The last two attempts at repulsing the infidels, the seventh and eighth Crusades led by King Louis IX, ended in disaster and the King himself died of the black plague in Tunisia during the campaign.

If the Christian—and mainly French—supremacy in the Middle-East was short-lived, the consequences of the Crusades were lasting and affected life in Western Europe in many different ways. A number of the powerful and enterprising feudal lords never returned and several French kings took advantage of their absence or death to consolidate their power and extend their territories.[30] France eventually emerged in the 12th century as the strongest monarchy in Europe. And, in spite of the mutual hatred, distrust and violent fighting between Christians and Moslems, lasting contacts between East and West were established.

The Crusaders brought back home a number of oriental customs as well as fruits, flowers such as the tulip, and above all, a taste for luxury, fine furniture, silks, rugs, jewelry, perfumes, spices and richly adorned weapons. Numerous oriental motifs, both floral and animal, as well as decorative patterns, arabesques and volutes were adopted by Romanesque sculptors and are characteristic of a

---

[30] Philip I among others. He was barred from taking part in the Crusade because of excommunication: he had carried off the wife of one of his vassals. Philippe II Auguste found it expedient to abandon the Holy Land where he had left his rival, Richard-the-Lionhearted, in order to plot against him at home (see below).

number of churches from that period. Arabic numerals replaced the
cumbersome Roman numerals at the beginning of the 12th century
and new trade routes with the Middle-East were permanently established. The widespread demand for merchandise which was shipped
along them resulted in the enrichment of not only different cities
and ports, but also of the Hospitalers and the Templars. The Hospitalers or Knights Hospitaler of St. John of Jerusalem, a military
religious order which focused on the protection of the sick and the
needy, still exist as a society, known as the Knights of Malta: they
resided on this Mediterranean island from 1518 to 1798, at which
time they were expelled by Napoleon.[31] And, whereas the physical
presence of the Western knights was brief, they gave to the Christian
communities in the Holy Land dating back to the 1st century A.D. a
tremendous spiritual boost. Today's pilgrims still view with awe and
admiration Romanesque and Gothic churches which were erected by
the crusaders and have withstood the test of time.

12th and 13th Century Capetians

As we have seen, Philippe-II-Auguste, son of Louis VII by his
third wife, was left with the monumental task of reducing the menacing power of the Plantagenets, Henry II and his sons, and the so-
called "Angevin Empire". At the time he was crowned as a fourteen-
year-old youth, Philip expressed the wish "to make the monarchy as
strong as in the time of Charlemagne." For some ten years he had to
face Henry II himself and astutely plotted against him by befriending
his perfidious son Richard-the-Lionhearted. When the latter became
king of England, he turned against Richard and conspired in his
absence with his younger brother John Lackland. When Richard
eventually returned from the Holy Land, a decisive confrontation
took place. Richard built on Philip's threshold a superb and menacing fortress, the Château-Gaillard (its ruins can still be seen in Les

---

[31] The Templars will be further discussed in Chapter IV and in the Appendix.

Andelys in Normandy), but, fortunately for the French king, he was killed by a bowman's arrow in 1199. Philip then took up hostilities against John Lackland who had succeeded Richard on the English throne. The Château-Gaillard fell in 1204 (year of Aliénor's death) and Philip became master of practically all of his enemy's territories on French soil. He dealt a final blow to John when he defeated a formidable coalition of English and Germans at Bouvines (1214). This battle is considered to be the most important single victory in French history.[32]

Philippe Auguste's son Louis VIII died young, but his grandson, Louis IX known as Saint-Louis, was to achieve the grandeur of France. Out of his concern for honesty and justice he returned some of the territories in southwest France to the English, though he was far from being a weak king: French royalty actually reached its medieval apogee under his reign. Raised with love and strictness by a remarkable mother, Blanche de Castille,[33] granddaughter of Aliénor, who was as wise as she was pious, Saint-Louis grew up humble and modest. He would wash the feet of the poor in a Christlike gesture and personally administered justice; he also reformed the judicial system throughout France. In order to achieve uniformity and centralization, he minted royal coinage which replaced that of his vassals. He fortified Carcassonne and had a secure port built in Aigues-Mortes. We also owe to him the incomparable gothic gem, the "Sainte-Chapelle" in the heart of Ile de la Cité, which has kept its magnificent stained glass windows intact for many centuries. It used to shelter one of the most revered relics in the Christian world, Jesus' crown of thorns at the time of the crucifixion (see below).

Though he was a chivalrous knight and, as noted above, set out for two Crusades, Saint-Louis loved peace and adjusted by treaty a number of conflicts over borders. He enjoys the reputation of having been the best of all French kings, with the possible exception of Henri IV.

---

[32] John Lackland's discomfiture forced him, in England, to accept and sign the Magna Carta.

[33] The only queen in the Middle-Ages to have personally nursed her son.

WHAT TO SEE

- Paris: The Louvre, the Sainte-Chapelle
    Château de Vincennes
- North of Paris: Ruins of Château-Gaillard in Les Andelys.
- Provence: Aigues-Mortes
- Languedoc: Carcassonne

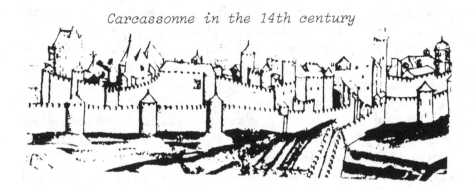

Carcassonne in the 14th century

Aigues-Mortes

Chapter 3

THE MIDDLE AGES: ARCHITECTURE, ARTS AND LETTERS

The Romanesque

The Romanesque art and architecture in the Middle Ages are practically entirely of religious inspiration. While, as mentioned above, feudal lords built fortified castles for security, not for beauty or leisure, the genius of the master-builders expressed itself in innumerable cathedrals, churches and abbeys which from the end of the 10th century on clothed France, according to the chronicler Raoul Glaber, in "a white cloak of new churches".

The first style which spread throughout Europe, known as "Roman" in French and Romanesque in English,[1] kept the basic plan of a Roman basilica, but was constructed entirely of stone (see sketch). It is characterized by semi-circular arches ("arcs en plein cintre") and vaults. The vault of the nave, at times a cradle-vault, ("voûte en berceau", often reinforced by "arcs doubleaux"), at other times

---

[1] In England it was called the "Norman" style, as it appears after William the Conqueror's invasion (Canterbury, Winchester, Durham, Lincoln).

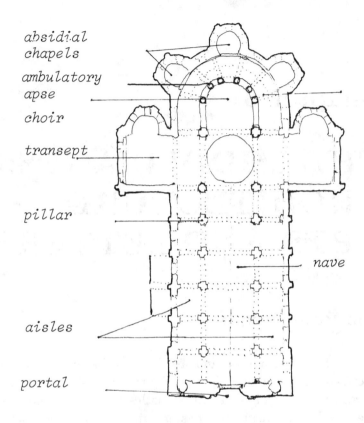

absidial
chapels

ambulatory

apse

choir

transept

pillar

nave

aisles

portal

Plan of a Romanesque church

Plan of a Romanesque portal

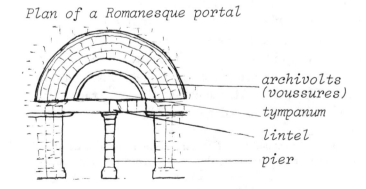

archivolts
(voussures)

tympanum

lintel

pier

an arris vault or at times a vault with cupolas, exerted a strong lateral pressure and had to be supported on the inside by massive pillars and on the outside by equally massive buttresses or "contreforts". The weight of the vault also required the support of thick walls which could not be weakened by large openings. Because it had few and small windows, the Romanesque church would have had a rather somber appearance, were it not for the rich sculpture and at times sumptuous mural paintings (unfortunately very few have been preserved in their original splendor).[2]

The sculpture, mainly on the capitals and the façade of the church, particularly on the portal and its tympanum which was the spot most visible to throngs, had as a goal, however, not so much decoration, as instruction. The medieval cathedral or abbey church is a book carved in stone which we often no longer know how to read. In those days when the masses of people were illiterate, it offered the faithful a course in history, in religion, with emphasis on the Old and New Testaments, and in ethics. It spoke of the rewards awaiting the "just" and the terrible punishment of those who would not live according to God's commandments. The Devil with his snares is forever present and the scene of the Last Judgment is one of the favorite motifs on tympanums and mural paintings of the 11th and 12th centuries.

Romanesque sculpture is characterized by the depth of the religious feeling and at the same time the keenness of observation and the truth in the representation of everyday reality in innumerable scenes of knights on horseback, peasants tilling the soil, wine-harvesters picking grapes, craftsmen at work and pilgrims en route to shrines.

---

[2] Many medieval churches were lavishly painted on the inside and often on the outside as well. Some statues and sculptures still bear traces of polychromy. Most of the colors have disappeared in the course of the centuries, but many frescoes were unwittingly covered by priests and abbots with thick layers of plaster. The few that have survived, such as in Auxerre and Berzé-la-Ville in Burgundy and in St. Savin-sur- Gartempe, not far from Poitiers, give, however, an idea of their scope, the lesson they carried to the faithful and the warmth they lent to the church (see also the very unusual polychrome capitals in Chauvigny, near St. Savin).

Autun, capital: "The Tempta-
tion of St. Anthony"

Romanesque façade
in the Limousin

For us, it bears witness to the medieval mores and way of life, as well as to the flora and fauna of the time.

In the days they were built, cathedrals assumed the role of mass media and availed themselves of all the audio-visual means of instruction at their disposal. Thus, the drama originated in the church. The so-called "mysteries" and "miracles" gave the faithful a lively presentation of important religious events, and Passion plays are to these days performed in traditional manner and garb throughout the Christian world.[3]

Medieval art and mind were alien to modern positivism. The visible world surrounding man in the Middle Ages was to him but a replica of the invisible world and was filled with objects endowed with a spiritual meaning. These were ruled by a complex interaction of so-called "correspondences", which he painstakingly attempted to decipher. Romanesque art is, in spite of some realistic scenes, far removed from naturalism and is strewn with symbols. Numbers were also believed to possess a mystical and religious meaning.[4]

When the Romanesque artist abolished perspective, it was not so much because of his ignorance, but because he felt that this very perspective gives a false idea of the true dimension of things (e.g. of the distant sun). He magnified objects of great spiritual importance, such as the hands of Christ sending off his apostles on a mission as can be seen on the tympanum of Vézelay (see fig.).

Romanesque sculpture is part of the church structure and entirely subordinate to it: the rigid statues, feet together and arms glued to the body, are as straight as the columns which they adorn and to

---

[3] Among the best known are the Oberammergau Passion Play and the infinite variety of shows staged in Spain during the Holy Week (la Semana Santa) and at Christmas. With time, the Devil became a favorite character, and because of increasing profanity, drama was banned from the inside of the churches and moved first to the "parvis" (square in front of the church) and then away into halls owned by the brotherhoods staging the plays.

[4] E.g., three for the Trinity, the three virtues, the "trivium"; four for the four Gospels, the four seasons, the quadrivium, etc.; 3 x 4 gave the key number of 12 (apostles, months and zodiac signs, twelve peers) and 3 + 4 is seven, the number considered as special, even magical, from the dawn of time.

which they are soldered. How expressive and diversified, however, are the faces! These were great artists, the mostly anonymous builders and sculptors of the Middle Ages. One of them, Gislebert, did sign his masterpiece, the impressive Last Judgment on the tympanum of St. Lazare in Autun, which throngs of lepers (St. Lazarus was the patron saint of those afflicted with the dreaded disease) could admire, as they attended mass from a place outside the cathedral: they were not allowed inside (see fig.).

WHAT TO SEE

Among many others famous Romanesque churches and abbeys:

- Paris: St. Germain-des-Prés**
    Musée de Cluny***
- Normandy: Caen:
    Abbaye-aux-Hommes
    Abbaye-aux-Dames
- Poitou: Poitiers:
    Notre Dame-la-Grande***
    Baptistère St. Jean
    St. Hilaire
- Not far from Poitiers:
    St. Savin-sur-Gartempe*** (mural paintings)
    Chauvigny (polychrome capitals)
- Burgundy: Vézelay***
    Cluny**
    Autun***
    Tournus* near Cluny
    Berzé-la-Ville: mural paintings
- Center: Conques**: Ste. Foy
    Le Puy: Cathedral and St. Michel de l'Aiguille
- Provence: Arles: St. Trophime**
    Cistercian abbeys of Sénanque,** Le Thoronet**

- Southwest: Moissac***
    - St. Bertrand de Comminges*
    - St. Sernin in Toulouse*
- Pyrénées Orientales: St. Michel de Cuxa*, St. Martin du Canigou**, Serrabone, Elne
- West: not far from Le Mans: Benedictine Abbey of Solesmes, famous for Gregorian chanting
- New York: The Cloisters***, erected from remnants of a French monastery, the St. Michel de Cuxa abbey in the Pyrénées Orientales.

The Gothic

From about the middle of the 12th century, a new style gradually started replacing the Romanesque: it was called Gothic,[5] French or "ogival" which means in French "pointed", as it was characterized by the broken or "pointed" arch. This style, based on a better comprehension of stresses, solved the problem of the weight of the vault and allowed it to rise to hitherto undreamt of heights. Since heavy walls were no longer needed to support the vault they became the framework for increasingly large openings, windows or "roses." These were filled with a plethora of radiant, multicolor stained-glass which lent the church an aura of quiet serenity. The massive counterforts were replaced by flying buttresses, such as can be seen at Notre-Dame in Paris: the cathedral looks from the side like a timeless ship fleeing into space with the help of winged oars (see fig.).

What strikes an onlooker in a Gothic church is its lightness, luminosity, and verticality: the eye is continually carried upwards. The structure points to heaven and expresses the Christian ideal of reaching higher, always higher, getting as close to God as human means

[5]The term was most likely used at the time of the classical revival to express scorn; since the style originated in the Ile-de-France, the contemporary designation was simply "art français".

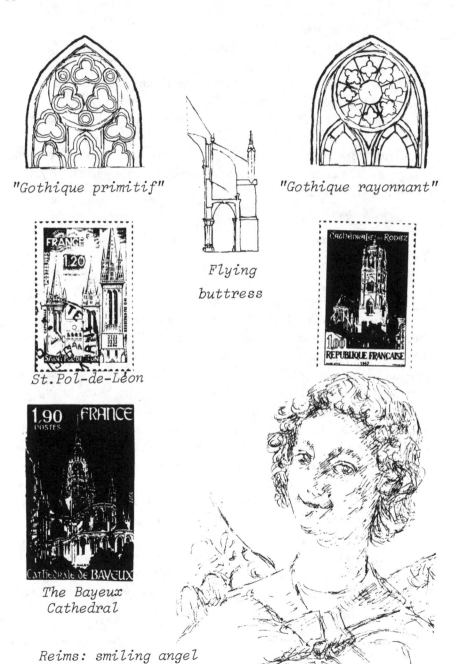

"Gothique primitif"

Flying
buttress

"Gothique rayonnant"

St. Pol-de-Léon

The Bayeux
Cathedral

Reims: smiling angel

will permit. Some of the Gothic churches actually seem to have an extra-terrestrial dimension: such are the Mont St. Michel, the cathedrals of Reims and Amiens, the choir of Beauvais and the Sainte-Chapelle in Paris.

Although Gothic can technically be divided into three periods, the early one or "gothique primitif", the simplest, purest and most harmonious of the three (St. Denis, the prototype,[6] Notre-Dame de Paris, Chartres, Sens), the "radiating" or "geometrical Gothic" ("gothique rayonnant"), which marks the apogee of the style (parts of Chartes, Amiens, Beauvais, Laon, Mt. St. Michel, the Sainte-Chapelle), and the "flamboyant" Gothic, which prevailed during the last two centuries of the Middle-Ages (see below), all the Gothic churches share the same qualities of elegance, lightness, logic of the structure and mystical thrust upwards. While some of the decorative elements remain symbolic, with a variety of patterns, geometric, floral, bestial and human, a large part of them are a sort of visual encyclopedia and represent the sum total of man's knowledge of the time. Interior painting was replaced by stained glass, which bore special meaning, as it diffuses light and light is symbolic of God himself. One has to see a Gothic cathedral bathing in the beautiful soft hues of masterfully put together stained glass windows to fully appreciate and understand the artistry and craftmanship of medieval builders and decorators (Chartres, la Sainte-Chapelle).[7]

Whereas the Romanesque abbey churches were mostly the work of monks, the Gothic cathedrals, located in larger cities, were the achievement of the entire urban population, including burghers, notables, aristocrats, royalty and even...oxen, which are so touchingly sculpted on the towers of the cathedral in Laon. Various guilds, which made significant contributions to the construction in work and money, and were also immortalized in the churches they helped build

---

[6] Built in 1140. The abbot, Suger, made a special stay at Cluny in order to study the architecture of that abbey, where the pointed arch was used for the first time in a church.

[7] We see today a great revival of this trade; modern stained glass craftsmen in France study and use the techniques of their medieval counterparts.

(e.g., the "vignerons" or vintners' stained glass window in the "Queen of Cathedrals," Chartres).

From the middle of the 12th century on we witness a proliferation of churches dedicated to "Our Lady". This was due to the development of a fervent cult of Mary and her increased role in iconography. This in turn had a bearing on the change of attitude toward women as they started enjoying widespread respect and a privileged status.[8] There was also a change of emphasis from a stern Christ-the-Judge to an understanding and compassionate Christ-the-Redemptor, a Christ who forgives and redeems men through his suffering; and to the suffering of Mary, the Lady of Sorrows, the indulgent and sweet Mother who offers her intercession for the salvation of the weak and wretched humanity. Men's feelings toward God slowly shifted from fear and awe to love and compassion.

Innumerable statues of the Virgin and her life, such as scenes of the Annunciation (one of the most beautiful can be seen on the portal of Reims) adorn Gothic churches. A comparison of Gothic sculptures with those of the Romanesque period give a measure of the evolution that had taken place. The stone figures, though still subordinate to the church's structure, steadily gain in independence, until they appear as detached and free. They also come alive both in expression and gesture. The wrappings of the Virgin carrying her infant son show the natural curve of the body and the fold of her tunic. The faces of kings, prophets and saints are not only humanized, but at the same time imbued with a hitherto unknown serenity, such as can also be seen on the "smiling Angel" at Reims and the "beau Dieu"—beautiful God—who blesses the faithful at the entrance of the Amiens cathedral.[9]

---

[8] This attitude was echoed in the "courtly" literature of the time (see below).

[9] Many of these statues were painted. Numerous traces of polychromy are still visible, such as gold on the "Vierge dorée" (Golden Madonna) at Amiens.

WHAT TO SEE

- Brussels: City Hall
- England: Westminster Cathedral
- Germany: Cologne Cathedral
- Italy: Venice, Palace of the Doges
    Milan, cathedral
- Spain: Cathedral of Burgos
- France: Cathedrals and abbeys (among many others):
    Amiens***
    Auxerre*
    Bayeux**
    Beauvais**
    Chartres***
    Laon
    Le Mans**
    Mt. St. Michel***
    Paris: Notre-Dame***, Ste. Chapelle***
        Le Palais de Chaillot: Musée des monuments français
        Musée de Cluny
    Reims***
    Rouen***
    St. Denis***
    Senlis*
    Sens*
    Strasbourg***
    Bourges: the palace of Jacques Coeur**

Education

In the early Middle Ages education was entirely in the hands of the Church, and was dispensed at first in monastic schools, and later in "cathedral" schools in cities founded by Charlemagne. Some of these learning institutions attained great renown—such as the cathedral school of Notre-Dame which became the University of Paris. It spilled out of the too limited Ile de la Cité to the left bank of the Seine and to the hill of Ste. Geneviève, to the "Latin Quarter," so called because Latin was the language in which courses were taught. The Latin Quarter has kept its name and some of its traditions to this day. The students and faculty, strongly imbued with ideas of freedom and autonomy eventually formed a "corporation" which on various occasions clashed with the municipal authorities. In order to prevent such happenings, Philippe-Auguste gave a royal charter to the University: it had already become famous thanks to such renowned masters as St. Anselme and especially Abélard,[10] whose "disciples" came to listen to his teachings from the four corners of the world.

In 1222, the University was placed under the direct dependence of the Holy See and later received from the pope himself its definitive charter with the right of "suspension". This gave both master and students a powerful weapon which they could use in retaliation. Thus, in 1229, the University of Paris proceeded with "suspension", left the city and temporarily "established" itself in England (while, according to some sources, giving its origins to the University of Oxford). The University of Paris steadily increased in size and reputation (Roger Bacon and Dante were students, as well as the famous 15th century poet Villon). It counted among its scholars such celebrities as the German Albertus Magnus and the Italian St.

---

[10] Abélard (1079-1142) the author of *Sic et Non*, a critical analysis and interpretation of Church texts, is known for his passionate and unhappy love affair with the niece of Cannon Fulbert, Héloïse. Secretly married to his teen-age pupil—she was one of the rare women of her time to get such advanced education—he had a son by her, Astrolabe. The unfortunate lovers were cruelly separated, and Héloïse retired to a monastery of which she later on became the abbess. Their deeply moving lifelong correspondence has inspired a number of artists and writers, such as J.J. Rousseau. Their "Gothic tombs," erected at a later date, can be seen at the Père Lachaise cemetery in Paris. Abélard's work met with the wrath of St. Bernard and was condemned by the Church. He was offered refuge by Cluny where he died. It is Abélard who assured the independence of the University of Paris by settling on the left bank of the Seine.

Thomas Aquinas who, in his master-work the *Summa Theologica*, achieved both a reconciliation of Christian dogma with the philosophy of Aristotle, and a kind of encyclopedia of all the knowledge of the time.

Most medieval students led a life of hardship. They lived in miserable quarters, often went hungry and took on, like many young people in our own time, all sorts of odd jobs to survive. In 1257, a charitable man, Robert de Sorbon, confessor of Saint-Louis and director of the Institution,[11] founded and endowed a college where underprivileged students of theology were supplied with lodgings, food and books (his example was later followed by other benefactors). Thus the Sorbonne was born, and its name was used for a long time as a broad designation for the University of Paris.

Soon up to 20,000 students, grouped in "Nations", settled in the Latin Quarter and formed a community whose traditions are at the base of today's campus-life. In side streets merchants catering to this community, such as ink and parchment vendors, bakers and laundresses, established their shops. The entire "campus" made yearly visits to neighboring fairs (e.g. the Lendit in Saint-Denis, which is still held yearly with modern "tanners" and textile vendors) in a noisy and colorful parade of pageantry. Students have always been a source of practical jokes and puns and perpetrators of protests and demonstrations. The 16th century writer Rabelais left us some vivid illustrations of their wit and spirit.

The University comprised four faculties: Theology, Medicine, Law and Arts, the latter being a kind of general instruction for young people between the ages of 14 to 20, which ended in the successful candidate's earning the title of "bachelier" (bachelor) and a diploma, "le Baccalauréat".[12] The curriculum, the *Septem artes liberales* (or seven liberal arts), was divided into two parts: the *trivium*, realm

---

[11] His principle was: "Vivere (to live) socialiter et collegialiter et moraliter et scolariter."

[12] The "bac" is still in French secondary schools the final test and certificate before higher studies and gives an education roughly equivalent to the American junior college.

of dialectic, where grammar, rhetoric and logic were taught, and the *quadrivium* which offered the study of arithmetic, geometry, astronomy and music.[13] The instruction was oral, with students taking down the master's lectures on tablets—professional copyists' work was also available.

The current term for the instruction dispensed at medieval universities was scholasticism, and the method was mainly the use of syllogism. The texts studied were those of the Christian tradition, as well as of some classical Latin authors, such as Virgil and Cicero, whose rhetoric and eloquence were held in high regard. Solving the contradictions between Christian dogma and the philosophy of antiquity was one of the chief preoccupations of 13th century scholars.

Several other French universities became famous, mainly for specialized fields of instruction: Toulouse for law and Montpellier, where Rabelais was a student, for medicine. But the University of Paris specialized in theology and remained the great center which made of France the capital of medieval learning.

WHAT TO SEE

- Paris: Bibliothèque Nationale
  Archives Nationales
  The Sorbonne
  The Père Lachaise cemetery (tomb of Abélard and Héloïse)
- Montpellier: The University
  The statue of Rabelais

---

[13]The "baccalauréat" gave access to the three other faculties of "higher learning": medicine, law and theology. The Virgin Mary was considered as patroness not only of arts, but of intellectual disciplines as well. On a number of tympanums, including that of Chartres' façade, she is prominently associated with the seven liberal arts.

Literature in the Middle Ages

French literature from the 9th to the 13th century reflects, as could be expected, the various preoccupations of medieval society. The oldest texts are "hagiographic", which means that they pertain to the lives of saints (such as Ste. Eulalie, St. Alexis, St. Léger). The next and by far the most important genre is the "chanson de geste" (from the Latin "gesta"—deeds), poems narrating the heroic deeds of real or imaginary knights. Some hundred different "chansons de geste" have survived. These epic poems, recited to music by traveling minstrels, were the work, as mentioned above, of "trouvères" in the north and "troubadours" in the south.

The most beautiful and most famous of these poems is the *Chanson de Roland* or *Song of Roland*. Its earliest version dates back to the end of the 11th century and is said to have been sung by the soldiers of William the Conqueror at the time of his conquest in England. It was known to every minstrel and endlessly recited to feudal lords in castles and to throngs of commoners along the numerous pilgrim routes which led to Compostela.[14] The story it tells is the defeat of Charlemagne's nephew Roland at the hands of the infidels in the Cap of Roncevaux (Roncesvalles) and at the same time his inspiring spiritual victory. The poem expresses the chivalric ideals of heroism, honor, feudal loyalty, devotion to the fatherland, respect for bonds of friendship and boundless faith in God. Roland has the typical mentality of the knight from the time of the Crusades. He is rash, fearless, proud, imprudent, arrogant and vengeful, and at the same time loyal, sensitive and deeply moving. There is no place in his life, nor in the poem, for love or women: Roland's fiancée Aude makes but a brief appearance in the story to fall dead when the news of the rear-guard's defeat and her beloved's death reaches her (see Appendix).

From the 12th century on, new elements appear in literature and they again reflect the changing tastes, preoccupations and mores of

---

[14] We witness today a great revival of pilgrimages to Santiago de Compostela.

the feudal society which has become more refined, more elegant and more polite. The knight is now entirely subdued by his lady: he owes her allegiance, love, respect and blind obedience. As noted above, the newly developed cult of the Virgin Mary is linked with this new attitude toward woman and her rise in society. The knight is still fearless and heroic, but fights less frequently for his lord or his homeland than in defense of the weak and helpless, such as widows and orphans, and by his prowess hopes to become worthy of the demanding beauty whom he has vowed to love. The stories unfold in a fantastic, totally unrealistic world, in enchanted forests where magicians (such as Merlin), fairies (such as Morgane), lions and all kinds of exotic animals lurk and strive to ensnare the valiant wanderer. The knight overcomes the unbelievable dangers by being a sort of superman, at the same time dauntless and astute.

This so called "courtly literature" (*roman courtois*), inspired by the "Matter of Britain" (*matière de Bretagne*) stemming from Celtic legends is woven around the central figures of King Arthur and his "Round Table of twelve peers" in Camelot. His beloved, beautiful wife Guinever (Guenièvre) has given her heart against her own will to the so far irreproachable Launcelot: the mood is now for fatal love, a bewildering and blinding passion stronger than man's will, love as a tragic destiny, such as is depicted in perhaps the most poetic and moving of all courtly romances, *Tristan et Yseult* (*Tristram and Isolde*). This poem has inspired scores of writers, artists and composers and still exerts its fascination on 20th century readers. Its authors were protégés of no other but queen Aliénor,[15] who in her youth had lived in the southern tradition of courtly love. As was mentioned, she exerted her influence on French literature not only directly, but also through her daughter Marie de Champagne, who in turn patronized France's greatest medieval writer, **Chrétien de Troyes**, author of such well known works as *Yvain*, *Lancelot* and *Perceval*.

---

[15]She extended her patronage to the first French poetess, Marie de France, author of the famous short poems called *lais*. One of them narrates the story of Tristan ("Le Chèvrefeuille").

Love in all its manifestations is also the subject matter of the first part of a long poem from the middle of the 13th century, *Le Roman de la rose*, which centers on the analysis of all the nuances of passion. The second part of this curious poem, written by an author of a different generation, reflects, however, an entirely new, misogynous spirit and constitutes a mordant satire of society as well as a sum total of all medieval knowledge.[16] This second part, far removed from the knightly ideals of "esprit courtois" is close in inspiration to the bourgeois literature of the time, as found in the *Roman de Renard*, the *fabliaux*[17] and numerous comic plays[18] and farces which attain their apogee in the hilarious 15th century *Farce de Maître Pathelin*: it is to our day frequently performed and always meets with thundering applause.

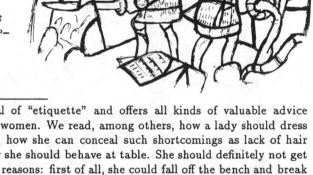

Chartres: stained glass window picturing Roland

---

[16] It is also a manual of "etiquette" and offers all kinds of valuable advice frequently destined for women. We read, among others, how a lady should dress to enhance her beauty, how she can conceal such shortcomings as lack of hair and bad teeth, and how she should behave at table. She should definitely not get drunk, and this for two reasons: first of all, she could fall off the bench and break a limb or two; and, secondly, in a state of inebriation she might be tempted to reveal secrets which could result in great harm or even catastrophy.

[17] Many had a lasting reputation and were not only widely read but also served as an inspiration to 16th, 17th and 18th century authors, such as *Le Vilain mire*, on which Molière based his *Doctor in Spite of Himself.*

[18] The drama, as mentioned above, slowly evolved from strictly religious plays to representations of historic deeds, such as the life of Jeanne d'Arc.

Avignon: Palais des Papes

Château de Chinon, where Templars were held prisoners

Chapter 4

THE LAST TWO CENTURIES OF THE MIDDLE AGES

France in the 14th and 15th Centuries

Philippe-le-Bel (Philip-the-Fair, grandson of Saint-Louis), who ascended the throne at the end of the 13th century (1285-1314), had none of the virtues and scruples of his great predecessor, but was more astute than any of the previous kings. Though he left a reputation for greed and violence, his reign was marked by a further strengthening of the French crown. Since Philip was always short of money, he tried to levy taxes on the clergy, which brought him into open conflict with Pope Boniface VIII. The pontiff eventually died from the shock caused by an attempt on his life perpetrated by the ruthless king's emissaries. Philip then had a French cardinal elected pope and transferred the Holy See to Avignon,[1] where he could keep an eye on its activities. The popes remained in this sunny Provençal city for the next seventy years or so, and when they

---

[1] This radiant city on the Rhône river is also known for its bridge and the very popular folk song "Sur le pont d'Avignon, l'on y danse, l'on y danse."

returned to Rome, they left behind not only an imposing palace (a visitor's "must") but also excellent memories: the city's exemplary administration, the enrichment of the entire region through new trade and a flourishing wine-production (highly recommended is the renowned Châteauneuf-du-pape). In order to obtain financial aid and other support of his people, Philip was the first king to call the Assembly of the Estates-General (1302).[2]

He governed with the help of "légistes" or "lawyers" and patronized the "Parlement", a sort of supreme court, which was an instrument of royal power and exerted a powerful influence until the end of the ancien régime (this institution eventually gave rise to a new social class called "noblesse de robe").

Since further funds were needed both for his costly administration and continual warfare, Philip turned his attention to a new prey, the Templar Knights, and decided to seize the vast riches which the order had amassed from the time of the Crusades.

All the Templars were arrested by night and by surprise in their powerful citadels in Paris[3] and elsewhere, accused of heresy and idolatry and submitted to torture. Extorted confessions led to their condemnation and to the confiscation of all their belongings. The knights themselves were burned at the stake. From the flaming pyre, the unfortunate prior, Jacques de Molay, is said to have cursed Philip and all his posterity. Philip himself died suddenly at the age of forty-six, felled by a mysterious illness which afflicted him during a hunt. And the bloody history of his thirteen "accursed" descendants is but a web of crimes, debauchery and misfortunes which also befell France during the some hundred and fifty years that followed.

Philip-the-Fair's three sons all reigned for a very brief time and left no male heirs.

At the death of the last one (1329), Philip's nephew became king

---

[2] These were to play an extremely important role at the time of the French Revolution.

[3] The so-called "Temple" in Paris became a prison. Louis XVI and his family were kept prisoners there during the French Revolution before the King's beheading.

The Hundred Years' War:
the surrender of Calais
(sculpture by Rodin)

Charles VII
and
Agnès Sorel

Jeanne d'Arc

after Fouquet

of France: this marks the ascent to the throne of a lateral branch of Capetians, the Valois. England's Edward III, grandson of Philip through his daughter Isabelle, claimed his rights to the French succession, whereupon French barons invoked the Salic law (loi salique) which barred women from transmitting the crown. The dispute gave rise to a long conflict between the two countries which lasted until 1453 and is known as the Hundred Years' War. It was for France the most dismal time of its history, filled with bloodshed, treachery, pestilence, famine and devastation.

The English started with a series of advantages: they still owned the Guyenne in southwest France, allied themselves in the course of the war with the powerful dukes of Burgundy, and inflicted upon the French three crushing defeats[4] at Crécy, Poitiers[5] and later on at Agincourt (Azincourt). Charles d'Orléans, the famous fifteenth-century poet and father of king Louis XII, was taken prisoner during this battle and spent twenty five years in captivity in England. At one time, not only did France lay in ruins, but everything indeed seemed lost: the English had reconquered most of their territories and Charles VII was disowned by his own perfidious mother and insane father (Charles-VI-le-Fou).

The French throne was to go to the English king and the English were already occupying Paris. Charles VII, scorned even by those who had not deserted him, was forced to withdraw to the tiny territory still under his rule, which earned him the contemptuous title of "Roi de Bourges".[6]

But in the midst of all the despair, France was saved thanks to the intervention of Joan of Arc (Jeanne d'Arc), known also as Joan of Lorraine (she was born in Domrémy in Lorraine) or as the Maid of Orleans. Prompted by visions and "voices" from heaven, she set

---

[4] 1346, 1356, 1415.

[5] 2 King Jean-le-Bon (John-the-Good) was taken prisoner during this battle and held in captivity in London. He was released and returned to France, but as his son, whom he had left as a hostage, escaped, he went back to England where he died.

[6] Before he was officially anointed king of France, he was simply called "dauphin".

out to free her country. Driven by an indomitable spirit, she eventually gave the French the necessary example and courage to fight and reduce the enemy.[7] Her arrival at Chinon, where she recognized Charles who had disguised himself and was hiding among his courtiers, her victory at the besieged key-city of Orleans, her role in the anointment of Charles at Reims, which gave him official and spiritual stature and rallied to his side the French people, are universally known and have inspired countless artists, poets, and playwrights.[8] Equally well known is her imprisonment, the calamitous propaganda trial that followed and her death at the stake on the marketplace in Rouen, where in recent years an ultra-modern church has been erected in her honor.

While Charles did nothing to save the life of the heroine, he benefited from the memory she left behind and the unity the French nation had achieved thanks to her. By 1453 the English had been expelled from France and only Calais remained in English hands (it was reconquered a hundred years later).

But it was not until the reign of Charles' son, Louis XI, the "bourgeois" or "spider-king", an unsympathetic, superstitious, cruel and sly little man, that decisive steps toward the consolidation of the kingdom were taken. Louis XI, who resided in somber medieval fortresses and dressed like a simple burgher, managed to reduce the powerful and brilliant Duke of Burgundy, Charles-the-Rash,[9] and annexed his vast and prosperous territories.

By the end of the 15th century, when Louis XI's son Charles VIII married Anne de Bretagne, the last important feudal province was also reunited with the French crown.

---

[7] The English soldiers were called at the time by the French "les godons" from the swear word constantly on their lips.

[8] E.g., Schiller, G.B. Shaw, Claudel, Péguy and Anouilh; operas by Verdi and Tchaikovsky; a 1948 film starring Ingrid Bergman.

[9] "Charles-le-Témeraire," also called "Charles-the-Bold," lived in magnificent pomp at the great foyer of arts and letters in the capital of Burgundy, Dijon.

WHAT TO SEE

- Paris and Orléans: Statues of Jeanne d'Arc
- Avignon: Palace of the popes, bridge
- Bourges: Palais Jacques Coeur
- Chinon: Château
- Dijon: Palace of the Dukes of Burgundy
- Domrémy: Jeanne d'Arc's birthplace
- Loches: Château: "donjon" royal prison (specially for Louis XI's enemies); royal apartments, hall where Jeanne d'Arc visited Charles VII; tomb of Agnès Sorel, Charles VII's mistress
- Reims: Cathedral, museum of Palais du Tau
- Rouen: The "old market place"
- Near Tours: Plessis-lez-Tours: Château of Louis XI
- near Angers: Château de Plessis-Bourré (built by Jean Bourré, finance minister of Charles VII, Louis XI and Charles VIII)

Life, Arts and Letters in the 14th and 15th Centuries

The last two centuries of the Middle Ages, marked by warfare, devastation and several terrible outbreaks of the black plague, reduced the population of some parts of France by a quarter, but did not hinder progress in several different domains: in the 15th century six more universities were added to the preceding three (Besançon, Aix en-Provence, Nantes, Poitiers, Bordeaux, Caen) and a prototype of capitalism was introduced by Jacques Coeur. While cities gained increased independence and wealth, the gap between rich and poor became more and more noticeable. Many starved to death, but life at certain courts reached a luxury hitherto unknown. Fashions, men's as well as women's, were indeed extravagant: this was the time for

Chinon: Royal apartments where Jeanne d'Arc found Charles VII

"Hennin"

"Poulaines"

the most sumptuous fabrics and furs, for bizarre two-colored outfits and long pointed shoes or "poulaines"[10] (which had to be lifted with the help of attached strings to facilitate walking) and for highpiled coiffures crowned with equally pointed hats or "hennins".

The split between the idealistic and the realistic approach to life was also more pronounced in arts and letters. Daily encounters with violence and death resulted in the famous "danse macabre". Witchcraft, magic and satanic cults associated with crime (as in the case of Joan of Arc's fellow soldier Gilles de Rais, the Bluebeard of many bloodcurdling stories), were common manifestations of the spirit of the times, side by side with extreme religious fervor and mysticism. There was also a tendency to satirize and to laugh off everything in the old "Gallic" tradition of "esprit gaulois", as exemplified in the *Farce de Maître Pathelin*.

This triple inspiration can be detected in the work of one of France's greatest poets, François Villon, who was born in the year of Jeanne d'Arc's trial (1431) and who eventually vanished without a trace some time after 1460, having most likely met with a violent death.

Charles d'Orléans wrote elegant lyric poetry during his twenty-five-year-long captivity in England—some of his rondels, put to music by Debussy and Poulenc, have excellent recent recordings. The vocal polyphony of the 13th century ("ars antiqua") reached new heights and acquired new techniques in the compositions of Guillaume de Machaut (1300-77), one of the originators of "ars nova". In the 15th century, the polyphonic song became divorced from religious music. We owe to Josquin des Prés, who revived the old lyric tradition of the troubadours, some of the most beautiful "chansons" and "motets" of the period.

In architecture, the predominant style is the flamboyant Gothic, characterized by exaggeration, extreme refinement and an increasingly abundant and complicated decoration over a more sober structure by "arcs en accolade" resembling tongues of flame, such as can

---

[10] The fashion is supposed to have come from Poland or "Poulogne" ("Pologne" in modern French).

Louis XI

The "donjon" of
the château de Loches

Villon's "Epitaphe"

Dijon: Palais des Ducs

"Danse macabre"

be seen on the portal and the stone-lace "jubé" of St. Cécile in Albi, the Hôtel-Dieu in Beaune and the churches of St. Maclou in Rouen and St. Germain-l'Auxerrois in Paris.

As far as sculpture in concerned, it gains total autonomy from architecture and finds its most striking expression in wooden carvings of religious inspiration. The most prestigious foyer of art and stone sculpture in the 15th century was the court of the Dukes of Burgundy. The tombs of the Dukes in their Dijon palace and in the church of Brou (Bourg-en-Bresse) are unparalleled masterpieces and "musts" on a tourist's list (the tomb of the Burgundian Philippe Pot can today be admired at the Louvre).

Insofar as painting is concerned, mural frescoes were no longer used in churches where they had been replaced by stained glass windows, but continued to decorate private residences, such as the papal palace in Avignon. The art of miniature painting ("enluminure") reached new precision and beauty in the works of the Limbourg brothers ("Les Très Riches Heures du Duc de Berry") and of Fouquet ("Les Heures d'Etienne Chevalier"). The latter also excelled in a genre new to France, the portrait on wood of lay persons, mostly kings and influential aristocrats (e.g. Charles VII, Jovenel des Ursins, Agnès Sorel).

The paintings of the Maître de Moulins, the best French "primitif", and Enguerrand Quarton's[11] *Pietà* of Villeneuve-les-Avignon are also remarkable works of art. Tapestries were yet another art form which steadily gained in popularity: without them no château between the 15th and 18th centuries could be properly decorated. The oldest, the "Apocalypse of Angers",[12] is already a masterpiece. But the most beautiful are perhaps those which represent the quest and hunt of the elusive Unicorn: one such series can be viewed at the Musée de Cluny in Paris, another at the Cloisters in New York.

---

[11] Also known as Enguerrand Charenton.

[12] Tapestries (like stained glass windows) have made a comeback in the 20th century: a display of Jean Lurçat's masterful series "Le Chant du monde" can also be seen in Angers.

WHAT TO SEE

- Paris: The Louvre: the Pietà of Villeneuve-les-Avignon
    portrait of Jean le Bon by Girard d'Orléans
    tomb of Philippe Pot
    portrait of Charles VII by Fouquet
    Church of St. Germain l'Auxerrois
    Musée de Cluny: tapestries, medieval art, furniture
- Albi (S.W.): Cathedral of St. Cécile
- Angers: Château; tapestries
    Lurçat's tapestries in St. John's Abbey church
- Autun: Musée Rolin, the Nativity of Le Maître de Moulins
- Beaune (Burgundy): The Hôtel-Dieu
    The Musée du vin (formerly palace of Dukes of Burgundy)
- Bourg-en-Bresse: Church of Brou
- Chantilly: Château
    Museum: "Les Très Riches Heures du Duc de Berry"
    Other 15th century miniature paintings
- Dijon: Palace of the Dukes of Burgundy
    The nearby "Chartreuse de Champmol"
- Rouen: Church of St. Maclou
- Villeneuve-les-Avignon: Musée de l'Hospice
    Works of Enguerrand Quarton
- New York: The Cloisters Museum

"La Dame a la licorne" (Musée de Cluny)

"Gothique
flamboyant"

Church of Brou

Chapter 5

THE SIXTEENTH CENTURY AND THE RENAISSANCE

The Italian Wars • François I • Henri II • The Wars of Religion

In the second part of the fifteenth century, a number of events took place which changed the face of the world as it was known at the time and had far reaching consequences for the centuries which lay ahead. Distant travels and explorations, as well as the discovery of new lands,[1] led to novel perspectives and the creation of new trade routes. The fall of Constantinople to the Turks (1453) brought to the West, along with fleeing refugees and scholars, texts and manuscripts containing a vast knowledge of pagan antiquity. The revolutionary "heliocentric" theory of the Polish astronomer Nicolas Copernicus (1473) totally upset the hitherto accepted conceptions of the universe. The perfecting of the printing press by Gutenberg (the first French "imprimerie" was opened in 1470) allowed for the wide dis-

---

[1] Few people need to be reminded of the date of the discovery of America in 1492.

Anne de Bretagne and her
Château de Fougères

Charles VIII

Azay-le-Rideau

semination of texts which had previously been available only in costly manuscripts, and led to the free study ("libre examen") of such writings as the Bible and the Gospels. At the beginning of the sixteenth century men felt that the Middle Ages were far behind and that they could enjoy the opportunity of living in a great, brand new world.

As far as the political history of France is concerned, the first part of the sixteenth century is dominated by events connected with the "Italian wars". Both Charles VIII, son of Louis XI, and Louis XII, son of Charles d'Orléans (they each in turn married the heiress of the last remaining powerful feudal province, Anne de Bretagne), pursued the idea of claiming, because of vague rights of blood, the Kingdom of Naples and the Duchy of Milan, and undertook warfare in Italy. The great Renaissance king, François I, cousin and son-in-law of Louis XII, who ascended the throne in 1515, decided to continue the efforts of his predecessors. But, after some initial good luck and an important victory at Marignan, he soon found himself confronted by a formidable foe, Charles V (Carlos Quinto or Charles-Quint) who was in 1519 elected Holy Roman Emperor and became the ruler at the same time of Spain, Austria, the Nederlands, Lorraine, Artois and Flanders, Italy, a part of Germany, the Spanish "New World" and that part of Burgundy[2] which had not been snatched away by Louis XI from Marguerite de Bourgogne, daughter of Charles-the-Rash (Charles-le-Téméraire). François I was defeated at Pavia and sent as a prisoner to Madrid. His former ally Henry VIII of England having deserted him, François looked for help in his fight with Carlos wherever he could find it, including the Turkish sultan. The war eventually came to an end during the reign of his son, Henry II, but rivalry between the French kings and the Hapsburgs or the "House of Austria" was to continue for a long time to come.

While France was forced to abandon all its territorial claims in Italy, the "Italian wars" brought about a further unification of the French people and the concept of a "French nation" became solidly implanted in the minds of both the kings and the inhabitants of the

---

[2] In a treaty signed upon his release from captivity, François promised to return Burgundy to the Hapsburgs, but he later reneged on this agreement.

Cognac: François I's birthplace

François I after Clouet

Amboise, Clos-Lucé: Leonardo da Vinci's residence

Blois: octogonal stairway after da Vinci's plans

country. In order to achieve more uniformity, French replaced Latin as the official language of the courts. The impact of the Italian wars on the artistic and cultural life of France was, however, of even greater importance.

François I was not only a great fancier of women[3] but also a lover and patron of arts and a Maecenas in the true sense of the word. Dazzled by the artistic treasures of Italy where the Renaissance had been flourishing already for some time, he decided to bring his backward country up to Italian standards. To this end he invited and incited with gifts of gold and money prominent Italian masters to come, live and create in France and he was successful in attracting Cellini, Rosso, Il Primaticcio and Andrea del Sarto to France. The works of these artists gave most of its luster to Fontainebleau. Leonardo da Vinci also accepted François' invitation and spent the last years of his troubled life in the King's company and vicinity. He resided at the manor of Clos-Lucé below the château of Amboise which he could reach by an underground passage. According to legend, Leonardo died in François' arms and bequeathed him on his deathbed the most famous painting in the world, the Mona Lisa, known to the French as "La Joconde". François had previously purchased the "Virgin, Child and St. Anne" and had amassed a number of other masterworks which can today be admired at the Louvre.

The French landscape also changed rapidly in this first part of the sixteenth century, as somber feudal châteaux-forts with their tiny windows and thick walls intended for defense were replaced by elegant and sumptuous "châteaux de plaisance" in the new Renaissance style of architecture. The Loire valley, and in particular the green and picturesque Touraine, called for good reason "the garden of France," proved to be a choice spot for the erection of new royal and aristocratic dwellings.

It is in this region that François decided to have his favorite

---

[3] He was a real ladies' man and is said to have written, while musing over the inconstancy of women, this distich on the window of the château de Chambord: "Souvent femme varie/Est bien fol qui s'y fie" (Women are fickle, a fool is he who trusts them).

hunting lodge built, the well known Chambord castle which was begun in 1519 by 18,000 workmen and finished in a matter of several years. François also acquired Chenonceaux and built St. Germain-en-Laye, where Louis XIV was to be born in the following century. At the same time he had important changes made at Blois and at Fontainebleau, where he resided in full splendor of the Renaissance. He traveled from château to château with a brilliant court and the most beautiful ladies in the country. He loved festivities, hunting, luxurious appointments, dazzling clothes and jewels. His two famous portraits by Clouet and Titian show a strong willed face with a large nose and intelligent eyes with a pensive expression.

But François was more than a warrior and a gallant gentleman: he was above all an enlightened monarch with a keen interest in literature and intellectual matters. He surrounded himself with scholars, made possible the reprinting of texts from classical antiquity and founded in 1530 the Collège de France. This center of humanistic studies, where Hebrew, Greek and Latin were taught according to the most recent methods, was to be totally independent of the tyrannical censorship of the Sorbonne. The Collège de France celebrated its four-hundred-and-fiftieth anniversary in 1980 and is still the most prestigious learning institution in the world.

François I was sympathetic to the Renaissance with all it meant and was open to new ideas including the "courants evangéliques" which enjoyed the protection of his sister, Marguerite de Navarre.[4] The free study of the Bible and the Gospels made accessible by the invention of the printing press opened the question of their interpretation and eventually led to the Reformation and a profound split in the Christian world.[5] François I showed at the beginning a tolerant

---

[4] Marguerite de Navarre (or d'Angoulême) was not only a protectrix of artists and writers, but also achieved a high degree of renown as a writer and a poetess.

[5] The rulers of most Scandinavian countries, Germany and the Netherlands accepted the Reformation often not so much for ideological reasons, as in order to get hold of the Church's possessions and have the money hitherto levied for Rome channeled into their own treasury. As is well known, Henry VIII of England had his own reasons for breaking with the pope who refused to sanction his divorce at the time Henry wished to marry Anne Boleyn.

Henri II after Clouet

Catherine de Médicis
(16th c. anonymous painter)

Diane de Poitiers (French School)

attitude toward the Protestants, and it was not until blasphemous posters were displayed in Paris and glued to the doors of his own château in Blois that he decided to react. A first crackdown eventually resulted in the massacre of the "heretic" Vaudois in Provence.

François' second son, who inherited the crown in 1547[6] and who reigned under the name of Henri II, was much less tolerant. In this he was influenced by the Guises, a family of staunch Catholics who had become extremely influential, and even more so by Diane de Poitiers, the great love of his life. His romance with this famous woman, some twenty years his senior, is one of the most unusual love affairs in French history. It had far reaching repercussions on the political life of the country and is brought to mind in scores of buildings and art treasures of the period. While married by his father to the unattractive Catherine de Médicis with whom he had ten children, he had eyes only for Diane.[7] Her initial D adorns practically every decoration and piece of masonry executed for the King during his reign. The day he was killed in a tournament, at the age of forty, by a splinter of wood which lodged in his eye, Henri II was wearing, as usually, the colors of "his lady", black and white. Diane was sixty at the time.

Meanwhile, the Reformation had made tremendous progress in France under the leadership of Calvin who eventually established himself in Geneva and ruthlessly persecuted the Catholics who happened to fall under his hand. Many aristocrats and men of high position openly became "Huguenots".[8] The royal persecution which became fierce at times, as is often the case, only strengthened the Protestants' will to persevere. The real confrontation did not start until 1559, at the death of Henri II, which gave Catherine de Médicis the opportunity to play the political role she had always coveted. The participants of the anti-Catholic "Conjuration d'Amboise", who

---

[6]The dauphin had died of a sudden illness.

[7]He gave her the château de Chenonceaux, which after his death Catherine made Diane exchange for Chaumont.

[8]The word comes from the German "Eidgenosse", or member of a group bound by oath.

Charles IX

Diane by Jean Goujon
(formerly at the château
d'Anet, today at the
Musée du Louvre)

Henri III

Henri IV

had plotted the kidnapping of the sickly young dauphin (he was married to Mary Stuart and reigned for a brief few months as François II), were dealt an exemplary punishment; their corpses were hung from a balustrade at the château d'Amboise which can still be seen today by visiting tourists. When François II's brother Charles IX became king at the age of ten, Catherine was running the kingdom with the help of the Guises and the so-called "religious wars" broke out with unsurpassed violence. The worst atrocities such as torture, burning and wholesale butchering of adversaries were committed on both sides. While Catholics were executing Huguenots, Protestants were vandalizing Catholic churches, beheading statues and breaking stained glass windows. Some of the most outstanding masterpieces of Romanesque and Gothic art, such as Vézelay, became the victims of a destruction which was to find its equal only once more in French history, at the time of the 1789 Revolution.

While apparently trying to reach a reconciliation with the Protestants, Catherine seems to have panicked and in 1572 persuaded Charles IX to order the terrible massacre of Huguenots on the feast day of Saint Bartholomew, which was to mark the wedding of his sister Marguerite with the future Henri IV. The ill-famed "Saint-Barthélémy" is one of the most tragic events in all French history. The young king is said to have died of remorse and grief two years later and without posterity.

A third son of Catherine, Henri III, then ascended the throne. He left a sad reputation and the dubious record of having been the worst king of two countries, France and Poland, where he had been elected to the throne.[9] As soon as he received the news of his brother's

---

[9] At a swearing-in ceremony at Notre-Dame in Paris in September 1573, Henri had to accept the conditions set for his employment as king of Poland. When he came to the article concerning religious freedom, which had been passed by the Polish Diet, he tried to miss the clause in question, but had to give in after being sternly reminded "Si non jurabis non regnabis," "If you do not swear, you will not reign" (according to Adam Zamoyski, *The Polish Way*, Franklin Watts, N.Y., 1988). Some Polish influences which lingered for many years in the court ceremonial at Versailles date back to Henri III. Poland was at the time the largest kingdom in Europe, extending from the Baltic to the Black Sea. The "polonaise,"

death, he left Cracow secretly by night, and reached Paris with the apparent intention of making concessions to the Protestants. His plans were countered by the Duc de Guise, who was himself eyeing the crown. Henri III got rid of this awesome rival by perpetrating the most famous murder in French history.[10] Barely a year later, Henri III himself was stabbed to death by a fanatic monk. Just before he died, the childless Henri designated as successor to the throne his cousin and brother-in-law, Henri de Navarre. This Protestant prince, who eventually reigned as Henri IV, was forced to wage a several years long war and convert to Catholicism in order to become king.[11]

Henri IV is known to have been the "father of his people" and the best ruler France ever had. He also signed the most important act of toleration in French history, the Edict of Nantes which made the freedom of religion not only a privilege, but the right of every French citizen.

Letters, Architecture and Art in the 16th Century

The Renaissance—"re-awakening"—which swept through all of the Western world, was brought about by a number of facts mentioned above. It was a period marked by the release of vital energy in all domains, by curiosity, adventurousness, enthusiasm, exuberance, optimism and boundless faith in scientific progress and in man's potential.

which became the opening dance at royal balls throughout Europe in the 17th century, was first performed at a celebration of Henry III's arrival in Cracow.

[10] He underhandedly invited Guise to the château de Blois, where he had him repeatedly stabbed by his guards. The chamber in which the sinister event took place is visited yearly by thousands of tourists.

[11] He is reputed to have said: "Paris is well worth a mass." Henri IV's crowning marks the ascent to the French throne of the Bourbon-Capetians, who are descendants in direct line of Saint-Louis.

The spirit of the Renaissance is often referred to as *humanism*, which is characterized by a shift from other-worldly to secular concerns, by the admiration for classical antiquity, by the cult of beauty, the respect for man and a new interest in the enjoyment of life to its fullest. Man became the center of attention and the newly exonerated human body served as an inspiration to artists in all the disciplines. Nude figures, which adorn the exterior as well as the interior of most Renaissance buildings, were the favorite subjects of sculptors and painters, while poets went so far as to sing each individual detail of a woman's face and body in short, sometimes daring poems called "blasons" which enjoyed great popularity at the time. Pleasure, no longer reprehensible, became an art in itself, as society experienced an unprecedented "joie de vivre". Man felt that both his spirit and his body had been liberated from former constraints: he felt, indeed, confident in his greatness and strength, saw no limits to his possible achievements and envisaged the advent of a perfect society marked by freedom, tolerance and progress in all domains.

The "wish to return to the sources" and the rediscovery of the pagan antiquity made possible by the influx of classical texts after the fall of Byzantium led to the study of Hebrew, Latin and Greek and brought about the vogue of ancient philosophies, such as neoplatonism, epicurism, stoicism and skepticism. These currents are all reflected in the French literature of the period, which is best represented in the works of Rabelais during the first part of the century, of the Pléiade poets toward the middle of the century, and of Montaigne in the late 1500's.

Rabelais' satirical novel, known today as *Gargantua and Pantagruel*,[12] relates the lives of two lovable giants and embodies the spirit of the early Renaissance. Still medieval in its pedantic quest for encyclopedic knowledge, its misogyny, coarse humor, vulgarity, and verbal ingenuity, it is truly a Renaissance work by its love of

---

[12] Rabelais has left a lasting imprint not only on Western thought, but on the vocabulary as well. Most of us understand what is meant by "Rabelaisian humour" and, while the English speaking world talks about a "Gargantuan appetite", the French call an enormous meal "un repas pantagruélique".

life, its rejection of asceticism, of the folly of warfare and of all forms of political and religious tyranny, its optimism and faith in man's intrinsic goodness, as seen in the utopian dream of the "ideal" abbey of "Thélème.[13]

The Pléiade, a group of seven poets of which the best known is Ronsard, was named after a constellation of seven heavenly bodies in the sky. These poets rejected the lingering medievalism in French poetry and tried to impose a new poetic system based on classical, mainly Greek, themes and forms. They also tried to enrich the French language by coining new words so as to make it suitable for the expression of the highest poetic thought. They proclaimed the dignity of the poet who is, according to them, filled with inspiration and enthusiasm[14] or god-possessed, and therefore immortal. Following in the footsteps of the Italians, particularly Petrarch, they launched the vogue of the sonnet, which has been held in high esteem for centuries in France.

In the latter part of the 16th century, at a time when the ferocity of religious wars and the unyielding fanaticism on the part of both the Catholics and the Protestants had dampened the original optimism of the first Renaissance, **Montaigne** published one of the most significant books in world literature. His *Essais* (1580) or "Trials" mark the birth of a new literary genre, the essay. While the subject of this loosely constructed work is the study of himself, Montaigne's meditations touch upon all and anything that concerns man in his baffling diversity. Montaigne constantly asks the question "Que sais-je?" (What do I know?), and does not attempt to find an answer. But he examines, describes, ponders, compares, and illustrates with concrete examples drawn from the vast knowledge he succeeded in accumulating during long years of observation and extensive reading. Montaigne had embraced in turn epicurism, stoicism and skepticism, but the evolution of his thought eventually led him to a philosophy of acceptance and he concludes on a serene note of faith in the goodness of Nature. While Montaigne never tries to preach or teach, the *Es-*

---

[13] See Appendix.
[14] From Greek "entheos", filled with god (Theos-God).

sais are a powerful lesson in tolerance and understanding, based on the concept of relativity of human needs, beliefs and behavior, such as can be seen in two of his famous essays, "Of Cannibals" and "Of the Education of Children." They both strike an amazingly modern note (see Appendix).

The architecture of the French Renaissance, which has basically followed the Italian models, is embodied in a variety of buildings, such as townhalls, but is best represented in the innumerable châteaux scattered throughout France and most impressively concentrated in the Loire valley, where some 120 of these graceful structures can still be viewed today. These châteaux feature three distinct "Renaissance styles". The earliest, sometimes called "style Louis XII" is often a mixture of a predominantly Gothic structure with some Italian Renaissance decorations. Such are the Louis XII wing of Blois and Amboise. The second, referred to as "1re Renaissance française" evolved during the reign of François I: many of these châteaux are endowed with a multiplicity of Italian Renaissance elements (pilasters, loggias, galleries, balconies, niches, etc), though without any visible concern for regularity and symmetry. But they still keep the French high roofs and the basic plan of a château fort, as well as some vestiges of its defense system, such as watchtowers, machicolation and sentry walks. Some of the best known châteaux belonging to this period are Blois;[15] Azay-le-Rideau, a real gem situated on a tributary of the Loire; Chenonceaux, the bone of contention between Catherine and Diane; and Chambord with its exuberant, exaggerated and overloaded roofs, its multiplicity of chimneys, turrets and lanterns which led Chateaubriand to compare it to a "beauty with windblown hair". The third style, called "2e Renaissance française" tends toward truly classical regularity and symmetry, with façades divided into stories according to the meticulously calculated "orders" established in antiquity. The stress on verticality has made way for a new balance between vertical and horizontal lines and, while the Gothic seems to invite movement, this type of Renaissance building

---

[15]The François I wing, with its "Loggia façade" and octogonal stairway conceived by Leonardo da Vinci.

with its essentially flat surfaces tends to appear as static. Parts of the Louvre belong to the later Renaissance, and particularly graceful is Pierre Lescot's Cour Carrée, which is naturally one of the monuments in Paris known to nearly every visitor to France. Yet another superb historic structure closely associated with the Renaissance is Fontainebleau, which cannot be omitted from a tourist's itinerary, and which is called by the French "la maison des siècles", since it was used as a residence by every single reigning French monarch and bears the important imprint of the three great kings of the 16th century: François I, Henri II and Henri IV.[16]

While Italian architects, as mentioned above, had been invited to France to launch the new building style, several of their French counterparts also achieved considerable renown during the Renaissance, particularly Pierre Lescot and Philibert Delorme (or de l'Orme), who was the choice of François I, Catherine de Médicis and Diane de Poitiers and who is responsible for parts of Fontainebleau, Catherine's gallery at Chenonceaux, her no longer existing Palais des Tuileries (it was at one time connected with the Louvre) and Diane's château d'Anet. He is also believed to have sketched the plan of Rabelais' ideal Abbey of Thélème.

Among the many sculptors of the 16th century, Jean Goujon deserves a special mention: his bas-reliefs adorn, among others, Lescot's façade of the Louvre, the Musée Carnavalet and the Fontaine des Innocents in Paris. He also created a number of versions of the goddesss Diana the best known of which is now at the Louvre. Some of the most striking sculpture and statuary of the time can be admired at the French kings' necropolis of St. Denis: the traditional "gisants" of monarchs and queens, resting side by side in royal garb, feet together and hands folded in prayer, have now been replaced by practically nude corpses carved in stone, only partly covered by the folds of their shrouds, and immortalized in the last convulsions of

---

[16] Napoleon also loved Fontainebleau; the château houses scores of souvenirs of the Emperor. A museum devoted to the Bonaparte family was added in one of the wings in 1986.

agony[17](see fig.).

As far as painting is concerned, the French artists are definitely overshadowed by the Italians: two of the most prominent ones, Rosso and Primaticcio, decorated Fontainebleau and were the initiators of the so-called "School of Fontainebleau", which set the tone for French painters for some ninety years, well into the beginning of the 17th century. In the art of portraiture, the outstanding name is that of the Clouets—father and son—who immortalized in paintings and drawings not only the Valois kings and kin, but all the notables of the period as well (François I, Henri II, Catherine de Médicis, Diane de Poitiers, François II, Charles IX, Henri III, Elisabeth de Valois, Admiral Coligny and the Guise family, among many others).

In music, Clément Janequin assured the continuity of what had been called the "golden age" of French music at the time of Josquin des Prés. Janequin composed, outside of several masses, psalms, and motets, over three hundred "chansons" or songs which became widely disseminated thanks to the invention of printing. Another 16th century composer, Roland de Lassus, put into music some of the works of the Pléiade poets and particularly those of Ronsard.

WHAT TO SEE

- Châteaux of: Anet*
    Amboise* and Clos-Lucé
    Azay-le Rideau**
    Blois***
    Chambord***
    Chantilly***
    Chaumont*
    Chenonceaux***
    Cognac (birthplace de François I)

---

[17] Such are the tombs of Louis XII and Anne de Bretagne, of François I and Claude de France (by Bontemps) and Henri II and Catherine de Médicis (by Germain Pilon).

Fontainebleau***
St. Germain-en-Laye (near Paris)
- Paris: The basilica of St. Denis (16th century royal tombs)
- The Musée Carnavalet—sculptures by Jean Goujon
- "Fontaine des Innocents"—sculptures by Jean Goujon
- The Louvre: façade built by Lescot
  sculptures by Goujon
  "La Joconde" and other paintings by Da Vinci
- Ecouen: (Ile de France)
  Musée de la Renaissance
- In the Dordogne: Montaigne's château
- In Chinon: statue of Rabelais
- Near Chinon: La Devinière, house where Rabelais was born,
  and museum

Montaigne

Sully

Henri IV's statue on Pont-Neuf

Château de Sully s/Loire

by Quesnel

Chapter 6

THE SEVENTEENTH CENTURY: THE AGE OF ABSOLUTISM AND CLASSICISM

The Beginning of the Century: Henri IV

Henri IV's all too brief reign inscribed itself in golden letters in France's history. His wise minister, the Protestant Sully, is to a great extent responsible for the remarkable reputation the King has been enjoying for almost four centuries, since it is also known that Henri devoted much of his time to innumerable love affairs and richly deserved his nickname of "Vert-galant". Married to the equally love-hungry daughter of Catherine de Médicis, Marguerite de Valois[1] —"la reine Margot"—who, as is said, could not stand her

---

[1] The French Court had originally hoped to marry her off to the King of Portugal and in 1559 sent to Lisbon a certain Jean Nicot to engineer the union. Nicot failed in his mission, but managed to ingratiate himself with Catherine de Médicis by initiating her to the virtues of tobacco, which was called at the time "nicotiane", or "Médicée" or else "the queen's herb." It was supposed to cure

husband's strong odor of garlic[2] and looked for amorous adventures wherever she could find them, the King was able to divorce her, since she had given him no heirs. After the sudden death of his beloved Gabrielle d'Estrées, whom he had intended to make his new spouse, he accepted a "marriage of reason" with the unattractive Marie de Médicis. The new queen gave birth to several royal children.

Henri's chief preoccupation was, however, the well-being of his country: an equestrian bronze statue of the King, prominently displayed in the middle of the Pont-Neuf which he had widened and completed, still reminds Parisians as well as all visitors to the capital of the great merits of his reign. Swamps were drained, agricultural techniques improved and France became endowed with the most modern network of canals and roads in the world. Bridges were built and roads were lined with rows of elm trees which shielded troops and travelers from the discomforts of sun and heat. Even today drivers in France during the summer months find it much more pleasant to take the old "routes nationales" than the scorching new "autoroutes" (expressways). Mulberry trees, on which the silk worm feeds, were planted in the south and this gave rise to a flourishing silk industry in the Lyon region. The King also encouraged navigation and sea ventures and it was with his blessing that Champlain established in 1608 the city of Québec on the St. Lawrence river. Henri also showed genuine concern about the lot of his people and tried to improve the life standard of the common man: he expressed the wish that each Frenchman have "a chicken in the pot on Sundays" (this famous saying was to be later repeated by one of the presidents of the United States of America).

---

toothache and headaches and help heal wounds.

[2] Right after his birth at the château de Pau in the Béarn, Henri's father smeared his lips with garlic juice and put a drop of local wine saying: "Thou shalt be a true Béarnais."

WHAT TO SEE

- In the southwest of France: the château de Pau in the Béarn, birthplace of Henri IV.
- In Paris: The Pont Neuf
  The Louvre: "La Grande Galerie" which was built by Henri IV to connect the Louvre with the Tuileries and which today shelters masterpieces of European painting.

Louis XIII • Richelieu

At the time when Henri IV was felled by the murderous dagger of Ravaillac in 1610, his son by his second wife was only nine years old. The personal reign of the new king, Louis XIII, was preceded by the regency of his limited and frivolous mother,[3] a time marked by ineptitude, scandal and a resurgence of intrigues plotted by the most influential and power hungry feudal families in the country. The Queen Mother's shameless favorites Concini and his wife were eventually put to death on the young King's orders. When Louis took the reins of the kingdom in his own hands, he realized that his prime objectives were to consolidate the royal power and to subdue at the same time the turbulent nobility and the Protestants who had created since the Edict of Nantes a sort of "state within the state."

After much hesitation, the King put his trust in the minister who eventually was to play the most important role of all ministers in French history: the renowned cardinal Richelieu. Richelieu paved the way for the absolutism that was to mark the French monarchy for the next hundred and fifty years and prepared the never-to-be-equalled glorious reign of Louis XIV.

---

[3] One of Marie de Médicis' very few merits lies in the fact that she commissioned Rubens to glorify the royal family in a series of masterpieces which are now displayed at the Louvre.

Louis XIII, called Louis-the-Pious, or Louis-le-Juste, was timid, withdrawn and overly religious. It seems that history has as yet not pronounced its final judgment on him as a person. Misogynic, and yet capable of sublime though unfulfilled love, such as his enraptured feelings for Mlle d'Hautefort and Mlle de La Fayette, the King habitually neglected his Spanish wife Anne of Austria, and distrusted her, probably with good reasons.[4] At one time the Queen actually faced the danger of being tried and sentenced for treason. Things changed completely in 1638 when "the miracle" happened and Anne gave birth, after more than twenty years of marriage, to the royal couple's son and heir who was to become the most famous of all French kings, Louis XIV.[5]

The last word has probably not been said, either, about Richelieu: implacable, calculating, capable of the lowest of deceits, ruses and hypocrisy, he stopped at nothing to achieve his goals. Cruel and unforgiving, hated by all including those who served him, he was, more for his "blood stained" hands than for the color of his ecclesiastical gear, called the "red Cardinal" by generations of writers, particularly the Romanticists. Richelieu inflicted exemplary punishment on those who dared disobey his orders or endlessly plotted his assassination: he leveled the most formidable fortified castles of his enemies and publicly executed members of even the most prominent and prestigious families.[6]

But Richelieu's true goal was to serve the monarchy and bring prosperity and power to the country. His ministry brought about not only military and political victories to France—he eventually

---

[4] In the long war that opposed France and Spain she did seem to favor her native country and attempted to give secret information to her brother, the Spanish monarch. Her romance with the handsome Duke of Buckingham which underlies the plot of Dumas' *The Three Musketeers* continues to inspire writers and historians of our day. Richelieu may have indeed been in love with the Queen, and, feeling rejected, ceaselessly accumulated evidence against her.

[5] Two years later, a second son was born to Anne and Louis, Philippe d'Orléans, called "Monsieur."

[6] Richelieu had prohibited dueling, and in order to defy the Minister, Montmorency openly fought a duel on the Place de la Grève: he was beheaded.

humbled and contained the all powerful Hapsburgs—but also internal order and stability together with respect for the Crown. He subdued the Huguenots at the famous siege of la Rochelle (1628) and reduced the aristocracy's influence to such an extent that it did not take much effort on the part of Louis XIV to turn the proudest heads of the kingdom into his obedient personal attendants and servants.

Richelieu was, moreover, a true Maecenas and a great lover of art and literature. He displayed a particular interest in the theatre and his encouragement doubtlessly had a bearing on the unsurpassed dramatic production in 17th century France which boasts such names as Corneille, Racine and Molière. The Cardinal attempted to make Paris the artistic and literary capital of the West and in 1635 founded the French Academy which is still the most prestigious of all literary institutions in the world.[7] Due to Richelieu's efforts, the French language achieved a supremacy all over Europe which was to last for several centuries, although the "classical" need of clarity and conciseness led 17th century doctrinaires to purify and prune it to the point of eventually impoverishing it.

In spite of innumerable conspiracies and attempts on his life, the most famous and heartbreaking of which ended in the execution of Louis XIII's young favorite, Cinq-Mars, Richelieu died a natural death in 1642, several months before his King's demise. On his deathbed, he recommended as his successor another cardinal, the Italian Mazarin who, in a much less brilliant way, was almost as instrumental as his predecessor in bringing the royal power to its apogee.

Mazarin was practically the exact opposite of Richelieu: he did not brandish his power, seemed accommodating and, as a good diplomat, hardly ever said "no." But he was perseverant and tenacious and surpassed in cunning, deviousness and intrigue the most skillful statesmen in history. Since Louis XIV was only five at the time of

---

[7] The "Académie" is made up of forty prominent literary figures or "Immortals". Being admitted to this illustrious body can occur only at the death of one of its members. Almost 350 years after its foundation, the Belgian born Marguerite Yourcenar was the first woman ever to be invited to become an Academician.

Richelieu by Champaigne

Louis XIV by Bernini

Château de Rambouillet

1675 — 1975

his father's death, Anne of Austria was named regent and Mazarin became the right hand of the Queen Mother. He soon also occupied an important place in her heart and many historians believe that the couple was actually united in secret wedlock.[8]

The Reign of Louis XIV

Mazarin appeared to many members of aristocracy a weak man and the time seemed ripe for overthrowing the arbitrary power of the royal government. The so called "Importants"—members of the most illustrious families in the kingdom—decided to make an attempt at regaining their past influence. The first protest was launched by the Parlement and resulted in an internal struggle called "la Fronde" or "sling", which lasted roughly from 1648 to 1652 and resulted in the complete victory of the throne, the regent and the prime minister. When the latter died in 1661, Louis XIV, whose childhood had been deeply marked by various humiliations endured during the Fronde,[9] decided not to share with anybody what became the most absolute rule in all French history. Louis' supreme authority is often considered as best encapsulated in one of his lapidary sayings: "L'Etat, c'est moi" ("*I* am the State").

Before his death, Mazarin managed to engineer the marriage of Louis XIV with the Spanish infanta Marie-Thérèse of Austria, although the young monarch was enamored with Mazarin's own niece, Marie Mancini. The Spanish princess was short and homely and Louis never felt genuine love for her. He consoled himself with scores of favorites, the most notorious of which were Mlle de La Vallière and the unsuperseded charmer, Mme de Montespan.[10] They not

---

[8] At the time, the title of Cardinal was not necessarily bestowed upon an ordained priest, and Mazarin was not bound by vows of celibacy.

[9] At one time, the royal family was forced to flee from the Louvre palace by night.

[10] Her husband, a noted exception in the 17th century, did not feel flattered by

only played official roles at the court, but begat numerous royal children who were later "legitimated" by the King. In spite of his open liaisons with other women, Louis never neglected his own wife, and she gave birth to six offspring. Only one son survived, but he was the most important of all, the Grand Dauphin, heir to the throne. The Grand Dauphin had in turn three sons of his own, the oldest of which was blessed by the birth of two young boys. At that time the succession to the French throne seemed assured beyond any reasonable doubt: nobody could have foreseen that shortly before his death Louis XIV would lose to contagious disease his son, his grandson and the older of his two baby great-grandsons: the younger one was fortunately saved from the homicidal practices of the doctors—such as the bleeding of infants as well as of adults—by his governess and thus survived to become Louis XV.

Louis XIV's reign is known as "le grand règne" and lasted for 72 years (1643-1715). The Sun-King's glory was reflected not only in the grandiose lifestyle and truly indescribable magnificence of this court, first at the Louvre and then at Versailles, but also in all French arts and letters of his time. The unifying element in the architecture of the Versailles palace which best embodies Louis' aspirations is the ever present symbol of Apollo, who represents the Sun-King lending his light to the world. The three major artists who were instrumental in the planning of this most famous château in the world, Le Vau, Le Brun, and Le Nôtre, were actually discovered not by Louis XIV, but by his superintendent of finance, Nicolas Foucquet, who had hired this remarkable team to erect and decorate his sumptuous residence in Vaux-le-Vicomte.

Foucquet had been appointed by Mazarin, and, following in his protector's footsteps, amassed tremendous riches which were made accessible to him by the office he held. He was, however, not only immensely wealthy, but also discriminating: the very embodiment of elegance, good taste and refinement. Among others, La Fontaine,

the attention the King bestowed upon his wife. He dressed in mourning clothes and lamented in public the loss of his spouse, until the irate Louis had him banished from the court.

Molière and the great Lully were invited to write and perform for this connoisseur of arts and literature. In order to inaugurate his delightful residence in Vaux which was close to completion, Foucquet unwittingly gave a magnificent reception intended to dazzle and amuse the young King: instead, it filled the monarch with envy and wrath. Prompted by the jealous Colbert who coveted Foucquet's position, Louis had the Superintendent arrested almost immediately after the festivities.[11] Following a lengthy lawsuit which left dismal impressions of the King's sense of justice in the memories of the social elite of the time, and which Mme de Sévigné retold step by step in a series of witty and fascinating letters, Foucquet was sentenced to banishment. Louis, showing his vengefulness and the implacable side of his character, commuted the sentence to life imprisonment and the Superintendent ended his days in the gruesome fortress of Pignerol. His death, shrouded in unclear circumstances, is often linked by historians, researchers and fiction writers with the mysterious story of the "Masque de fer" ("Man in the iron mask"), whose identity has never been established, and who spent a number of years in this awesome prison. Several such sinister enigmas, like the sudden death of "Madame,"[12] the twenty-six-year-old sister-in-law of the King, and the frightening "affaire des poisons" in which Mme de Montespan herself was implicated, show the dark side of this dazzling reign and have prompted a number of authors to write about what is called the "envers (the ugly side) du grand siècle."

Louis confiscated Foucquet's possessions and took in to his service the artists who had worked for the Superintendent: they became the shining stars of his court and helped enhance the splendor of his reign. The King became a Maecenas himself and it is to a great extent due to the royal patronage that French literature attained during this period an unparalleled perfection. Louis' entire entourage, including his delightful sister-in-law, the English princess Henriette, and the

---

[11] Foucquet's disgrace may actually have been contemplated by Louis several months earlier.

[12] Henriette d'Angleterre, daughter of the unhappy king of England Charles I and Louis XIII's sister, Henriette de France.

inquisitive and vivacious Mme de Montespan, took an active part in the artistic and literary life of the country, encouraged and inspired artists, poets and composers and held in their palaces performances of dramas written by the foremost playwrights. Many of Molière's comedies were premiered in royal or aristocratic residences.

Louis' love of art, women, hunting and festivities and the multifarious court ceremonials he had imposed on others as well as on himself did not distract him in any way from the work of government, which he took very seriously. The King never seemed bored with it or overwhelmed by its responsibilities and considered it a mission: he was, in his own view, a "monarque de droit divin", a divinely appointed instrument of God's will and the representative of God on earth.[13]

Louis was particularly interested in foreign affairs, in diplomatic policy and in the waging of wars, for he saw in victorious battles the consecration of his glory. He also attempted to give France economic stability and independence. Since he distrusted the nobility—he had put members of the once proud and insubordinated aristocracy at his personal service—his ministers were chosen from among the bourgeoisie. The most capable, hardworking and influential of them was Colbert, who did a superb job of economic and fiscal consolidation. His mercantilist policies or "colbertisme" were designed to impede imports by the imposition of high tariffs and by bans on the shipment of foreign goods. At the same time, he subsidized French shippers and manufacturers and created government-owned industries of certain luxury goods, such as the Saint-Gobain glass and the famous Gobelins tapestry works which are still in operation today.[14] He

---

[13] Every year, he touched with his own hands hundreds of people afflicted with scrofula: it was believed that the King was endowed with healing powers for that disease which is also known in England as the King's evil.

[14] In 1954, following the initiative of Guerlain, a dozen representatives of the greatest French "de luxe" crafts and industries banded together under the name "Comité Colbert" to renew the 17th century "visionary" minister's time honored concepts of good taste, quality and professional pride. In 1988 the Comité Colbert included 70 companies connected with the French "art of living": gastronomy, fashion design, interior decoration and the manufacturing of crystal,

also took interest in France's colonial growth[15] and helped rebuild the navy and merchant marine. Colbert extended his authority also over the arts, reorganized the Academy of Painting and Sculpture, founded the Academy of Science and the Academy of Architecture as well as an art academy for French students in Rome. But his main preoccupation, at which he worked indefatigably, was to fill the royal treasury, forever overextended by the staggering cost of the building of Versailles and other luxurious residences and continuous wars initiated by the King against other European states.

Louis XIV was, indeed, a very bad neighbor: he annexed in time of peace and without forewarning coveted territories while spreading death, carnage and terror. He also intermittently waged "declared wars."[16] It must be conceded that he strived for "natural frontiers" and gave France much of its present day shape.

The last years of Louis' reign were marred by a number of defeats at the hands of the Dutch, the Germans and the English. At the end of his seventy-two year long rule, Louis left France devastated, impoverished and exhausted. On his deathbed, the Sun-King cautioned his five-year-old great-grandson and heir to the throne against the errors he had committed and recommended that he pursue peace at all price. Though Louis failed to mention the importance of internal peace, his intolerance in matters of religion tore and ruined France and left perhaps deeper wounds than the wars he had sustained against foreign powers.

Religion played a very important role in the 17th century, during which French society was imbued with a strong religious spirit, despite the existence of a persistent "libertine" current (its manifestations became less and less open as Louis' absolute rule tightened its grip and dealt increasingly harshly with atheism). Catholicism

---

jewelry, perfume and leather goods.

[15]It is during Colbert's ministry that Cavelier de la Salle explored the Mississippi Valley and founded Louisiana, and that the colony of San Domingo was established.

[16]The war of 1702 was triggered by the "Spanish succession". The end result was the acceptance by Louis XIV of the Spanish crown for his grandson, Philippe d'Anjou, which marks the ascent of the Bourbons to the Spanish throne.

had found a new vitality in the Counter-reformation, and the 17th century gave France several of its best known saints[17] who changed not only the quality of spiritual life, but also the attitudes of the elite towards convicts and children born out of wedlock. Most of the aristocrats who lived in dissolution and even debauchery, such as the Grand Condé, his sister Mme de Longueville, who had been La Rochefoucauld's mistress, and his younger brother, the Prince de Conti, sooner or later converted and made their peace with God, at least in the face of death.

Within the ranks of the Catholics a violent conflict arose between the followers of strict morality with notions of predestination as exemplified by the Jansenists, with their center in the nunnery of Port-Royal, and the more mundane Jesuits who stressed the importance of man's free will. The Jansenists accused the Jesuits' casuistry of hypocrisy and laxity, and to ward off the persecution by the powerful Sorbonne, defended themselves with the help of one of the greatest minds of the century, the author of *Pensées*, Pascal. Pascal launched against the attackers a series of vehement and impassioned writings which appeared under the title *Les Provinciales*. Many members of the high aristocracy were attracted by the holiness and purity which emanated from the Abbey of Port-Royal and the exemplary life led by the "Solitaires", a group of men who had retired to Port-Royal-des-Champs and dispensed in their "petites écoles" an education of very superior quality.[18] The Jesuits, on the other hand, were concerned with setting moral standards which could be achieved not by an elitist minority, but by the vast majority of Christians under their guidance.[19] The King, who tolerated no disobedience in matters of

---

[17]St. François de Sales, founder of the order of Salesians, Sainte Chantal, grandmother of Mme de Sévigné and founder of the Order of Visitation, and the beloved St. Vincent de Paul who devoted his life to the most deprived, neglected and persecuted, such as "enfants trouvés" ("foundlings") and men convicted to the galleys. A famous film dating back to the 30s, *Monsieur Vincent*, is still regularly shown in art theatres.

[18]The famous playwright Racine had been a student of the "petites écoles."

[19]The Jesuits were excellent pedagogues and had established all over Europe schools for boys which were renowned for their outstanding instruction.

religion and was deeply convinced that all his subjects had a duty to share his kind of Catholicism in the name of the established doctrine "cujus regio, ejus religio",[20] took harsh measures against the Jansenists and eventually ordered the dispersion of the nuns and the destruction of the Abbey.

Louis acted even more brutally toward the Huguenots and made it a crime to remain a Protestant in a country where henceforth only Catholicism would be tolerated. In 1685, he revoked the Edict of Nantes granted by Henri IV and in doing so undoubtedly committed the worst error of his reign. The Huguenots were forced to convert and no means were spared against the recalcitrant ones, including the dreaded "dragonnades" and condemnation to the galleys. The most courageous and worthy Protestants chose not to change their faith under threat and fled abroad, bringing their valuable skills as artisans and craftsmen to neighboring countries,[21] while depriving France of its most industrious, solid and productive element.

The last years of the great reign were somber and depressing. The King, who had greatly loved women and distractions, turned to bigotry, partly under the influence of Mme de Maintenon, the widow of the burlesque poet Scarron and the governess of his illegitimate children with Mme de Montespan. Louis secretly married her, maybe as early as in 1683, the year of Marie-Thérèse's demise. Mme de Maintenon wielded a powerful influence during the next thirty years. It became fashionable to display austere mores, avoid festivities, linger in churches. The court was filled with "dévots" whom La Bruyère so aptly denounced as the most hypocritical brand of courtiers that ever existed. In spite of some measures which could be termed as generous—such as the erecting of the famous Hôtel des Invalides for the accommodation of disabled soldiers and veterans, and the melting of his solid gold dishes and service to cover the expenses caused by warfare—Louis had shown little concern for the well being of the masses of the French people: he had overburdened them with taxa-

---

[20] "The one who reigns imposes his religion."

[21] Some 5,000 French Huguenots who had emigrated to Berlin started this one-time small city on its path to prosperity and expansion.

tion and allowed to die of disease and starvation. As his corpse was being taken to the traditional royal necropolis of St. Denis, it was met on its way with insults, curses and jeers from the city's population who saw in the King's death a welcome relief from a loathsome reign and tyrannical oppression.

Literature, Architecture and Arts in the 17th Century • Classicism and Academicism

The powerful current called *Baroque*, which swept Europe at the beginning of the 17th century, affected French arts and letters to a much lesser degree than those in neighboring countries. The very word "baroque" (one of the several proposed etymologies traces its origins to the Portuguese "barroco" meaning irregular, or uneven) has always had a pejorative meaning in French, as it carries a connotation of overcharge, exaggeration and lack of taste. Until the first part of the 20th century authors writing in the "baroque" vein, such as Théophile de Viau and Saint-Amant were referred to as "irregular", "stray" or "misguided." Only quite recently has their original contribution to the world of letters been fully acknowledged and appreciated.

The Baroque in literature, which evolved within a society marked by the violence of religious wars and the turbulent years of Marie de Médicis' regency, is characterized by freedom, fancy, eccentricity, exuberance, profusion of detail and taste for the mysterious, the unexpected, the violent, the morbid and the macabre. It attempts to shock, calls for strong sensations and appeals to the senses. It also stresses the evanescent character of things and humans, and portrays, as Jean Rousset puts it, a "Protean" and multifaceted man in a universe of change and flux. *Classicism* on the other hand, which in France can be considered as a reaction to the Baroque,[22] appeals to

---

[22] The term "Baroque Classicism" is not used in French as the two words imply an opposition and a contrast.

the intellect and seeks out, underneath the "transitory," the *universal* and the *eternal* in man of all times and all places. Classicism, with its stress on reason, restraint, clarity of thought and expression, as well as hierarchy[23] and obedience, coincides with the advent of absolutism in France and reaches its apogee during the reign of the Sun-King. The author and the artist no longer try to astound or shock, but strive to please a refined and knowledgeable elite of "honnêtes gens"[24] by the perfection of their work, which must be sober, concise, logical, correct, social, impersonal, and above all, useful. They must display an interest in psychology and teach an edifying moral lesson, while following the strictest rules and regulations ever set by doctrinaires in the history of letters.

A seventeenth century playwright had to observe the so-called "three unities",[25] ban all violence, vulgarity and lowliness from the stage and avoid the mixing of comic and tragic elements.

Although Classicism did not succeed in stamping out either the *burlesque* with its coarse humor, or the lingering *préciosité* (which had been born in the salon of Mme de Rambouillet at the outset of the 17th century in an attempt to refine the crude speech and manners of French society and eventually degenerated into affectation, exaggeration and absurdity),[26] it did impose itself as the predominant aesthetics of the *grand siècle*[27] and gave to French literature

---

[23] A "hierarchy" was established for the different literary genres, with the epic and tragedy at the top of the list.

[24] The "honnête homme" was the prevailing type in Louis XIV's society. In contrast with the ostentatious "généreux" of the first part of the century, he was modest, polite, well read, extremely refined and the epitome of good taste.

[25] Of "time", "place" and "action." For the sake of verisimilitude, a single problem had to arise and get resolved in a single day (or roughly 24 hours), while taking place in a single well-defined locality or area (such as could be created on the stage within the scope of a single theatrical performance).

[26] The reluctance to call things by their names and the striving for originality led to the use of such ridiculous metaphors as "commodities of conversation" for armchairs, "thrones of modesty" for cheeks and "mirrors of the soul" for eyes.

[27] In the third part of the century, a literary controversy arose within the ranks of the "classicists": it was called "La Querelle des Anciens et des Modernes" and focused on the relative merits of authors of the classical antiquity and those of

some of its greatest names ever.

Descartes laid the foundation for the emergence of European rationalism. A great mathematician and scientist in his own right, Descartes the philosopher tried to prove the sovereignty of reason in his landmark treatise *Le Discours de la méthode*, where he affirms that man is capable of arriving at the truth by the sole activity of his "bon sens" or reason, if he knows how to "guide it properly". After making a clean slate of all the previously acquired knowledge by means of "universal doubt", Descartes arrives at one certainty: the very act of doubting implies that man thinks, and therefore exists. The "Cogito ergo sum" (I think, therefore I am) is one of the most often quoted sentences of all times (as mentioned above, many Frenchmen consider themselves as being "Cartesian" or disciples of Descartes, i.e. clear thinking and behaving logically, according to the rules of reason).[28]

Pascal who also was a genial mathematician and scientist, first tried his hand at literature in the *Provinciales*, written in defense of the persecuted Jansenists whose ideas he had espoused. In this work already he appears as an extremely brilliant prose writer. But his true glory rests in his unfinished collection of *Pensées* (Thoughts) which were to be an apology of the Christian religion. These are as widely read today as in the 17th century, not only because of the beauty and purity of style and the profoundness of the meditation on "man's fate", but because of its link with modern Christian existentialist ideas as well.

Pascal was a "moralist" in the 17th century meaning of the

---

contemporary writers. The "quarrel" continued well into the 18th century.

[28] See above, Part I. Alan Bloom's 1987 bestseller *The Closing of the American Mind*, upholds an accepted stereotype: "Every Frenchman is born, or at least early on becomes Cartesian or Pascalian...Descartes and Pascal represent a choice between reason and revelation, science and piety, the choice from which everything else follows...The opposition between *bon sens* and faith against all odds, set in motion a dualism that we recognize when we speak both of French clarity and of French passions." (Let us not forget that while Pascal was a great scientist, Descartes was a true believer in God, whose existence he made every attempt to prove in his *Discours*.)

word. So were many other great authors of the time, including **La Rochefoucauld**, renowned for the incisive spirit of his *Maximes*; La Bruyère, who sketched masterful, realistic and unflattering vignettes of 17th century French society in the *Caractères*; and the beloved **La Fontaine**, who has been enchanting entire generations of young and old readers with the wisdom and the incomparable poetic quality of his *Fables*.

And so were, naturally, the three great playwrights of the century mentioned above, since the theatre, too, was geared to didacticism: tragedy was supposed to bring about the Aristotelian "catharsis"[29] and comedy attempted to correct men by means of laughter: "castigat ridendo mores."

Whereas **Corneille** captured the spirit of the heroic aristocrat or *généreux* of the first part of the 17th century in lofty plays, such as *Le Cid* and *Horace*, the tragedies of **Racine** are the true embodiment of the classical ideal. *Phèdre* is in particular both in composition and in style a unique and unparalleled masterpiece. **Molière** is known as the father of modern comedy. He succeeded in proving the validity of some of the basic tenets of French classicism, since his "universal" types such as the Miser, the Hypocrite, the Social Climber, the Misanthrope, and the Hypochondriac appeal to theatregoers in the 20th century as much as they did in his own time. A number of Molière's plays, notably *L'Avare*, *Tartuffe*, *Le Bourgeois Gentilhomme*, *Le Misanthrope*, *Le Malade imaginaire*, *Les Précieuses ridicules* and *Le Médecin malgré lui* (*The Doctor in Spite of Himself*) are regularly included in the répertoires of major theatres throughout the world.

Two women—socialites and close friends—deserve a privileged place among the 17th century "greats": Mme de La Fayette, author of *La Princesse de Clèves*, who is credited with the creation of the modern "psychological novel", and **Mme de Sévigné** who became "an author in spite of herself" thanks to her fascinating and extremely voluminous correspondence. The hundreds of letters she

[29] The "purifying of emotions by art": in the case of tragedy, through the experiencing by the audience of "terror and pity" during the performance.

wrote, mostly to her beloved daughter Mme de Grignan, left us not only an intimate portrait of a 17th century "mondaine", but also an original account of events that took place in her time, and lively portrayal of life at Louis XIV's court.

As far as architecture is concerned, few truly baroque buildings exist in France (in Paris we find, for example, the church of Val-de-Grâce): the most beautiful square commissioned on the orders of Henri IV, the Place des Vosges, is characterized by classical symmetry and simplicity.[30] So are the Palais du Luxembourg, the Palais Royal and the Sorbonne. The most important architects of the 17th century were **François Mansart** who gave its origins to the word "mansarde" and built, among others, the château of Maisons-Laffitte and the Louis XIII wing at Blois, and Louis **Le Vau**, who erected Foucquet's Vaux-le-Vicomte in collaboration with the landscaper **Le Nôtre**. After Foucquet's arrest, both these architects were appointed by Louis XIV to work at Versailles.[31] The palace was eventually finished, after Le Vau's demise, by Jules **Hardouin-Mansart**. Hardouin-Mansart is also responsible for the Dôme of the Invalides in Paris and the Grand Trianon in Versailles. The powerful and grandiose, but at the same time elegant and harmonious "style Louis XIV" in architecture with its "giant order", classical flat roofs and frontons,can further be admired in the superb ensemble of the Place Vendôme, also by Hardouin-Mansart, and the Colonnade du Louvre designed by the Perrault brothers. Louis XIV chose to adopt their plans in preference to those of the great Bernini.

The Italian master did, however, leave an imprint of his stay in France, most importantly a very famous marble bust of Louis XIV; and his style also influenced, to a certain degree, not only the 17th century French "baroque" sculptor Puget, but also **Girardon** and **Coysevox** who are primarily responsible for the decorating of Versailles.

French painting flourished during the 17th century and boasts

---

[30] This elegant square in the Marais quarter has been recently restored to its original beauty after many decades of neglect.

[31] See above. Further detail in Appendix.

such names as Poussin, Le Lorrain, La Tour and Le Nain.

Nicolas Poussin, who spent most of his life in Rome, espoused the aesthetics of Classicism in reaction to the "chaos and exaggerations of the Baroque." His didacticism, choice of "noble genres" — religious, historical and mythological scenes which carry an edifying moral lesson and invite meditation on "reward and punishment"[32]— his use of geometrical, logical lines, stress on composition, careful proportioning and subdued hues[33] make him the classical master "par excellence." The Louvre alone possesses 41 of his paintings.

Claude Gellée, better known as **Le Lorrain** (he worked in Rome for some time as a pastry cook), created imaginary, idealized and truly enchanting landscapes, bathed in the rays of the rising or setting sun. The luminosity of his canvasses and the importance given to light and water have linked his name with the much more realistic art of 19th century Impressionists. The tricentenary of his death in 1982 was marked by the first exhibition devoted solely to his works: it opened in Washington, D.C. before going to the Grand Palais in Paris.

Also linked with Impressionism is the art of **Georges de La Tour**, whose nocturnal scenes in "chiaroscuro", frequently of religious inspiration,[34] feature a single source of light, such as a torch, lantern or candle, which lends to the tableau an almost mystical dimension (*Ste Marie-Madeleine, St. Jerôme, L'Adoration des Bergers* (shepherds), *St. Joseph, St. Sébastien*).

In an entirely different vein called "genre painting", the three **Le**

---

[32] Among his best known canvasses are: *Le Massacre des innocents, Les Bergers d'Arcadie* ("Et in Arcadia ego"), *L'Enlèvement des Sabines* (The Rape of the Sabine Women), *Orphée et Euridyce* (at the New York Metropolitan Museum) and *Sélène et Endymion* (at the Detroit Institute of Arts).

[33] The controversy which opposed two factions of French academicians in the 17th century, those who argued in favor of color and those who argued in favor of drawing or composition, was called "la Querelle des Rubénistes et des Poussinistes."

[34] La Tour, who also depicted "cardsharpers" and "soothsayers," was clearly influenced by the Italian school called the "Tenebrosi" and by Caravaggio's canvasses with spotlight effects.

126

Molière after Mignard

Pascal 1623–1662

CHARLES LE BRUN

LOUIS LE NAIN

Nain brothers who were influenced by the Flemish school, created realistic scenes of country life while endowing their humble peasants with a sense of dignity and an almost biblical greatness.

Several names stand out also in the field of portrait painting, notably that of Philippe de Champaigne (best remembered for this portrayal of Richelieu and the different members of the Jansenist community), **Mignard**, ("Mazarin", "Molière", and "Mme de Sévigné" among many others), as well as Rigaud and Largillière who left several commissioned portraits of the Sun-King.[35]

Charles Le Brun deserves separate mention, in spite of his superficial artificial and facile art. Discovered by Foucquet, he eventually became "first painter" at the court of Louis XIV and adorned the interior of Versailles with huge paintings of the King as a mythological god or as a victorious Greek or Roman hero. Le Brun was appointed by Colbert in 1663 to take charge of the Gobelins manufacture. An ardent admirer of Poussin, he rose to the position of head of the Academy of Painting and Sculpture and wielded a real dictatorship in the realm of fine arts.

The leaders of all the 17th century *Académies* were instrumental in carrying out the King's wishes and transmitting to the artists the royal patronage inherent in the "grand siècle" and translated it into the sphere of aesthetics. The French *academicism*, with its ideals of obedience to rules, restraint, order, symmetry, regularity, power and majesty, of which Versailles is the prime example, has exerted a true hegemony in the fields of French "beaux-arts" and "belles-lettres" well into the 19th century.

This hegemony became evident also in the realm of music at the time when the unscrupulous and cunning Italian composer Jean-Baptiste **Lully** became the head of the French Royal Academy of Music. Lully had ingratiated himself with the King by catering to his taste for ballet—Louis was an expert dancer himself and often appeared in court performances—and later for the opera. Lully sup-

---

[35] A superb exhibition of French 17th century art and documents entitled "The Sun-King: Louis XIV and the New World" was organized by the Louisiana State Museum and was featured also at the Corcoran Gallery of Art in 1984-85.

plied the music for several of Molière's "comédies-ballets" notably the ever popular *Bourgeois Gentilhomme*, but eventually abandoned the playwright, wishing to keep for himself the monopoly of all musical productions. This betrayal forced Molière to enlist the collaboration of another composer, Charpentier, who is responsible for the musical portions of his last comedy, *Le Malade imaginaire*.[36]

Toward the end of the century, French Classicism in music found a powerful expression in the works of **Couperin-le-Grand**, who succeeded in achieving a harmonious synthesis of the French and Italian musical traditions.

WHAT TO SEE

- Paris: Hôtel des Invalides
    Hôtel de Sully
    Musée Carnavalet (former residence of Mme de Sévigné)
        additions by Mansart; statue of Louis XIV by Coysevox
    Place des Vosges in the Marais
    Place Vendôme
    Place Dauphine on Ile de la Cité
    Palais-Royal (formerly Palais-Cardinal) built for Richelieu
        by Lemercier
    Sorbonne by Lemercier, tomb of Richelieu by Girardon
    "Institut" built by Le Vau (site of the Académie Française)
    Palais du Luxembourg, built for Marie de Médicis and
        decorated by Rubens, Poussin & Phillippe de Cham-
        paigne (today: the Sénat)
    Louvre: the "Colonnade" by the Perrault brothers
        the Cour Carrée
        paintings of the Royal Family by Rubens
        paintings of 17th century French masters

---

[36] Molière, who held the title role of the Hypochondriac in this play, was overtaken by convulsion during the final act of the fourth performance on February 17, 1673, and died almost immediately after, at the age of 51.

furniture, decorative arts
Bibliothèque Nationale (Hôtel Mazarin)
Val-de-Grâce church
Musée de la Monnaie (Hôtel Conti)
The Tuileries gardens designed by Le Nôtre

- Near Paris: Château de Maisons-Laffitte (Yvelines)
    Chantilly: château of the Grand Condé, museum, 17th
        stables and "live horse" museum
    Magny-les-Hameau: Musée des Granges de Port-Royal
    Maintenon: château (park by Le Nôtre)
    Rambouillet: château, museum and park
    Sceaux: Park by le Nôtre designed for Colbert (museum
        of the Paris region in 19th century château)
    St. Cloud: former residence of "Monsieur"
    St. Germain-en-Laye: château, birthplace of Louis XIV
    Vaux-le-Vicomte, near Fontainebleau: Foucquet's château
    Versailles: château, museum and park

- In the provinces:
    Brissac near Angers: château rebuilt in "style Louis XIII"
    Castres south of Albi: Musée Goya (formerly bishop's res-
        idence built by Hardouin-Mansart, park by Le Nôtre)
    Cheverny near Blois: château
    Château-Thierry near Soissons: birthplace of La Fontaine
        (museum)
    Rouen (Normandie): birthplace of Corneille (museum)
    Burgundy: Bussy-le-Grand, château of Mme de Sévigné's
        cousin, Bussy-Rabutin

*Château de
Maisons-Laffitte*

Louis XV by La Tour   Mme de Pompadour   Queen Marie
                              after Van Loo   by Nattier

Nancy: Place Stanislas

Chapter 7

THE EIGHTEENTH CENTURY: THE AGE OF ELEGANCE, ENLIGHTENMENT AND REVOLUTION

The Regency • Louis XV • Society in the 18th Century

The Sun-King had bequeathed to his successors at the same time a tradition of total absolutism, a sense of unprecedented grandeur, and a burden of irreducible debt which made of the 18th century a period of constant crisis.

As mentioned before, at the time of Louis XIV's death, his great-grandson and heir to the throne was only five years old and during his minority France was governed by the regent Philippe d'Orléans, son of Monsieur, Louis' younger brother. Philippe was not unintelligent; well aware of the need for change, he gave back to the Parlement the right of "remonstrance" which had been abolished by his uncle. But he was far from being truly dedicated to government. A handsome, affable, dissipated and debauched man, he loved sensual pleasures above all and spent much of his time on hitherto unprecedented orgies. Until he died in 1723 of apoplexy brought about by overeating, overdrinking and overindulging, his time was marked by insouciance and immorality. Finally liberated from old formalities and rigid etiquette, society's long repressed urge for fun and gaiety now found its fulfillment.

The Regency was marred by the unfortunate "Law affair". The Scot John Law—to some a genial adventurer, to others a crooked jailbird—was allowed to open a private bank in France which eventually became the Royal Bank and was granted monopoly of trading with Louisiana, the West Indies and Canada. In order to develop trade routes through New Orleans to the heartland of North America, Law started selling shares in the landed concession of the Mississippi Valley. The territory had to be colonized and since there were few volunteers, forced shipments of criminals and prostitutes were sent to the New World (the famous novel by abbé Prevost, *Manon Lescaut*, on which Massenet's opera is based, recounts the story of one such shipment). Law's entire system ended in bankruptcy and disaster, and as the "Mississippi bubble" burst, many Frenchmen lost their entire fortunes. To this day the capital city of Louisiana stands as a reminder of Philippe's unhappy regency.

Louis XV, according to custom, came of age at thirteen. He was married at fifteen to the Polish princess Marie Leszczynska,[1] six years his senior, but healthy, very devout, kind and intelligent. Louis was deeply in love with his wife who eventually became weary of bearing the King a child year after year. Louis XV then turned to innumerable mistresses, the most famous and influential of which was the beauteous "little bourgeoise" who received the title of Marquise de Pompadour. The most unfortunate of the King's favorites, Mme du Barry, was later guillotined for her flashy affair with the King.

---

[1] The French texts usually simplify the spelling of this name to Leczinska (and Leczinski).

Queen Marie's father, Stanislas Leszczynski,[2] was the dethroned king of Poland. Unable to help him regain his lost crown, Louis XV made his father-in-law ruler of Lorraine. The Duchy, which at his death reverted to France, still bears visible marks of the exemplary reign of this beloved mini-monarch, lover of peace, of his people, of literature and of all the arts. The Place Stanislas in Nancy is a true gem of 18th century architecture, sculpture and craftsmanship and is a must for all those who visit the Lorraine.

On his coming of age in 1723, Louis entrusted the government to his aging tutor, cardinal Fleury, and until his death the wise old man ran the country in an exemplary way: he brought it peace and economic recovery, while revitalizing its commerce and rebuilding its merchant marine.

The new prosperity France enjoyed at that time is visible today all over the country and mainly in Paris: one of the most famous squares in the world, the place de la Concorde[3] conceived by Jacques-Ange Gabriel, as well as innumerable luxurious private residences such as the Elysées Palace, bear witness to the beauty and elegance of 18th century architecture and the opulence of the capital's residents. Beauty and elegance were undoubtedly the very essence of the period in every aspect of life: charming interiors, much more intimate than those of the preceding century, graceful decors in the prevailing "Rococo" style, comfortable, curvilinear furniture, superb rugs, tapestries and china, especially from the royal manufacture at Sèvres. And, against this backdrop, beautiful men and women dressed in exquisite silks, brocades and lace; people in love with music, luxurious appointments, and capable of enjoying to its fullest the refinements of life and all things that bring delight to the eyes and all the senses.[4] The dream-like and sensuous quality of paintings by such artists as Watteau, Boucher and Fragonard render to perfection

---

[2] Stanislas is portrayed as one of the truly enlightened monarchs in Voltaire's most famous work *Candide*.

[3] It was at the time called Place Louis XV, then, as the guillotine erected in its center was doing its ugly job during the Reign of Terror, it became for a brief period the Place de la Révolution.

[4] Gastronomy, or the art of fine cooking, dates back to the 18th century.

the ambiance of this last century of the ancien régime, when it was "good to live," when the term "sweetness of life" used by Talleyrand had taken on a literal meaning. The fashion switched from grandeur and pomp to comfort, privacy and intimacy—as exemplified by the construction of Le Petit Trianon at Versailles—to whispered conversations in cozy boudoirs where love and "badinage" were the main preoccupation.

Instrumental in the shaping of mid-century taste was to a great extent Mme de Pompadour, be it in the matters of fashion, art or even literature. Intelligent, cultivated, witty, lively, and altogether charming—such as we see he painted by Quentin de la Tour in his most famous portrait of all—her task was to continually divert and amuse the usually bored King. A good actress in her own right (Louis had a theatre added to the Versailles palace with her in mind), she was a lover of drama and all forms of art and extended her encouragement and patronage to painters, such as Boucher, artisans, manufacturers of luxury goods and writers, including the *philosophes*.

Much less happy was her influence in the field of domestic and foreign affairs. After Fleury's demise Louis XV assumed, according to the pattern set by his great-grandfather, a personal rule. But he was ill suited to be his "own prime minister", and the "métier de roi" or "profession of king" held no interest for him. He increasingly relied on the counsel of his mistress and of various ministers, now peacemakers, now "hawks". The result was a haphazard both internal and external policy and a series of costly and disastrous wars, which ended not only in financial strain, but also in staggering territorial losses. France eventually had to give up Canada, the lands extending from the Appalachian mountains to the Mississippi, some islands in the Caribbean and practically all of its holdings in India.[5]

What prevailed at the court was corruption, debauchery and

---

[5]These territorial losses overseas were to a certain extent compensated at home by the reversion to France of Lorraine and by Louis' acquisition of Corsica in 1768. Even the most enlightened minds of the century had no understanding of the importance of colonies and Voltaire scornfully dismissed Canada as "quelques arpents de neige" ("several acres of snow").

scandalous spending: Mme de Pompadour and Louis XV are in turn credited with the famous or rather infamous saying: "Tout cela durera bien aussi longtemps que nous...après nous, le déluge" (This will surely last as long as we shall, after us, the deluge). The once "well beloved" King—he had been given at the beginning of his reign the the sobriquet of "Bien-aimé"—acquired little by little in the eyes of his people the image of an egotistical spendthrift and hated tyrant.[6]

Towards the end of his reign, Louis XV seemingly woke up from his habitual lethargy.[7] Ideas of the Enlightenment with an increasingly violent denunciation of tyranny and oppression, as expounded in the writings of Montesquieu, Voltaire, Diderot, and Rousseau, had been widely disseminated. The *philosophes* and many of the lucid thinking members of the nobility were demanding reforms and the King himself saw the need for action. But as every attempt at serious change in society met with the veto of the all powerful Parlement, Louis decided to abolish the traditional judiciary body and sent its members into exile. It was a daring move and would have doubtlessly been a salutary measure, had Louis XVI not had the weakness of revoking his grandfather's decree.

When Louis XV died of smallpox in 1774—he had to be taken to his burial place at St. Denis by night for fear of rioting—he left to his grandson a heavy legacy of fiscal and political problems. The country was ripe for revolution and the new young monarch totally unsuited for the handling of the difficult, almost insoluble problems that lay ahead of him.

---

[6] On today's Place de la Concorde , which was at the time place Louis XV, an equestrian bronze statue of the King had been erected, with, at the foot, allegoric figures representing the virtues. One day, the following verse had been inscribed on the statue: "Oh, la belle statue, oh, le beau piédestal!/Les vertus sont à pied, le vice est à cheval" ("Oh, the beautiful statue, oh, the lovely pedestal/Virtue is on foot, vice rides on horseback").

[7] There are numerous attempts today at rehabilitating Louis XV's reign which was traditionally regarded as perhaps the most disastrous in French history.

Louis XVI

Louis XVI was a man of good will and desirous of ruling well,[8] but he lacked intelligence and decisiveness and had no interest in government. One of the delights of his life was hunting and he indulged in his favorite distraction even on the day the Bastille was stormed, a detail which shows his poor judgment and total lack of understanding for the gravity of the situation. He also played at being a locksmith and achieved a high degree of skill in this craft.[9] Louis was extremely pious and very devoted to his children and wife, with whom he was deeply in love, too much so for his own good; he frequently gave in to her whims and followed her ill-conceived advice. He had been married at fifteen to the beauteous Austrian princess Marie-Antoinette—"l'Autrichienne"—who soon became the target of popular resentment. She alienated the French by her haughtiness —she disliked appearing in public and accepted only the company of a small coterie—her love of luxury and entertainment and her staggering expenditures. The new queen gave sumptuous festivities in the gardens of Versailles, in which she had erected a "Temple of Love." She spent a fortune on clothes and set the fashion for extravagantly full crinoline dresses and high coiffures topped with feathered hats, which made it difficult for socialites to get into their coaches. Marie-Antoinette was also in a sense a disciple of Rousseau, whose ideas were very popular with high society, and spent much of her time in the artificially rustic ambiance of her "Hameau", a farm she had set up in the parc of Versailles, where she amused herself at tending to perfumed and beribboned sheep and cows. Giving in to fashion, she had a "family portrait" painted by Mme Vigée-Lebrun, for which she posed, as a "good mother", in simple attire with her

---

[8] He actually cared about being popular and pleasing everybody. For example, during the Revolution he accepted to wear the tri-colored cockade. Earlier, he had agreed to wear a potato flower in his boutonnière to help the agronomer Parmentier in his publicity for the newly imported potato plant.

[9] In spite of his reputation of weakness the King showed superb strength of character and great dignity in the face of adversity, imprisonment and death.

The purchase of Corsica
in 1768

Louis XVI

US Bicentennial 13c

Young Marie-Antoinette
after Périn-Salbreux

three children. The general mood under the influence of Rousseau, Diderot and such painters as Greuze, was for a return to morality and rigid virtue and away from frivolity, as is visible in the decor and furniture at the end of Louis XVI's reign. All the arts of that period were markedly influenced by the excavating of the cities of Pompeii and Herculaneum, and Classicism was vigorously renewed with the paintings of David, whose favourite subjects were heroic scenes from Roman antiquity, such as *Le Serment des Horaces* ("The Oath of the Horatii") in 1784.

The need for change was becoming increasingly evident. The voices of the *philosophes* and cries for reform were making themselves more and more audible and found their strongest expression in the works of Beaumarchais, author of *Le Barbier de Séville*, whose *Mariage de Figaro* was to be later termed by Napoleon as "the Revolution in action."[10]

In the face of mounting difficulties Louis XVI was, regretfully, making increasingly disastrous decisions. Thus, under the pressure of a variety of counselors including the Queen, he dismissed Turgot, the only man whose wisdom and devotion could have perhaps saved France.[11]

He recalled the Parlement and, prompted by his foreign minister Vergennes, pledged support to the American revolution and sent military and financial help which France could ill afford at the time. While his step was in line with the prevailing ideas of freedom and good for the country's prestige, since France emerged from the glorious Traité de Paris (1783) as a champion of liberty and brotherhood (it also settled some old accounts between France and England), it resulted in no tangible territorial or political gains and plunged the government's treasury into full deficit.

Since in 1787-88 all lenders refused to provide the money needed to avert a full-fledged crisis, Louis XVI had to give in to demands

---

[10] Both of Beaumarchais' masterful comedies were made into operas: Rossini's *The Barber of Seville* and Mozart's *The Marriage of Figaro*.

[11] Among other reforms, the minister had abolished the "corvée royale" or duty of the peasants to repair roads without remuneration.

by the Parlement for the convocation of Etats-Généraux (Estates-General) which had not been assembled in over one hundred and fifty years of authoritarian rule. This historical event took place on May 5th, 1789, and marks the beginning of the French Revolution.

Arts in the 18th Century

The arts in the 18th century reflect, as was discussed above, the changing tastes and moods of the French society. After Louis XIV's demise the outburst of "joie de vivre" and new way of life was embodied in the lighthearted and thoroughly charming *Rococo* style, so named for its reliance on pieces of rocks ("rocaille") and shells ("coquilles") as motifs of decoration.[12] The Rococo featured graceful, less majestic, more intimate buildings and curved lines in the decoration of the interiors. Most of these were outfitted with delicately carved wall panelings, divided by the insertion of small paintings and with plaster embellishments, such as gilded scroll tracery. The furniture was curvilinear, the colors light and soft. The painter's palette was pastel and the dominant theme - love in all its manifestations.

Watteau is the prime exponent of Rococo style in painting. He portrayed members of theatrical troupes ("Gilles", "La Finette", "Arlequin", "Le Mezzetin", etc.) and members of high society in quiet dalliance, such as can be seen in his *Fêtes galantes*. The best known canvas of the series is undoubtedly the *Embarquement pour Cythère* (Pilgrimage to Cythera)[13] in which we see young and elegant couples, dressed in luxurious silks, on their journey to "loveland": they form a graceful arabesque, remindful of a minuet. The warm, though subdued colors, the soft texture of the background foliage,

---

[12] Rococo may also be related to the Italian term "barocco": it shares with the Baroque not only the above-mentioned decorative motifs but also fancy ornamentation and the impression of a never ending movement. It may even be considered as a variation of the Baroque on a much smaller scale.

[13] Cythera is the island and the birthplace of the goddess of love, Venus.

the romantic mood, the pearly clouds and the misty, shimmering landscape are pleasing to the senses. But the entire tableau is imbued with an aura of melancholy, hinting at the evanescent quality of love. Watteau is undoubtedly the most poetic of all 18th century painters.

Much more carnal and explicit is the work of **Boucher**,[14] head of the French Academy and favorite of Mme de Pompadour of whom he executed a famous portrait. Boucher also produced designs for tapestries, porcelain and stage settings. His rendering of sensuous and seductive bodies of nubile women, often associated with Venus and other mythological goddesses, are frankly erotic. And so are the still more frivolous canvasses of Pater, Lancret, and especially **Fragonard**. Their depictions of not only sophisticated flirtation and "first kisses", but also passionate love scenes and "peeping Toms" often border on pornography. Fragonard, the author of the suggestive "Swing" and a disciple of both Chardin and Boucher was, however, a real master of composition and has left a number of excellent portraits.

Among other portrait painters, **Quentin de la Tour** (not to be confused with the 17th century Georges de la Tour) reached the heights of popularity with his pastel renditions of the King, the Queen, Mme de Pompadour and all the other important figures of Louis XV's time, including most of the great *philosophes*. Nattier, who was a protégé of Marie Leszczynska, left us not only numerous portraits of members of the royal family, but also a term for a certain shade of greenish-blue called "bleu Nattier." **Mme Vigée-Lebrun**, mentioned above, rose to the position of "peintre ordinaire" of Marie-Antoinette and executed the best known picture of Louis XV's last mistress, Mme du Barry.

In contrast to the lighthearted and often superficial art of society painters stands the mastery of **Chardin** who continued to work in the realistic vein traced by Le Nain in the 17th century. He portrayed simple people, simple scenes and simple objects, to which his brush

---

[14] In 1986, the Detroit Institute of Arts organized the first exhibition devoted to the works of Boucher, which was also shown in New York and in Paris.

succeeded in lending a high degree of beauty and a poetic quality. He is an unsurpassed master of still life: but his lowly pots and kettles, eggs and potatoes, dead game and fish (such as "La raie"), strike us as so many gems glimmering in their jewel-like tones. Chardin's numerous genre pictures of children at play and women engaged in family or household duties (the most famous of which is probably *Le Bénédicite* - "Grace") often underscore the virtues and piety of middle class life and may appear as being didactic. Indisputably moralizing, though, are the "bourgeois" canvasses of Greuze,[15] with their "rural patriarchs", "prodigal sons", "blushing brides" and "innocent maidens" (which the artist somehow usually portrayed in unequivocally sensuous and even brazen poses). This melodramatic, contrived art, extolled by Diderot, was extremely popular in France well into the 20th century.

As we have already seen, a renewed interest in Roman antiquity, Roman aesthetics and Roman virtues—stoicism, patriotism, courage, moderation— found its expression during the reign of Louis XVI in the Neoclassicism of **Jacques-Louis David.** Later on, David espoused the philosophical and political ideals of the Revolution which he served with zeal, while reaping the benefits of his position as virtual dictator of the arts during that period.[16]

Among the many 18th century sculptors,[17] **Houdon** stands out as an extremely talented and prolific master who executed busts not only French notables (Voltaire, Rousseau, Diderot, Mirabeau, etc.), but also of some great Americans: Washington, Benjamin Franklin, Thomas Jefferson and John Paul Jones, to name a few.

Besides examples of 18th century architecture cited above, such as the Place Stanislas in Nancy by Héré and the Place de la Concorde and Le Petit Trianon by **Jacques-Ange Gabriel** (who is also responsible for the theatre and two wings at Versailles), let us mention

---

[15] See above.

[16] David became a member of the "Convention" and voted the King's execution. He immortalized many of the events and the prominent figures of the time.

[17] Clodion, the Coustou brothers, Lomoyne, Pajou, Caffieri and Mme de Pompadour's protégé, Pigalle.

Soufflot's projected church of Ste Geneviève in the Latin Quarter, which was called Panthéon during the Revolution and became the resting place for men of great merit, among which Voltaire, Rousseau, Victor Hugo, Zola and also the World War II Résistance hero, Jean Moulin.

As far as music is concerned, the most important French composer is Jean-Philippe **Rameau** whose operas (*Hippolyte et Aricie*, *Les Indes galantes*) have met in recent years in France with renewed acclaim. Rameau was an original theoretician and an innovator: his departure from hitherto accepted principles provoked yet another aesthetic controversy in the 18th century, called "la Querelle des Lullistes et des Ramistes." The German master Gluck made several trips to France, where he eventually found the protection of his former pupil Marie-Antoinette, as well as the friendship of the *philosophes*, and where his operas (*Orfeo*, *Iphigénie en Aulide*, *Iphigénie en Tauride*, *Alceste*) enjoyed a tremendous success.

Letters in the 18th Century • The Enlightenment

The 18th century has been called in turn the "Age of Reason", the "Age of Ideas" and the "Age of Enlightenment." Whereas all three terms capture some of the spirit of the period,[18] the word "Enlightenment" is most often used to express the mood, ideals and aspirations of French 18th century thinkers and writers.[19]

Two authors of the first part of the century not associated with the Enlightenment who have endured a lasting success, each in his

---

[18] The establishing of a comparison between their respective merits has been occasionally given in the past as an examination topic for degree candidates at American universities.

[19] Poetry did not flourish during the "age of reason" which boasts only one truly great poet, André Chénier. He was guillotined during the Revolution (see below), and his tragic love and death have inspired Giordano's opera *Andrea Chenier*.

own field, are the playwright Marivaux and the novelist Prévost.[20] Marivaux can be credited for bringing the Rococo style into literature, because of his constant preoccupation with love and all its manifestations, as well as the "pastel" charm of his world and the graceful quality of his dialogue.[21] Marivaux enjoys a great revival in modern day France and some of his plays never leave the répertoire of the Comédie Française. Abbé Prévost's psychological novel *Manon Lescaut*, already mentioned above and whose theme is total love *à la* Tristan and Yseut, is still widely read today, but is actually better known to the English speaking world through the operas based on its action and characters.

The *Enlightenment* is a term applied to a definite revolution in the history of thought and especially to its manifestations in 18th century France. It signifies, according to Columbia University professors Otis Fellows and Norman Torrey,[22] a "popularization and dissemination in literary form of scientific knowledge" and an "all pervasive philosophic and critical spirit." The *philosophes*—in its 18th century meaning the word is not synonymous with "philosophers"— had no use for abstract philosophizing: they had in mind practical goals, such as the welfare of men through the improvement of society, through tolerance and through freedom from religious authoritarianism and any form of tyranny. The "esprit philosophique" is marked by rationalism, skepticism, anticlericalism, relativism, cosmopolitanism and the encyclopedic movement. All the great intellects of the period contributed to Diderot's *Encyclopédie*,[23] including Rousseau who later on parted ways with the *philosophes*: while the idea of progress and the perfectibility of man was the dominant spirit

---

[20] His *Manon Lescaut* has been interpreted by some critics as a "philosophical" novel in the sense that it portrays the revolt of the individual guided by nature against society.

[21] The term "marivaudage" with which Marivaux has enriched the French vocabulary refers to a refined, somehow affected or "précieux" way of expressing oneself.

[22] *The Age of Enlightenment*, Appleton-Century-Crofts, 1942, p. 1.

[23] D'Alembert in particular was closely associated with the effort to publish this awesome work.

of the age, Rousseau embraced the theories of primitivism and extolled the virtues of the "noble savage" and of simple life in harmony with Nature.

Although the *philosophes* envisaged a world of equality in the eyes of law, most were far from being revolutionary and hoped to achieve their aims with the help of reforms and by "enlightening" the minds of governments and reigning monarchs. Such was the attempt made in the first part of the century by **Montesquieu**[24] whose witty satire on the despotism and the unreasonableness of French institutions and conventions, *Les Lettres persanes* (a fictional correspondence of two Persian visitors to France), met with immediate success. But his *Spirit of Laws* (*De l'esprit des lois*) is one of the most significant works ever written, as it has influenced not only the first constitution of the French Republic, but also the Fathers of the American Constitution.

The towering figure who spans the century and who dominated the intellectual and literary life of his age, **Voltaire**, was also basically a conservative: he became immensely wealthy and surrounded himself with luxurious appointments and all the refinements available at the time. He disliked the lower classes and had nothing but scorn for primitive man: he even poked fun at the "unkempt hair" and the "dirty nails" of Adam and Eve. While Voltaire was a deist, not an atheist—he compared the world to a clock which would not be conceivable without a clockmaker—he did wage a relentless war against all organized religion and in particular the Catholic Church. He held up to ridicule practically everything that was respected by his contemporaries, religion, governments, institutions, laws and customs, without ever offering any viable alternatives to the existing evils,[25]

---

[24] On behalf of the city of Bordeaux, a descendent of the famous French philosopher presented the American people with a bust of his ancestor in ceremonies celebrating the bicentennial of the American Constitution. The bust is displayed between those of George Washington and General La Fayette in the exhibition hall at the State Department in Washington, D.C.

[25] *Candide* ends with a much debated moral: "Il faut cultiver notre jardin" (We must cultivate our garden).

which is why some critics have called him a "debunker".[26] But even if his values are negative and he is neither an original or a profound thinker, Voltaire is considered the most representative author of his era. He was an exceptionally prolific writer[27] who put his sharp wit and literary talent to work at every genre possible, including the theatre. Today few of Voltaire's works are widely read, with the exception of his "philosophic tales" and particularly his masterpiece of straight faced irony and brilliantly incisive style, *Candide*, which brings into sharp focus the ridicules and the shortcomings of his age (*Candide* was set to music by Leonard Bernstein).

If Voltaire was the "symbol" of the Enlightenment, **Diderot**, a confirmed atheist who had a boundless faith in Reason, in Nature, in Science and in Progress, was the recognized leader of the *philosophes*. He embodied their spirit and found a powerful tool for the dissemination of "philosophic" ideas in the *Encyclopédie* of which he became the editor and at which he worked indefatigably against all kinds of odds until its triumphant completion. A brilliant speculator, capable of astounding insights, Diderot was interested in everything: his versatility earned him the sobriquet of "Pantophile." He had a passion for literature and dabbled in practically all the genres, including the novel. He wrote several plays and extolled the "drame bourgeois", intermediate between tragedy and comedy. Diderot was also knowledgeable in art: he reviewed the "Salons" or exhibitions of new paintings held yearly in Paris in a series of often extremely perceptive articles, and can thus be considered the "father" of modern art criticism.

While Diderot was called by Rousseau "un homme prodigieux", the 18th century writer whose work was seminal and who seems truly prodigious to us today is **Rousseau** himself. The influence of this genial autodidact—Rousseau never had any formal schooling—has

---

[26] He was accused by the Romanticists of the 19th century of having killed their faith and taken away their hope, which eventually drove a number of them to suicide.

[27] Voltaire, a former pupil of the superb Jesuit schools, was a master of rhetoric and argumentation.

reached far beyond his own century and has actually changed our world's way of feeling, thinking and behaving. His input in such varied realms as politics, government, philosophy, mores, education, literature and even music cannot be overemphasized. It has been said that Rousseau was more than a literary man, more than a great originator of ideas and that he represents a whole aspect of humanity, an attitude toward life.

Rousseau's great motto was a return to Nature:[28] Nature is pure and it has been corrupted by society. His idealistic vision of primitive man, his stand against civilization with all its evils and his attacks on the demoralizing influence of the theatre, which was the mass media of the time and the most effective tool for the "philosophic" propaganda, inevitably pitted him against his former friends. The latter retaliated violently and Rousseau became not only an outcast, but also a victim of both open and surreptitious sarcasm, derision and persecution, particularly at the hands of the acrimonious Voltaire. This break with the other *philosophes* did not prevent Rousseau's works from enjoying an immense popularity: 18th century society immediately accepted his ideas and precepts. We already mentioned above the vogue of the "jardins à l'anglaise" or "English gardens,"— as exemplified in Marie-Antoinette's "Hameau" in Versailles— where nature flourishes free from the artificial symmetry imposed by man on the "jardins à la française", and the trend among aristocratic women to breast feed their babies. Rousseau's theories on the upbringing of children as expounded in his treatise, *Emile*, have played a decisive role in our own preference for a "child centered education", where the stress is put on personal experience and on laws of nature rather than on books.[29]

As far as literature is concerned, the highly emotive and passion-

---

[28] Rousseau is a precursor of some attitudes of modern-day ecologists.

[29] This seminal work, which claims that man is born good and children must not be corrupted by traditional book-oriented education opens, as do a number of Rousseau's works, with a strong, axiomatic statement: "Tout est bien, sortant des mains de l'Auteur des choses; tout dégénère entre les mains de l'homme" (All is good coming from the hands of the Maker, everything degenerates in the hands of man). Curiously enough, Rousseau abandoned his own five children at birth.

ate Rousseau who continually preached a return to "feeling", is a precursor of the Romanticists. The basic elements of Romanticism are already present in the very title of one of his late works, *Les Rêveries d'un promeneur solitaire* (rêverie, dream, feeling, nature, lyricism, solitude), while his *Confessions*, an outpouring of personal and sentimental accounts and often nostalgic recollections, are, indeed, a first both in mood and in genre.

Best known are, however, Rousseau's political ideas and his unparalleled contribution to the advancement of democratic thought: he never stopped insisting on the "legitimate and unalienable sovereignty" of the people and their "primordial right to govern themselves" through administrations chosen in free elections. Rousseau's direct link with the 1789 Revolution, which adopted as its motto the philosopher's ideals of "liberty, equality and fraternity" (still visible on today's French coins), cannot be overlooked. His works—the *Discours sur l'origine de l'inégalité* and in particular his *Contrat social*[30] —were the breviary of numerous prominent and influential French revolutionaries[31] who eventually brought to our world the most spectacular changes in the manner of government since the beginning of the modern era.

The influence on the spreading of revolutionary ideas of yet another great philosophe, the playwright **Beaumarchais**, has already been discussed earlier.

WHAT TO SEE

* Paris: Palais de l'Elysée
    Hôtel de Soubise (Archives Nationales)
    Hôtel Matignon
    Place de la Concorde by Gabriel

---

[30] This work starts again with a striking statement: "L'homme est né libre et partout il est dans les fers" ("Man is born free, and he is in chains everywhere").

[31] Such was, among many others, Saint-Just who delivered an impassioned speech on behalf of Louis XVI's death, while invoking Rousseau's arguments and imitating his oratory style.

Musée Nissim de Camondo (mainly furniture)

Bagatelle - château in the Bois de Boulogne built for the
Comte d'Artois (future King Charles X) in a matter
of two months by Bélanger (1777); the reason for
the hurry was a reception that the younger
brother of Louis XVI wanted to give in honor of
Marie-Antoinette

Louvre: period furniture, 18th century paintings, and
sculptures

The Panthéon by Soufflot (tombs of Rousseau and Voltaire)

- Ermenonville (near Paris): park where Rousseau's heart is
buried
- Ferney (near Gex and Swiss border): Musée Voltaire
- Fontainebleau: Royal apartments
- Grasse (Provence): Musée Fragonard
- Langres: Musée Diderot
- Lunéville: 18th century château of King Stanislas
- Montmorency (near Paris): Musée J.J. Rousseau
- Nancy: Place Stanislas
- Tournus (Burgundy): Musée Greuze
- St. Quentin: Musée Quentin (pastels by de la Tour)
- Versailles: Petit Trianon
Theatre
Apartments of Louis XV, Louis XVI, Marie Leszczynska
and Marie Antoinette
Marie Antoinette's "Hameau", her "Temple of Love"
- Geneva, Switzerland: "Les Délices", Musée Voltaire

The Revolution • The "Directoire"

The five years which elapsed between July 1789—date of the
storming of the Bastille—and July 1794, when the execution of Robespierre put an end to the reign of Terror, were the most violent in

French history and brought the most decisive changes not only in French society, but also in the way of thinking in the entire world.

This enormous and stupefying event, which surprised even those contemporaries who had advocated changes in the most vehement way and which continues to puzzle historians, scholars and sociologists of today, had both long and short term causes. The former include among others, the venality of office and tensions among the major elements of society such as the precluding of men of wealth and talent from entering the ranks of the nobility: it was noted that the aristocrats had become increasingly elitist and powerful and ready for another "Fronde". Another major factor was the wide acceptance of the criticism of traditional practices and of the notion that royal omnipotence was equivalent to tyranny, as expounded by the thinkers of the Enlightenment. The immediate causes were the acute financial difficulties encountered by the King's government and the economic depression that struck France after several years of bad harvests in the grainfields and in the vineyards, which resulted in the high cost of food and unavailability of bread.

On May 5th, 1789, as mentioned above, the King convened at Versailles a meeting of the Estates-General, consisting of the two privileged orders, the Nobility and the Clergy, and the Tiers-Etat, or Third-Estate, which comprised 98% of the entire population. But from the very start of the convention it became evident that neither the privileged orders nor the King himself were ready to listen to the innumerable grievances of the "people", or to give up their prerogatives: at best they seemed willing to accept some meaningless reforms. The members of the Tiers-Etat, which counted among its ranks not only such representatives as industrialists and professionals, but also progressive nobles like the notorious Mirabeau, then decided to deliberate separately and were joined by many clergymen and liberal aristocrats. Since the assembly hall at Versailles was not made available to them, they gathered in a nearby "tennis court" and there, in an ambiance of unprecedented enthusiasm, solemnly swore not to separate without giving France a new constitution: this famous "Serment du Jeu de Paume" (Oath of the Tennis Court) was immortalized by the most representative painter of the period, David (see above). The King, as usual, gave in and the deputies immediately set to work after changing the name of their body to "Assemblée Constituante" (Constitutional Assembly). It appeared that the country was going to obtain the necessary and desired reforms in a peaceful and orderly manner.

But tensions were running high and the mood was feverish. As time passed the unpredictable and contradictory decisions of the King aroused more and more suspicion in the ranks of electrified mobs, and eventually forces of violence were triggered which nobody was any longer capable of controlling.

When royal troops were brought in from the frontier to the capital and the minister Necker who had become a symbol of reform was dismissed, an angry populace, armed with hatchets and spikes marched on the Bastille demanding gunpowder, stormed the fortress and dealt in a blood-chilling way with the garrison who had surrendered. Although there were only seven prisoners detained at the time, this violent event seemed like an important victory, since the Bastille had always been considered a symbol of tyranny: during the ancien régime on the simple signing by the king of a "lettre de cachet", prisoners could be held indefinitely without the right to trial. The taking of the Bastille also showed the growing strength of the Parisian mobs which were going henceforth to dictate the course of action.

On August 4, the feudal system was abolished by the Assemblée Constituante (with a provision to compensate for some of the seigniorial losses), and on the 26th, as a preliminary step toward the new constitution, the Declaration of the Rights of Man and the Citizen was issued and approved by the King. This seemed to satisfy the vast majority of the population. But in the meantime there had been burning of castles and atrocities committed against landlords in the provinces, and the urban mobs were far from displaying a pacific mood. The King's younger brothers and scores of aristocrats took to a self imposed exile abroad, and acted wisely, for in October an angry group of women marched on Versailles demanding bread and forced the royal family to return to the Louvre, where it could stay under their watch. The King, who was torn between his willingness to cooperate with the reforms and the advice from his family abroad to invoke the help of Austria and Prussia in crushing the revolution from the outside, became a virtual prisoner of the Parisian mobs.

The next several months were devoted to the drafting of a new constitution, which transformed France into a constitutional monarchy, with as its head and chief executive a hereditary king with a power limited by the legislature. The latter was to rest in the hands of the "Assemblée Legislative", born from the Assemblée Constituante. The separation of powers also took into account the judiciary, and free justice was to be administered by elected judges. In an attempt at unification, the old provinces of the ancien régime—there had been 35—were replaced by 83 "départements". At the instigation of the unscrupulous but brilliant bishop Talleyrand,[32] the Church's property and land were seized and put on sale to repay the national debt. Priests were henceforth to function as public officials, elected by the entire population, Catholic or not, and paid by the state, which required them to become "assermentés" or "oath takers", i.e. take an oath of allegiance to the new constitution. This last measure deeply divided the minds of the French people and seemingly appeared as a stumbling block to the King, who was a devout Catholic and therefore very reluctant to sign the new constitution.

In June 1791, the King decided to flee abroad: the royal family, with the help of the Swedish envoy Count Fersen, slipped out of the palace by night in disguise, and headed toward the border. Near Varennes[33] Louis was recognized and forcibly brought back to Paris under the insults of hostile mobs. This attempted escape, which was interpreted as a desertion, had deplorable consequences for the image of the King—and the monarchy in general—in the eyes of the people.

---

[32] This Machiavellian statesman, renowned for his wit, savoir-faire and perfect manners, served with unparalleled cynicism—and ability—all the governments that came to power during his lifetime, and is one of the most colorful figures in history. Lafayette was at the time commander of the National Guard.

[33] This episode is the focal point of a movie with Marcello Mastroianni, *La Nuit de Varennes*.

The end of 1791 and beginning of 1792 were marked by chaos. Partisans of the ancien régime were disobeying the new government officials: the King was objecting to most of the measures taken by the Législative; priests were refusing to take the oath of allegiance, and peasants were unwilling to accept in exchange for their products the new paper money or "assignats" which seemed totally worthless. As a result, the urban populations were starting to experience famine. Things were further complicated by the fear of foreign intervention and at one point, believing that Austria and Prussia would imminently invade, the Assemblée Législative declared war on these two countries. The French troops were poorly organized—many officers from the nobility defected to the enemy—and suffered a number of setbacks. While Austria invaded Flanders and Prussia the Lorraine, the Assemblée declared in June 1792 that the "Fatherland was in danger" ("La Patrie en danger") and started an all-out mobilization. On August 10, the people of Paris with the help of national guards who had marched into the capital from the south while singing the "Marseillaise",[34] again attacked the Tuileries palace. The royal family, which had taken refuge at the Assembly, was then imprisoned in the dark citadel of the Temple.[35]

In September the French troops fortified by masses of volunteers scored an important victory over Austria and Prussia at Valmy. During the same time, at the instigation of the blood-thirsty Marat, thousands of nobles and "disloyal" priests were massacred in Paris.[36] The Assemblée Legislative gave way to a new body called "Convention" after the Philadelphia convention which had drawn up the democratic constitution for the United States. Monarchy was abolished and France was officially proclaimed a republic.

---

[34] This revolutionary hymn, composed in Strasbourg by Rouget de Lisle, was first sung by the soldiers enlisted in Marseille. It became the French national anthem.

[35] This was the fortress that had been constructed and occupied by the military order of the Templars (see above).

[36] Bernanos' play *Dialogues des Carmélites* centers on a moving episode of this time of persecution and executions of members of religious orders. Poulenc's opera bearing the same title had a brilliant run at the New York Met in 1987.

May 5, 1789

A "sans-culotte"

Danton

Louis XVI was tried for treason and sentenced to death.[37] He protested his innocence to the very last and set an example of heroic behavior before he was guillotined on January 21, 1793. Louis tried to comfort the members of his family whom he was leaving at the Temple, his wife, son and daughter and to give them courage. He died without flinching as a good Catholic, after having confessed to a "non-constitutional" priest. From the scaffold he attempted to address the witnessing crowds, but his voice was covered by the humming of drums. Both the King and the Queen achieved in the face of misfortune a grandeur they had not possessed as monarchs. Marie-Antoinette, who had been so frivolous and had erred in happier times,[38] showed love, concern and devotion to her martyr husband. Soon after his death she was separated from her children and transferred to the Conciergerie which had become a prison during the Reign of Terror. After an infamous trial, she, too, was condemned to death and died with great dignity on the guillotine on October 16th (the painter David drew a famous sketch of the Queen on her way to the execution). The fate of the young Dauphin—Louis XVII—who allegedly died at the Temple of malnutrition and mistreatment continues to be one of the most haunting mysteries in French history.[39]

In the provinces, the royalist guerrillas, mainly in the Catholic and conservative province of Vendée, continued to harass the republican forces: the military repressions that took place in that area surpass in cruelty the wildest imagination. As the war with foreign countries continued and seemed to imperil the very existence of the new republic, a split occurred within the ranks of the revolutionaries, i.e., between the truly democratic and moderate Girondins and the

---

[37] The death sentence was voted by the margin of one ballot (361 to 360) cast by Louis' cousin Philippe d'Orléans, named for his populist attitudes "Philippe-Egalité". He was later on guillotined himself.

[38] Only much later was her love correspondence with the handsome Count Axel Fersen discovered in Sweden.

[39] A number of historians argue, while presenting convincing evidence, that the little boy had been smuggled out of prison and replaced by another child, whose skeleton did not correspond to what was known of the Dauphin's height and build.

An execution during the Revolution

Marie-Antoinette on her way
to the guillotine (after David)

A revolutionary woman

Robespierre

Montagnards[40] who wanted to establish the reign of Terror. The Montagnards won; and after organizing a Parisian mob against the Girondins, they had them condemned to death and executed in June 1793.[41] Headed by the notorious trio Danton, Marat[42] and Robespierre, the Montagnards instituted a revolutionary government and gave the "Comité du Salut public" and the "Tribunal révolutionnaire" despotic powers.

During the Reign of Terror perhaps the saddest and bloodiest pages in French history were written. No one was safe from suspicion, imprisonment and slaughter. Hundreds of carts loaded with victims left daily the overpopulated prisons for the guillotine on Place de la Révolution (today's Concorde) amidst the cheering of bloodthirsty mobs who enjoyed executions like the most amusing of spectacles. Other heads were rolling in churches as, in an orgy of vengeful destruction, revolutionary vandals were beheading statues of saints and biblical kings, gems of Romanesque and Gothic art.[43]

When the danger from the outside waned after the general mobilization and French troops had been victorious on all the fronts, Danton wanted to stop the Terror, but was countered by Robespierre, a peculiar disciple of Rousseau who wore a wig and dressed like an aristocrat (he was called, because of his personal integrity, "l'Incorruptible"). Robespierre, who was a deist and instituted the worship of the Supreme Being, had set high ideals for himself and the future French society. But he was more than a fervent revolutionary,

---

[40] The Girondins were so called because many of their leaders came from the department of La Gironde. The Montagnards, or "Mountaineers", occupied the high rows at the Assemblée Legislative.

[41] The wife of one of the Girondins, Mme Roland, pronounced at the time she was going to be guillotined these famous words, "O Liberty! how many crimes are committed in thy name!"

[42] The odious Marat was stabbed to death in his bath by a heroic partisan of the Girondins, the young Charlotte Corday (see the well-known painting of the scene by David at the Brussels Museum of Art). Charlotte Corday was subsequently guillotined.

[43] The "heads" from the façade of Notre-Dame in Paris were unearthed only recently, and, since the cathedral had been entirely reconstructed by Viollet-le-Duc, they are now displayed at the Musée de Cluny.

and, like a true fanatic, refused to apply the very democratic principles that he was apparently advocating: according to him "there ought to be no liberty for the enemies of liberty." Robespierre had Danton arrested and guillotined together with the idealistic young Desmoulins, and became a true dictator. Blood continued to flow and heads continued to roll, among them, those of the famous scientist Lavoisier and the greatest poet in the 18th century, André Chénier. Eventually, in 1794, Robespierre was overthrown and guillotined by the "Thermidorians", so called because the event took place on July 27, or 9th of thermidor[44] according to the new calendar. The Thermidorians adopted a new constitution. A new government called the Directoire, composed of two councils of 250 and 500 members respectively, became the top authority. The Directoire, which lasted until 1799, solved the problem of consolidating the institutional achievements of the Revolution: it abolished slavery, created the "grandes écoles", including St. Cyr and Ecole Polytechnique, made the Louvre a national museum and instituted the metric system, still in effect in all of Europe and today also in Canada.

WHAT TO SEE

- Paris: Musée Carnvalet
  Place de la Concorde
  Panthéon
  Conciergerie (in Palais de Justice on Ile de la Cité)
  Louvre: David's canvasses and fragments of the *Serment du jeu de Paume*
- Cholet (Vendée): Museum of the Vendée repression
- Versailles: Musée

---

[44] The revolutionaries tried to do away with all traditions and established a new calendar: the year had 12 months with descriptive names such as "germinal", "floréal", "prairial", "fructidor", "brumaire" (month of fogs), "ventôse" (month of winds), each one divided for the sake of equality into 3 decades of 10 days. There were also new "sans culotte" feast days, such as the feast of Virtue, of Genius, of Work, of Rewards, etc.

158

Marat stabbed to death
in his bathtub
by Charlotte Corday

Chapter 8

THE NINETEENTH CENTURY

The Consulate and the Empire

In 1799, on the very eve of the nineteenth century, which was to be characterized by numerous changes, a multiplicity of forms of government and a wide variety of contrasting intellectual and literary currents, the Directoire constituted after the fall of Robespierre came to an abrupt end. It was a victim at the same time of its own incapacity, the destructive rivalry within its ranks and the onslaught of both dedicated republicans and monarchists, who were hoping for the return of the Bourbons to the throne. One of the "directors", Sieyès, called on a young, but already well-known and very popular general, Napoleon Bonaparte, to put in order the corrupt legislative councils. The famous 1799 "coup d'état du 18 brumaire"[1] overthrew the Directoire and established a Consulate, with Bonaparte at its head as First Consul.[2]

---

[1] According to the revolutionary calendar. This date in the present-day calendar would be November 9.

[2] His brother Lucien, as president of the "Conseil des Cinq Cents", was also instrumental in bringing Napoleon to power.

Bonaparte had just unexpectedly returned from Egypt: he had properly assessed the situation in France and foreseen the important role he could play in the future of the country. He was already the object of adulation following his many brilliant victories over the English (Toulon, 1793) and especially the Austrians in the legendary Italian campaign (Castiglione, Lodi, Arcole, Rivoli). Napoleon's venture against the English in Egypt, where he pronounced an often-quoted address to his soldiers,[3] eventually ended, despite a victory on land, in total retreat after the smarting naval defeat inflicted on the French by Lord Nelson at Abukir.

When Bonaparte became First Consul, he was barely thirty years old. Born in Corsica in 1769, he was one of the eight children of a lawyer from Ajaccio and his wife Letitia, who was to play an important role throughout the Napoleonic reign. It was a very close knit family, and in spite of some critical opinions regarding his character expressed by his brothers,[4] Napoleon the emperor placed his siblings and relatives on as many European thrones as he could find or create.

Ambitious, calculating and stopping short of nothing to achieve his goals, Bonaparte was not only ingenious as a strategist, but also capable of truly brilliant insights. He did not hesitate to enlist the help of unscrupulous and ignominious, albeit intelligent and cunning men, willing to serve any kind of régime, such as Talleyrand who became his foreign minister and the odious Fouché who headed the police force. Even though he had collaborated with the Revolution, Bonaparte despised the republicans and the liberals. He believed only in force and was implacable toward his critics and his foes.[5]

---

[3] "From the top of those pyramids forty centuries of history are looking at you."

[4] His brother Lucien wrote, in a letter addressed to another brother, Joseph, as early as 1792: "Napoleon is filled with ambition...in a free state he could be a dangerous man....He has an inclination to be a tyrant, and if he ever were to become a king, his name would make posterity shudder with horror" (June 24).

[5] His spies infiltrated all the strata and circles of society. Fearing an attempt on his life, Napoleon had the last descendant of the great Condé family seized in foreign territory and executed without ever having proof of his involvement in any plot. In 1809, in retaliation for having been excommunicated by Pope

But he had a unique flair for publicity and the talent to impress and rally crowds. Though he did not spare them, Napoleon's soldiers worshipped him and remained completely loyal to him in all adversity and even in the darkest moments of defeat and downfall.

Bonaparte was also a remarkable administrator, and, as he later recalled in the *Mémorial* he wrote during his exile on St. Helena, it was he who gave France the administrative, judicial and economic stability it was to enjoy for decades to come. He had the wisdom to maintain and consolidate the achievements of the Revolution in the fields of social relations, economic institutions and government. The law did not discriminate between noble and commoner, rich and poor. Bonaparte maintained the division of France into departments and instituted "préfets" at their head: these remained in office even when there was a change of power and became, during the next hundred and fifty years, one of the most stabilizing features in the French state. Napoleon instituted public, tuition free secondary schools ("lycées"), where superior methods of instruction have been forming the French elite ever since. He also founded the "Banque de France", the "Légion d'honneur" and extended amnesty to royalists and to the priests who had refused the oath of allegiance. Most importantly, he signed in 1801 a "Concordat" with the pope which put an end to the hostility of the Roman Catholic church towards the Revolution. Archbishops, bishops and all clergy were to be named and paid by the state, but invested by the authority of the Holy See. Fearing that it might fall into the hands of the English, Bonaparte sold Louisiana to the United States in 1803. In France, he encouraged industry, especially the manufacture of cotton, as well as agriculture.

His greatest achievement[6] according to Napoleon himself was, however, the stability he gave to the family through his "civil code",

---

Pius VII, he had the pontiff arrested and kept in captivity, first in Italy, then at Fontainebleau, until his abdication.

[6] "Ma vraie gloire n'est pas d'avoir gagné soixante batailles...ce qui vivra éternellement, c'est mon Code civil" he wrote in St. Helena. (My true glory is not to have won sixty battles...what will live eternally is my civil Code).

promulgated in 1804 and which was known for a long time as "Code Napoléon". He ensured the rights of children, made divorce practically impossible and regulated the relations between husband and wife, while giving the husband all the prerogatives, such as jurisdiction over inheritance, sale of joint property, and even the wife's dowry and personal money. Bonaparte himself at the time had no children, though he was married to Joséphine de Beauharnais, the attractive Creole widow of an aristocrat victim of the Revolution, who was six years his senior.

Meanwhile, warfare against England and the continental powers continued. After the decisive victories of Marengo and Hohenlinden in 1801, a treaty was signed at Lunéville with Austria, which surrendered Italy and the west bank of the Rhine, and subsequently at Amiens with England; but peace was to last only for a very brief time.

In 1802, Bonaparte was proclaimed "Consul for life" and in 1804 "hereditary" Emperor of the French by the senate. On December 2nd of the same year, wishing to follow in the footsteps of Charlemagne, he had Pope Pius VII brought in from Rome to proceed with his coronation as Napoleon I at the cathedral of Notre-Dame. But, in an unprecedented and arrogant gesture which was also symbolic of the "self-made man" he was, Napoleon took the crown from the hands of the Pontiff and placed it on his head himself. He then crowned his wife Joséphine. The scene was again immortalized by Jacques-Louis David, the revolutionary painter who had become the favorite of the new despotic régime.

Despotic is, indeed, the best term to define the rule under the First Empire. Napoleon did not share power with anyone and, like Louis XIV before him, personally made all the decisions, tolerating no opposition or discussion even from those who were close to him. Hundreds of people were held in prison for long periods of time without trial and the strictest censorship was imposed.

Napoleon wanted to have a brilliant court, but his generals, who were forced to attend all the gala events at the Tuileries, were better suited to the front line than to refined conversations in the salons.

Napoleon

The Place and Colonne Vendôme

Bonaparte's victory at Arcole

The newly created "aristocracy" was despised by the old, genuine one, who preferred to retire to their provincial châteaux than attend the reputedly boring functions at court. The Emperor himself was neither gracious nor entertaining and the cynical Talleyrand at one time expressed the regret that "such an intelligent man would have such poor manners."

Napoleon was, however, far from being uncouth and had a keen interest in architecture and art, which were to him also means of bringing luster to his reign. The Neoclassicism launched earlier by David suited to perfection the taste of the new emperor who added monuments inspired by imperial Rome to Paris: the church of the Madeleine; the Colonne Vendôme (a copy of Trajan's column), built with the melted bronze from Austrian cannons taken in the battle of Austerlitz; the Arc de Triomphe de l'Etoile (which was not completed until 1836); and the Arc de Triomphe du Carrousel (a copy of Constantine's Arch of Triumph), which Napoleon topped with the famous horses from the San Marco basilica in Venice (they were subsequently returned to Italy). The Emperor had brought back to France all the art he could lay his hands on during his numerous campaigns abroad, and, while some of them had to be restituted to the original owners in 1815, many remained in Paris and today constitute the bulk of the unparalleled treasures of the Louvre. The paintings of the time often depict great heroic scenes of the Napoleonic epic in the neoclassical vein, which is evident also in interior decoration and the massive "style Empire" furniture, inspired by Greek, Roman and Egyptian models.

Having established a "hereditary" reign, Napoleon decided at the apogee of its glory that he could no longer do without an heir, and for this reason, in 1809, divorced the now sterile Joséphine[7] in order to marry the niece of Marie-Antoinette, Archduchess Marie-Louise. Her

[7]She had two children from her first marriage and her daughter Hortense married the Emperor's brother Louis who became king of Holland. Napoleon left Joséphine as a parting gift the lovely Château de Malmaison, near Paris, where she resided until her death in 1814. The château is now visited both for its beautiful gardens and the many souvenirs of the Emperor which are housed in the building, today a state-owned museum.

father, the Austrian monarch, agreed only reluctantly to the union of his daughter with a man he considered an "usurper". Marie-Louise, though she never cared for her husband and remarried very soon after his death, did present him with a son in 1811. The child, whose official title was "le Roi de Rome" and who was forced to live in Austria as the Duke of Reichstadt after Napoleon's downfall, was affectionately called by the French "l'Aiglon",[8] —the eagle was the Emperor's emblem. This tragic young prince, separated at the tender age of three from a father he idolized all his life, died of tuberculosis at the Schönbrunn castle in 1832. His body, buried for over a century in Austria, was brought back to Paris on the orders of Hitler during World War II and now rests next to the granite sarcophagus of Napoleon at the Invalides.

The war with England and other powers, which had been interrupted by the treaties of Lunéville and Amiens, broke out again in 1803 and was to last intermittently for 11 years, until the end of Napoleon's reign. The French were again the masters on land, whereas the English controlled the seas. Napoleon's armies distinguished themselves by a series of brilliant victories which are kept alive in the memory of Parisians by the names of a number of streets and bridges, such as Rivoli, Arcole, Ulm, Austerlitz, Iéna, Friedland and Wagram.[9] But admiral Nelson again inflicted, this time at Trafalgar, a smarting defeat upon the French fleet in 1805 and Napoleon did not succeed in enforcing the "blocus continental" which he imposed and which called for the closing of all continental ports to England. Despite these failures, Napoleon had become, by 1810, the virtual master of all of Western Europe. He had put an end to the old "Holy Roman Empire", made satellites of the new Kingdom of Italy and of the Swiss Confederation and became protector of a newly created "Confederation of the Rhine". The Emperor also forced the Russians, who had at the end of the 18th century partitioned

---

[8] The "Eaglet". Edmond Rostand, the author of *Cyrano de Bergerac* wrote a moving play about Napoleon's son, entitled *L'Aiglon*.

[9] In London, not surprisingly, there is a Trafalgar Square and a Waterloo Station.

Poland in collaboration with Prussia and Austria, to recognize an independent "Grand Duchy of Warsaw" under his own protectorate. He had his brother Louis crowned king of Holland and made of his brother-in-law Murat first the ruler of the grand duchy of Berg, and then the king of Naples. His stepson became viceroy of Italy and his youngest brother, Jerôme, king of Westphalia. For yet another brother, Joseph, Napoleon had reserved the throne of Spain, and for this reason held the Spanish royal family in captivity in France for a number of years. This last step proved to be disastrous. The nationalistic Spaniards, helped in their resistance by the well trained English troops of Sir Wellesley, who was to become later Duke of Wellington, harassed and decimated the ranks of the French soldiers by an exhausting and costly guerrilla warfare (immortalized in the paintings of Goya), which was to last until the end of the Empire. Another unfortunate decision was the undertaking, in 1812,[10] of the Russian campaign against the tsar, which ended in one of the worst military debacles in world history. Unable to remain in Moscow, which had been burned and evacuated by the time he reached the city, Napoleon finally ordered a retreat in the frigid Russian winter, which decimated his army. Barely one sixth of it was eventually able to escape to Poland and then return to France.

In spite of this fiasco and an ever worsening situation in Spain, whose example was kindling resistance in all the rest of Europe, Napoleon still managed to win several important victories over Prussia and Austria, but eventually his armies were defeated in the bloody battle of Leipzig (1813). Even then, however, the Emperor refused the peace terms offered him by the coalition of his enemies.

Leaving his brother Joseph, who had been driven out of Spain, to replace him in Paris, Napoleon fought on several fronts. But his popularity had been waning, and, when the allies invaded France and marched on the capital, Joseph Bonaparte fled to Blois with Empress Marie-Louise and the young heir to the throne. The tsar and the king of Prussia entered Paris in March 1814 and were convinced by the

---

[10] Practically everyone is familiar with the *1812 Overture* by Tchaikovsky, where the sounds of the Marseillaise can be distinguished among the tolling of bells.

scheming Talleyrand that only the return of the Bourbons to the French throne would bring peace to Europe. Napoleon was deposed and forced to abdicate. He signed his abdication at Fontainebleau, which had always been his favorite residence and which still houses innumerable souvenirs of the Emperor. At the foot of the famous "Horseshoe stairway", he bid an emotional farewell to his troops who shed tears of grief.[11] Then he departed for his first exile on the island of Elba.

WHAT TO SEE

- Paris: The Arc de Triomphe de l'Etoile
  The Arc de Triomphe du Carrousel in the Jardin des
      Tuileries
  The Church of La Madeleine
  The Colonne Vendôme
  The Invalides: the tombs of Napoleon and of his son
- Near Paris: Château de Malmaison, Josephine's residence
  Château de Fontainebleau: numerous souvenirs of the
      Emperor, the throne room, the "abdication room",
      the cradle of the Roi de Rome, etc. The new
      museum devoted to the Bonaparte family.
  Château de Rambouillet: Napoleon's apartments and
      bathroom
  Château de Versailles Museum: new galleries devoted to
      the Consulate and the Empire
- Ajaccio, Corsica: Napoleon museums in the house where he was
      born and in the City Hall

---

[11] He told his soldiers: "Continue to serve France, its well-being has always been my only concern."

The Restoration • The "Hundred Days" • Louis XVIII • Charles X

The younger brother of Louis XVI was called from exile (he had left France during the Revolution in 1791), and made his entry into France on April 24, 1814 to become Louis XVIII (as was mentioned earlier, Louis XVII was the young dauphin who had most likely died during his imprisonment at the Temple). He agreed to rule as a constitutional monarch, signed a "Charter", and, while alone holding the executive power, retained Napoleon's civil Code and most of the political and social gains brought about by the Revolution. Louis also attempted to muster a reconciliation of different French political groups, royalists, republicans and Bonapartists, although the hostility between them was to remain alive for a long time to come. He delegated Talleyrand to sign a permanent treaty at the Congress of Vienna in 1815, and the skillful diplomat managed to turn the meetings into a personal triumph for himself and the country he was representing which, in spite of its defeat, was allowed to keep its 1792 boundaries. Talleyrand was, however, unable to prevent the occupation by Prussia of the Western bank of the Rhine and a new partition of Poland among its neighboring powers.

Before the Congress had ended its meetings, Napoleon decided to make a last attempt at regaining power. He secretly departed from Elba, returned to France and marched on Paris, while rallying to his cause practically all the troops that had been dispatched to stop and fight him.[12] He entered the capital and was cheered by throngs of loyal and enthusiastic crowds, as Louis XVIII fled in panic. Then the "cent jours" ("Hundred Days"), a new Napoleonic reign, started on March 20: it was to end on June 29th. A formidable European coalition army had been formed against the Emperor under the command of the Duke of Wellington and one of the most decisive battles in world history was fought on June 18th. This time Napoleon's fate

---

[12] The most popular figure of this period is that of General Ney, who was later brought before a firing squad for having joined Napoleon's forces and who is still considered today by many as a martyr of loyalty and patriotism.

was sealed: his defeat at Waterloo, near Brussels, put a definitive end to his ambitions. Confronted in Paris by the treacherous Fouché and Talleyrand, who had secretly negotiated with Louis XVIII, the Emperor had no other choice but to surrender to the English who whisked him away to the distant South Atlantic island of St. Helena. There they held him prisoner until his death. Before he succumbed to sickness in 1821 (possibly cancer of the stomach),[13] Napoleon wrote his *Mémorial* and dictated notes to his attendants while creating a haunting legend of the "fallen eagle", the tragic hero who had envisioned and unsuccessfully tried to achieve the greatness and happiness of his country. This "Napoleonic legend", which rapidly spread in France, was to play an important role during the decades that followed.

When Louis XVIII returned once again to take the reins of the reborn kingdom, he had to face the tensions between an ever more reactionary aristocracy, increasingly radical republicans and an ambitious, power-hungry bourgeoisie. The obese and gouty monarch who bore close resemblance to his unhappy older brother was, however, more intelligent than he was initially given credit for. Having understood the need for a liberal régime, he fulfilled his pledge of a moderate program and granted political and religious freedom to his subjects. He brought to France both peace and economic recovery. But his younger brother, who succeeded him upon his death in 1824 and reigned as Charles X, was imbued with the conservative spirit of the ancien régime. The new king attempted to revert to pre-revolutionary France and wanted once again to rule by "divine right". He insisted on being crowned with great pomp at Reims.

Charles X returned the Jesuits to power, increased the authority of the Church (among others, the opening of stores on Sundays was forbidden), and favored the "ultramontain" attitude which gave the pope greater authority over the decisions of the French clergy. He also compensated the émigrés for the lands that had been confiscated in 1792. These steps resulted in a wave of anticlericalism and general

---

[13] A number of researchers in recent years believe that the Emperor was poisoned.

discontent. While the powerful Romantic movement was bringing about a revolution against strict rules and limitations and spreading ideas of freedom in all domains, the Bonapartists were also becoming more and more active and vociferous.

In spite of a happier policy in foreign affairs—France participated side by side with England and Russia in the liberation of the Greeks from Turkish domination and a "punitive" expedition to Algeria eventually resulted in the conquest of the North-African country by the French—Charles was steadily losing ground at home. Forced by the multifarious forces of opposition into a yet more conservative and less tolerant attitude, the King reestablished censorship of the press and was about to change the electoral law in order to favor the conservatives, when, in July 1830,[14] a three day uprising, called "Les Trois Glorieuses"[15] broke out in Paris and resulted in his downfall. Charles was replaced by the "bourgeois king" Louis-Philippe, an Orléans, son of the "regicide revolutionary" Philippe-Egalité (see Chapter 7).

The July Monarchy and the Second Republic

The "middle class" king had to cater to the bourgeoisie who had chosen him. Dressed like a well-to-do businessman, he lived without pomp with his wife and his ten children, some of whom went for schooling to a mere public "lycée". He did away with the principle of "divine right", maintained the Charter, gave the Chambers the right to propose laws and abolished Catholicism as the official state religion. He found in Guizot an able minister who was instrumental in bringing about industrial and economic growth (his motto was "enrichissez vous"—"get rich") and encouraged the construction of

---

[14] That same year saw the first performance of the great Romantic composer Berlioz' *La Symphonie fantastique*.

[15] Delacroix's famous painting *La Liberté conduisant le peuple* has immortalized these events.

railroads—the most important breakthrough of the time[16]—the flow of investments and the building of factories.[17] He pursued a policy of peace with France's neighbors, exchanged visits with the British ruler, Queen Victoria, and, generally speaking, tried to please everybody and particularly the rich bourgeoisie: he consistently refused to extend suffrage to the less affluent citizens. Eventually, the opposition launched an all-out attack on all fronts simultaneously, by the republicans and socialists in cooperation with the urban proletariat, by the intellectuals and the legitimists,[18] who could not forgive the King for his disloyalty to the Bourbons and wanted the descendant of Charles X to return to the throne, as well as by the partisans of an ever stronger Bonapartist movement. To the latter Napoleon seemed like a giant, a hero and a martyr (the Emperor's notes from St. Helena were piously disseminated by his admirers), while the reigning force appeared to be extremely dull and totally inefficient.[19]

A victim of scorn and satire—Daumier delighted in ridiculing the King in the mordant and ingenious sketches of his head, to which he gave the shape of a pear—Louis-Philippe was finally deposed during the next revolution, which broke out in February 1848. He was forced to abdicate[20] and the Second Republic was officially proclaimed.

---

[16] The train—"demon of speed" as Victor Hugo called it—was considered by many at the time as a calamity: it was feared that its vibrations would cause women to miscarry and prevent hens from laying eggs. In 1987–88, the Vouvray wine growers protested against the passing of the TGV express trains through their region; a compromise proposal calling for the construction of a tunnel met with the objection that the fermentation of bottled wine maturing in the underground cellars would suffer from the shocks caused by the motion of the train.

[17] The conditions in these factories were generally terrible. The work day lasted from 12 to 15 hours and even children as young as 5 and 6 years old were employed in such industries as weaving.

[18] Mainly members of the old aristocracy, the army and the Church.

[19] Many Romanticists had made of Napoleon a sort of idol and Béranger's nostalgic songs of the Emperor's glory were sung in all strata of society. Louis-Philippe brought back from St. Helena the body of Napoleon in order to appease his enemies and had it buried in great pomp at the Invalides. He also completed, in 1836, the Arc de Triomphe de l'Etoile.

[20] The present day contender to the throne, the Comte de Paris, is a descendant of Louis-Philippe.

Joséphine's
Château de Malmaison

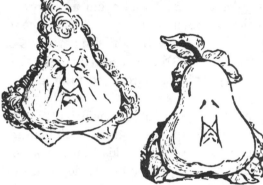

Daumier: Caricatures of
Louis-Philippe

Balzac by David d'Angers

The Napoleonic legend was so popular, that when elections were held for the presidency of the new republic, the candidate who won the majority of votes by a huge margin was Louis-Napoléon Bonaparte, son of the ex-king of Holland and nephew of the Emperor. He had already attempted, in 1836 and 1849, to overthrow the Orleanist régime with the help of the army and now began, immediately after his inauguration, to prepare the overthrow of the republic. In December 1851, he reestablished the empire in a famous coup d'état, and proclaimed himself Napoleon III.[21]

The Second Empire

In spite of his promise to "serve the French people", Napoleon III was an ambitious and unscrupulous opportunist. He was also an ingenious schemer and managed to be confirmed by a plebiscite thanks to a clever slogan "L'empire, c'est la paix" (Empire = peace). While the royalists and the old aristocracy immediately expressed their reservations, and such writers of stature as Victor Hugo, who went into voluntary exile on the island of Guernesey, tried to incite the people to revolt against "Napoléon le petit", most Frenchmen greeted his coming to power as a fulfillment of their hopes. The bourgeoisie wanted peace which would bring about continued prosperity, and the army a return of the prestige of the military. But the foreign powers looked at the new "usurper" with defiance and mistrust, and the new emperor, unable to find a true princess for a wife, married the lovely Spanish noblewoman Eugénie de Montijo, with whom he had earlier fallen in love (her beauty is admirably captured in the portraits of Winterhalter, some of which toured the U.S. in the 1970's). Louis-Napoleon and Eugénie immediately started a brilliant court, filled with entertainment and merriment. The festivities at the Tuileries attained a magnificence unseen since the days of Louis

---

[21] There was no Napoleon II: the name had been reserved for the son of Napoleon Bonaparte.

XIV. Paris became once again the artistic capital of the world where people from all other countries converged in order to enjoy themselves, listen to the music of Offenbach, applaud cancan dancers and avail themselves of the the services of an entire plethora of "demimondaines".[22] While the Emperor also had important changes made in other cities, Paris had truly become the apple of his eye. He was instrumental in giving it its present day shape, looks and character. Baron Eugène Haussmann, an able and energetic man, who was put in charge of the revamping of the city, demolished old and unhealthy neighborhoods, installed a network of sewers, created the central marketplace Les Halles (a picturesque landmark until it was in recent years moved to Rungis in order to make way for the Centre Pompidou), pierced the great arteries which constitute today's "grands boulevards", built eighty five miles of new streets, installed gaslights in the entire city and covered the pavements with asphalt. The beautiful parks of Bois de Boulogne and Vincennes also date back to this period, as well as the Opéra (which is today adorned with a ceiling painted by Marc Chagall). Napoleon III did more to the Louvre than any of its previous occupants: the palace was finally completed and connected on both sides with the Tuileries.

At the same time the "grands magasins" or department stores made their first appearance and since then have mushroomed all over France as well as abroad.

Napoleon was interested in art and with his Empress regularly visited painting exhibitions. The official "salons" favored the traditional "academic" approach, which produced very mediocre works, while stifling new endeavors, such as the budding current of Impressionism. The rejected artists, encouraged by the Emperor himself, eventually exhibited under the leadership of Manet their new vision in the Salon des Refusés in 1863.

---

[22] Ranging from the humble "grisette" to the demanding and expensive "lionne". The middle and late 1800s can be considered as the "reign of the courtesan" and a number of prominent writers pondered her "rise and fall" and her role in French society: Balzac (*Splendeurs et misères des courtisanes*), Dumas (*Le Demi-monde* and *La Dame aux camélias* on which Verdi's *Traviata* is based) and Zola (*Nana*), to name just a few.

The Second Empire began as a kind of dictatorship, with strict enforcement of censorship of the press and an elective system devised in a way that favored the administration's candidates. In a clever move, Napoleon rallied the clergy by material favors, thus depriving the royalists of their traditional ally. Though he did finally institute universal suffrage (only men however, voted in France until 1945) and considerably relaxed censorship and all forms of political repression— he even transformed the empire into a constitutional monarchy in 1869—his popularity steadily waned, especially after important initial victories in foreign policy and on distant fronts turned into a series of disasters. French colonies in Algeria, Indochina, Senegal and the Levant flourished. In the fifties France's prestige was enhanced by the defeat of the Russians in the Crimean war (victories at Alma, Sebastopol, Malakoff) and the successful French intervention in Italy (Magenta, Solferino). But in the sixties France lost diplomatically both in Poland, while supporting the Polish people's unsuccessful revolution against the Russians, and in the unfortunate Mexican venture which ended in the execution of the French protégé Maximilian by the forces of Benito Juárez. In 1870, Napoleon unwittingly got himself trapped into declaring a war on Prussia which ended catastrophically: over 100,000 French troops were captured by the Germans at Sedan and the Emperor himself was taken prisoner.

In Paris, the Palais Bourbon was immediately invaded by republican demonstrators and the IIIrd Republic was proclaimed. Napoleon III took the road to exile in England, where he died. Meanwhile, the war against Prussia continued to go badly. Paris surrendered in 1871, the German troops marched down the Champs-Elysées and, in the treaty signed in Versailles' "Hall of Mirrors", France surrendered Alsace and Lorraine and agreed to pay an enormous indemnity. Since, during the general elections that followed the disaster, the National Assembly in Versailles headed by Thiers was clearly dominated by monarchists, the city of Paris set up its own government, the Commune, and called for an insurrection. What ensued was a brief, but extremely bitter and bloody fratricidal confrontation, in which Marshal MacMahon's troops ultimately routed the undisciplined ranks of the "communards". This struggle and the repression that followed left lasting scars in the minds of the French people and in the capital itself where many historic buildings were set on fire. Among others, Catherine de Médicis' Tuileries palace was gutted and eventually declared as being beyond repair. It was torn down to make room for today's "Jardin des Tuileries" which opened a beautiful perspective from the Louvre on the Place de la Concorde.

WHAT TO SEE

- Reims: Musée du Tau, coronation cape of Charles X
- Paris: The Louvre: additions of Napoleon III
      The Garnier Opéra
      The "grands boulevards," the outer boulevards and a
            number of squares (Etoile, Bastille, Nation)
            planned by Haussmann. The "grands magazins"
      Musée Hugo in the Marais
- Compiègne: Museum in château, souvenirs of Louis-Philippe

The Third Republic until 1914

In August, 1871, Thiers' provisional authority was made official by conferring upon him the office of President of the Republic. The new president secured the evacuation of German troops and managed to repay the huge indemnity imposed by the winning power earlier than had been agreed upon. Thiers and MacMahon, who replaced him two years later, were both monarchists and it appeared that a new restoration was imminent. This was averted by the split between the two royalist factions, the partisans of the Orleanists, who supported the heirs of Louis-Philippe, and the legitimists, who hoped for the return to the throne of the grandson of Charles X, the Comte de Chambord. The latter lost this golden opportunity by his stubborn adherence to ultra-conservative views: he wanted to restore the white flag of royalty and abolish the tricolor, in use since the Revolution. Eventually, in 1875, after a series of constitutional laws, the republic as state form was finally enacted by a one-vote majority. The royalists did not disarm, however, and it was not until 1879, when MacMahon resigned, that the victory of the republicans was complete. They immediately settled some old scores: the 14th of July was adopted as a national holiday, the Jesuit Order dissolved, a system of free, secular education instituted and divorce, which had been prohibited during the Restoration, made lawful again. An amnesty was also granted to the participants in the 1871 Commune rebellion.

The constitution of 1875 established the office of a president, elected for seven years and vested with executive power, and a two-body Assemblée Nationale, composed of the "Chambre de députés" and the "Sénat", and endowed with great powers: it could at any time issue a no-confidence vote against the Cabinet of the prime minister, who was then forced to submit his resignation. The triumph of the legislative over the executive resulted in unparalleled ministerial instability, characteristic of the IIIrd and IVth Republics, and which was to last until 1958.

In 1887, the threat of a new coup d'état loomed again over the Third Republic. All the opposition, including the Bonapartists, had rallied under the banner of a popular minister of war, General Boulanger. But at the very moment when he could have seized power, the General changed his mind and fled to Belgium where he committed suicide. This, and the fact that Pope Leo XIII intervened to end the Catholics' opposition to the republican regime, did not prevent further hostility and confrontations. The most violent crisis erupted with the well known Dreyfus affair, when an army officer of Jewish origin was unjustly convicted of treason and sent for lifelong imprisonment to Devil's Island. The country was equally divided into two camps, the anti-Dreyfusards, made up of conservative elements, and the Dreyfusards who were leftists like Jaurès, republicans like Clémenceau or intellectuals like Emile Zola. The latter fought a sort of sacred war for the rehabilitation of Dreyfus who had become a symbolic victim of oppression and created a chasm between two opposing ideologies. Eventually, Dreyfus was exonerated and the French army purged of its conservative elements. Religious congregations were attacked and suppressed, their property was confiscated and some 10,000 Catholic schools forced to close. The Radical Republicans, who had come into power, put an end to the Concordat and established the Law of Separation of the Church from the state. In 1905, the Socialists eventually withdrew from the leftist bloc and later, after 1911, at the end of the radical ministry of Clémenceau, a more moderate republican government under Poincaré assumed power. Throughout this period, French society continued to enjoy, despite some economic catastrophes such as the infestation of the vineyards by the phylloxera, an ever improving life standard.

The lot of the workers and manual laborers who had reached the bottom of misery, so vividly described in Zola's fiction (*Germinal, L'Assomoir, Nana* among others), became more bearable. In 1884, trade unions were allowed to assemble and several years later the CGT (Confédération Générale du Travail), which is still today the most important union in France, was founded.

The new current of social Catholicism was also born out of a powerful Catholic revival. In 1910 the church of Sacré-Coeur, begun in 1876, was finally completed. In 1867, under Napoleon III, there had already been a World Exhibition in Paris, but that which was held in 1889, date of the centenary of the French Revolution, surpassed all expectations and drew 25 million visitors, though this republican venture was boycotted by the crowned heads of Europe. It was highlighted by the famous iron tower built for the occasion by Gustave Eiffel. Considered a horror by many Parisians at the time, it remained and has been ever since the beloved and most popular landmark in the French capital. During the festivities, a miniature copy of the Statue of Liberty, which had been offered by the French government to the United States in 1866, was unveiled on the Pont de Grenelle. The next "Exposition" (1900) left Paris two of its most popular exhibition halls: the Grand Palais and the Petit Palais.

The French upper classes continued to enjoy a carefree life, filled with pleasures and made easier by the many technological inventions of the preceding years. The modern bicycle and the automobile had made their appearance, the first "salon de l'auto" took place in 1898, and Paris was now endowed with a complete network of an underground communication system, the "métro".

In 1909 Blériot flew a plane from Calais to Dover. All the arts were flourishing and the first years of the 20th century richly deserve their name of "la belle époque". It was brutally interrupted by the outbreak of World War I, which was to bring about drastic changes in the way of life and the map of the world.

Letters, Arts and Sciences in the 19th Century

The richness and variety of the different literary and artistic currents which emerged, intertwined and evolved in the course of the 19th century even more rapidly than the changing political scene, allows here only a very general and simplified overview of the most important trends, such as Neoclassicism, Romanticism, Realism, Naturalism, Symbolism and Impressionism.

As was discussed earlier, the return to the "noble simplicity and quiet grandeur" of the neoclassical ideal extolled by the German Winckelmann and embodied in the works of **David** suited to perfection the taste of Napoleon I, who also favored the French 17th century classical literature. After David's death one of his disciples, the legendary **Ingres**, carried the sacred torch of Neoclassicism with its quest for the "ideal beauty" well into the middle of the 19th century.

Ingres, who was also a career violinist, achieved great renown and success in his day and has always been admired not only for his masterful touch and the purity of his lines, but also for his incredible versatility.[23] He left a number of outstanding portraits, including several of Napoleon I.

Whereas Classicism lingered on for several decades in the realm of visual arts, it was dealt a decisive blow by the rising tide of *Romanticism* in the field of literature as early as the first third of the century: the year 1830 marks not only the July Revolution and the deposition of Charles X, but also the "battle of *Hernani*". At the time of the first performance of this *drame* by Victor Hugo[24] which mixed all the genres, the long-haired Romantic poets engaged in a fist-fight with the "old fogies" and succeeded in conquering "the sterile cap of the three unities" and freeing the theatre from all classical constraints.

The roots of Romanticism can be traced, as will be remembered, to the 18th century, to Rousseau in France and a group of German writers, particularly Goethe, whose novel *The Sorrows of Werther* influenced an entire generation. The contrast between Classicism and Romanticism is illustrated in the simplified table on the next page.

From the rather large group of Romantic writers, Chateaubriand,[25] Lamartine, Vigny and Musset, whose plays are enjoying an unprecedented success on the contemporary French stage, **Victor Hugo** stands out as the uncontested leader who wielded a powerful influence not only in literary, but in social and political matters as well. Hugo was a true force of nature whose overwhelming literary

---

[23] Some of his canvasses like *Le Songe d'Ossian* and *Francesca da Rimini* are linked to Romanticism in subject matter as well as in treatment. Ingres did become, however, the symbol of Academicism and his monumental *Apothéose d'Homère* can be considered as a manifesto of Classicism. Pictured at the feet of Homer are his numerous disciples and followers, and among them Raphael, Poussin, Molière and Racine. Other famous paintings by Ingres include *La Grande Odalisque*, *Le Bain turc* (The Turkish Bath), *Oedipe et le Sphinx*, *Jupiter et Thétis*, *Stratonice*, *Le voeu de Louis XIII* and *Jeanne d'Arc*.

[24] *Hernani* inspired Verdi's beautiful opera bearing the same title (*Ernani*).

[25] Chateaubriand spent his childhood in a somber medieval castle, Combourg, and was lodged in one of its towers, where howling winds and haunting dreams were his only companions. The castle, not far from St. Malo in Brittany, is open to tourists.

production spans the century and comprises poetry, theatre and fiction. Although Hugo is known in France mainly as a poet, some of his novels have become world classics particularly *Notre-Dame de*

CLASSICISM	ROMANTICISM
general, universal, "eternal" man	individual, a "certain man"
social, mundane: appeal to elegant elite	anti-social: the Romanticist is a solitary man at odds with society, who finds refuge in nature
impersonal, objective; respect of rules; discipline, symmetry, equilibrium, restraint, reason, intelligence, logic	personal, subjective, "confession", freedom, even anarchy; lyricism, enthusiasm; exaggeration, imagination; instincts, passion, feelings, sensitivity; "internal conflict of man"
will power, control of feelings	melancholy and discouragement, ("Weltschmerz", "mal du siècle")
conciseness, precision	vagueness
clarity, lucidity	mystery, dreams
rejection of violence, of "extremes", of irrationality	unbridled violence, appeal of the supernatural, of death
inspiration drawn from pagan antiquity	contemporary subjects, nationalism, folklore
scorn for things "irregular," for the Middle Ages	love of strange things, of exoticism, appeal of the "dark ages" with their somber mysteries
strict rules of versification	freedom of versification
strict rules for theatre	freedom from all constraints: mixing of comic and tragic elements, of the "grotesque" and the "sublime"

Paris (*The Hunchback of Notre-Dame*) and *Les Misérables*, which, set to music in the 1980s, has beaten all records of attendance at the box office.[26]

Three prominent novelists, contemporary of the Romanticists can be classified as "Romantic realists." They endeavored to render reality in an objective, impersonal way without detracting or embellishing. **Balzac**,[27] the author of the awesome *Comédie humaine*; **Stendhal**, whose two masterpieces *Le Rouge et le noir* and *La Chartreuse de Parme* are still often screened on television in their most famous versions;[28] and **Mérimée**, to whom we owe not only several outstanding short stories (*Carmen* inspired Bizet's opera), but also the preservation of numerous Roman and medieval sites and monuments. In his capacity of "inspecteur général des monuments historiques", Mérimée entrusted Viollet-le-Duc with the restoration of the amphitheatres of Arles and of Orange, the fortress of Carcassonne and the churches of Vézelay and Notre-Dame de Paris among many others.

Romanticism was, toward the middle of the century, superseded by Realism, best expounded in the works of **Flaubert**, who strove to render the life of middle class people in an unexalted way, based on exact observation and documentation. Flaubert is one of the greatest French prose writers, known for the perfection of his style, his search for *le mot juste* and the harmonious rhythm of his sentence. His masterpiece, *Madame Bovary* (1857) created a scandal; but unlike his unhappy contemporary Baudelaire, Flaubert was found innocent of the charges of immorality brought against him in a law suit.

---

[26] The prolific Dumas father and son were probably the most popular authors of the time: they created several hundred plays and novels, among which *The Three Musketeers* (see above). George Sand, the feminist who smoked and sported men's clothes, was yet another widely read novelist of the Romantic era. She is also famous for her flashy amorous adventures and was the great love of both Musset and Chopin.

[27] Balzac appears to be still the most popular author: 69% of today's French readers have read at least one of his works.

[28] *Le Rouge et le noir* with Gérard Philipe and Danielle Darrieux; *La Chartreuse de Parme* with Marthe Keller.

In the generation that followed, Realism was continued in an exaggerated form by Naturalism which was linked with a school of thought called Positivism and shared its faith in the unlimited progress of science. Science had, indeed, made remarkable strides in all the fields, notably in optics and medicine.[29] While we owe the most remarkable discoveries to **Pasteur**,[30] Darwin's work on the origins of species and Claude Bernard's *Introduction à l'étude de la médecine expérimentale* had a direct bearing on the direction taken by Naturalism in the field of literature. The chief exponents of this current, the Goncourt brothers[31] and **Emile Zola**, attempted to apply the "clinical" method to the so-called "experimental novel" and thus reach "scientific truth" in the study of all aspects of human relations. Zola, while comparing himself to a physician in a laboratory, tried to prove his theories on the influence of heredity in a series of novels, *Les Rougon-Macquart (L'Assommoir, Germinal, Nana,* which were mentioned earlier, are still widely read today.) Two other fellow Naturalists, the unsurpassed short story writer **Maupassant** and the beloved Provençal **Daudet** developed, however, an entirely independent and personal style.

A minor poetic school, contemporary with Realism, the Parnassians, whose motto was *L'Art pour l'art* (Art for art's sake), aimed at a poetry of formal perfection, divorced from any social or moral preoccupations.

The end of the 19th century was marked by a violent reaction against Realism and Naturalism, brought about by the literary current called Symbolism, whose ideal was precisely the escape from reality. Symbolism found its early expression in the works of Baude-

---

[29] An extremely important breakthrough occurred in 1898 when the Polish born Marie Sklodowska-Curie and her husband Pierre discovered radium (Nobel prizes in 1903 and 1911).

[30] Few people are unaware of Pasteur's gigantic contribution to science: pasteurization is an everyday word, and the story of his successful battle against rabies has become legendary. The Pasteur Institute in Paris celebrated its 100 years anniversary in October 1987.

[31] Edmond was the founder of a literary society, which awards the "prix Goncourt", the most coveted literary prize in France.

laire, Verlaine and the precocious young rebel and innovator, Rimbaud, who experimented with the "alchemy of words." **Baudelaire**, the ultimate poet according to many, whose *Fleurs du mal* still exert a certain fascination more than a hundred years after its publication, was greatly influenced by Edgar Allan Poe. Baudelaire felt that poetry ought not be explicit, but appeal to the imagination through the "invisible, the impalpable, the dream." He saw the world as a "forest of symbols" and explored what is known in psychology as synaesthesia, or correspondences between various sense perceptions, such as listening to perfumes, savoring music and smelling colors. The most musical of all poets, **Verlaine**, stressed the importance of sound and rhythm: "De la musique avant toute chose" he says at the very beginning of his "Art poétique." He favored vagueness, airiness and mistiness and tried to establish new relationships between the word and the image. The Symbolist *chef de file*, **Mallarmé**, believed that the poet must suggest rather than state and "paint not the thing but the effect it produces."

Symbolism is prominently linked with Impressionism in other art forms: the Impressionist painters left the mixing of color to the eye of the beholder just as the Symbolists left the connection and form of their lines to be completed by the reader, and Debussy set to music not only sixteen of Verlaine's poems, including "Clair de lune", but also Maeterlinck's symbolist play, *Pelléas et Mélisande* and Mallarmé's *L'Après-midi d'un faune*. His prelude rendering "sounds and perfumes in the evening air" echoes Baudelaire's line "Les sons et les parfums tournent dans l'air du soir" in the first stanza of his melodious, haunting *pantoum*, "Harmonie du soir".

Baudelaire was not only a great poet, but also a remarkable art critic who was first to appreciate such talents as Courbet and Manet; he felt, however, an especially strong link with the Romanticists, and particularly with Delacroix, whom he considered to be the most enlightening of humanity's "beacons" (*Les Phares*).

It was **Géricault**, who more so than any of his contemporaries, paved the way for Romanticism in painting. In spite of his preoccupation with line and composition and his attachment to classical form, he was inclined toward violence and strong emotions. He also had a feeling for movement and chose to paint the world of his own day rather than mythological heroes (*Le Cuirassier blessé, L'Officier de la garde*). The *Radeau de la Méduse*, his poignant representation of a macabre contemporary event, appeared shocking on account of the ghastly nature of the scene, its gory details and grisly connotations.[32]

After Géricault's premature death caused by a fall on horseback, **Delacroix** (believed to be the natural son of Talleyrand) became the leading Romantic painter: his technique, his choice of emotional and violent subjects (death, carnage, cruelty, genocide, martyrdom and desolation) and his preference for the medieval, the exotic and the contemporary make him the very embodiment of Romanticism. Delacroix's canvasses are imbued with movement, pathos and horror; he also portrayed wild beasts and oriental women, the "very essence of femininity" with the "eternal mystery of their eyes". Delacroix was successful in achieving fame in his own time, despite the protests and vituperations of the "Academicians": Ingres scoffed at the great Romanticist's "drunken brush". And Delacroix was, indeed, intoxicated with color, which to him *was* the line.[33] He exerted a profound influence on modern painting by his conscious use of color blobs, streaks and masses, based on the new theories expounded by the physicists of his time and pertaining to the color circle and the effect of "complementary" colors.

Romanticism in sculpture is best represented by the work of **Rude**, whose *Marseillaise* (or "Departure of volunteers") adorns one side of the Paris Arc de Triomphe.

Realism with naturalistic tendencies in painting was defined by **Courbet** in a 1855 manifesto, in which he stated that his aim was to present "the customs, ideas and appearance of his own time."

---

[32] The canvas depicts the discovery, in the middle of the ocean, of a pathetic handful of survivors of a shipwreck, the victims of a naval disaster apparently brought about by the negligence of the government. The mixture of livid corpses with bodies of the survivors, who managed to stay alive by throwing the weaker into the water and practicing cannibalism, breathes anguish, despair and revulsion.

[33] "La ligne nait du choc des couleurs" (line is born from the collision of colors).

Courbet's prosaic scenes from everyday life are devoid of any grace or beauty and are meant to carry a social message. His painting *L'Enterrement à Ornans* created a scandal because its matter-of-fact portrayal of a funeral: its total lack of spirituality and vulgar ambiance seemed to negate the immortality of the soul.

The talented caricaturist **Daumier** is another Realist who had the same dedication to humble subjects and was a socially minded republican. He is best known for his satirical political cartoons.[34]

Even before the middle of the 19th century, several French artists concentrated their attention on landscapes which they painted for the first time in open air. This *plein-air* painting was made possible by the invention of the tin-tube. **Théodore Rousseau** and members of the so-called Ecole de Barbizon portrayed for the most part the surroundings of Fontainebleau; Millet is best known for his peasant scenes such as *Les Glaneuses* (The Gleaners) and *l'Angélus*. **Corot**, who was perhaps the first to look at nature with a "photographic" eye,[35] studied the luminosity of a sunny day and its reflections in the shaded areas, and is a precursor of the Impressionists in his exploration of the effects of light. But with the advent of *Impressionism*, light itself and the way it affects our perception of objects became the real subject of painting.

Impressionism, the most widely appreciated of all artistic movements, is so well known that it hardly needs an introduction or explanation (see Appendix for further detail). We owe the word "Impressionism"—a term of critical derision like Gothic, Realism and Fauvism—to a painting by **Monet** displayed in 1874 and entitled *Impression de soleil levant* (Impression of Sunrise). Claude Monet became the leader of the group of young innovators; he was joined by Renoir, Pissarro, Sisley and influenced Cézanne, Degas and

---

[34] Both Courbet and Daumier were closely associated with the Commune during its brief "reign" over Paris. Courbet, who was in charge of the Louvre and other historic monuments, ordered the toppling of the Colonne Vendôme which had been erected to the glory of Napoleon's victory at Austerlitz. Thiers' government put it back and made Courbet pay for the cost of restoration.

[35] Photography had been invented by Niepce and Daguerre and perfected in the 1840s.

Manet. While **Manet** had actually paved the way for Impressionism by exhibiting several "scandalous" canvasses (*Le Déjeuner sur l'herbe, Olympia*) in the Salon des Refusés (see above), only his later works, like *Bar aux Folies-Bergères*, are close to the art of the Impressionists. Manet's sister-in-law, Berthe Morisot, who excelled in the representation of domestic scenes and the American Mary Cassatt are the two women most prominently associated with Impressionism.

Cézanne eventually parted ways with the Impressionists and moved to Aix-en-Provence where he painted the surrounding landscapes, particularly the Montagne Sainte-Victoire, as well as numerous still lifes with an emphasis on planes, masses and geometric forms such as spheres, cylinders and cones. He is a precursor of the 20th century Cubists.

Toulouse-Lautrec had only a loose association with the Impressionists and, unlike them, never painted outdoors but portrayed in a unique fashion the closed "underworld" of entertainers, dancers, prostitutes and cabarets, where he spent most of his time trying to forget through debauchery and alcohol the infirmity that afflicted him. Lautrec is the supreme colorist and has never been surpassed in the art of poster designing (*Jane Avril, La Goulue, Aristide Bruant*).

Whereas Impressionism in painting is, as was seen above, very close to Symbolism in literature, a group of painters who called themselves Symbolists and portrayed a world of myth and fantasy, emerged in the late 19th century. These artists, most importantly Gustave Moreau, Odilon Redon, and Puvis de Chavannes developed entirely distinct styles within the programmed "ideal, symbolical, synthetic, subjective and decorative." Their work may be considered a protest against materialism, empiricism and scientism.

The term *Post-impressionism* is used with reference to the young generation of painters who had been influenced by Impressionism, but pursued entirely new artistic goals. **Seurat** (*Un Dimanche d'été à la Grande Jatte, Le Cirque*) and a group of friends, among which Signac, called themselves Neo-impressionists and clearly defined their aesthetics. Their technique of dividing color and applying distinct touches in tiny dots or points to merge in the observer's eye led to the coining of the term *Pointillism.*

The two towering figures of Post-impressionism, who had been closely associated with Pissarro and Seurat in Paris and whose stormy friendship ended in rift and tragedy, are Gauguin and Van Gogh. **Gauguin** abandoned a lucrative career as a stockbroker to paint at first in Brittany, then briefly under the sunny skies of the Provence where he had followed Van Gogh, and finally, having turned his back on Western civilization and his own family, in Tahiti and the Marquesas Islands. There his art, influenced by Japanese prints and his study of stained glass techniques, found its fullfilment in the portrayal of naive life "in nature." It tends toward simplicity, brilliant colors and large flat surfaces which Gauguin encircled with vigorous outlines. His flattened compositions, from which he eliminated shadows and aerial perspective, in search of what he termed a "childlike, synthetic barbarity" (he cautioned against painting too close to nature, claiming that "art is an abstraction"), has markedly influenced 20th century painters.

Van Gogh, whose *Sunflowers* (*Tournesols*) and *Irises* brought in 1987 the highest price ever paid for paintings until that year and whose talent was never recognized in his own time, is such a celebrity today that his tragic life and his unique art are almost universally known. Though he committed suicide at the age of 37, Van Gogh left an enormous *oeuvre.* The objects and fantastic landscapes he painted with violent tones used to their utmost intensity—trees, flowers, clouds, stars—become alive in swirling, dancing lines vibrating with anxiety and are rich in emotive, often disturbing associations. He is considered by some critics as a precursor of 20th century Expressionists.

Late 19th century sculpture is best represented in the works of Barye, who depicted mostly animals; the "Impressionist" Carpeaux whose *La Danse* adorns the Paris Opera; and by the beloved **Rodin** who does not need an introduction: his masterpieces can be admired

Napoleon III

*George Sand as sketched
by Alfred de Musset*

Alfred Sisley

in all the major cities in the world and numerous campuses throughout the United States.[36]

Nineteenth century architecture was in no way seminal: Garnier's
Opera lacks originality and embodies the lifestyle and taste for luxury
of the "belle époque",[37] but Labrouste's Bibliothèque Ste Geneviève
and the reading hall of the Bibliothèque Nationale deserve mention
for the ingenious use the the architect made of the new material at
his disposal—metal—and brought it to its fullest structural potential,
while achieving a balance between the pleasing and the functional.
The possibilities of metallic construction were further illustrated, as
we know, by the erection of the Eiffel Tower in 1889.

In music, Romanticism is best represented in the works of Hector
Berlioz (*La Symphonie Fantastique, Les Troyens, Roméo et Juli-
ette, La Damnation de Faust*), though two other non-French composers, the Polish Chopin and the Hungarian Liszt, both of whom
created in France, ought to be mentioned. The second part of the century abounds in gifted composers who achieved considerable renown:
Gounod, best known for his opera *Faust*; **Saint-Saëns** (*Danse
macabre, Le Carnaval des animaux*); César Franck; Lalo; Charpentier; Chausson; Chabrier; Massenet (operas *Les Pêcheurs de per-
les, Manon, Le Cid, Thaïs*); **Bizet** (*Carmen, l'Arlésienne*); Delibes;
d'Indy; and Gabriel Fauré. The versatile **Debussy**, who was considered in turn a Classicist, a Romantic and Impressionist-symbolist,
was eventually accused of being a "revolutionary." The German born
Jacques Offenbach, who so admirably rendered the lively, carefree
mood of the mid-to-late 1800s in a series of extremely popular light
operas (*La Belle Hélène, Orphée aux enfers, Gaîté parisienne, La
Vie parisienne* and the more serious *Contes d'Hoffman*), has already
been mentioned above.

---

[36] Best known are *Le Penseur* (The Thinker), *Le Baiser* (The Kiss), *Les Bourgeois de Calais, Balzac, Eve,* and *La Cathédrale.*

[37] It was, in 1861, the largest stage in the world, which could accomodate 450
performers at the same time.

A poster by Toulouse-Lautrec

Centenary of the 1875
Constitution

1889

Rodin

WHAT TO SEE

- Paris: The Louvre: 19th century art
  The Grand Palais and Petit Palais
  The Garnier Opera
  The Bibliothèque Nationale reading hall
  Musée d'Orsay: 19th century art (opened in 1986)
  Musée Balzac (in the 16th arrondissement)
  Musée Delacroix
  Musée Victor Hugo
  Musée Gustave Moreau
  Musée Rodin
  Musée Zola (opened in 1987)
  Museums devoted to works of the Impressionists:
        the Orangerie and Musée Marmottan (Monet)
  Statue of Balzac by Rodin (on Boulevard Raspail)
- Berry: Nohant: château of George Sand (souvenirs of Chopin
  and other Romanticists)
- Brittany: Chateaubriand's château de Combourg
  Pont-Aven: Museum
- Burgundy: Dijon: Musée Rude
- Normandy: Monet's house in Giverny
  Rouen: Musée des Beaux-Arts
- Provence: Aix-en-Provence: Musée Cézanne
  Cagnes-s/mer: Renoir house and museum
  Marseille: Musée des Beaux-Arts (works of Daumier)
  Nice: Musée Masséna
  St. Rémy-en-Provence: Asylum where Van Gogh was
  confined
- S.W.: Albi: Musée Toulouse-Lautrec.
- Various other art museums in major provincial cities:
        Avignon, Carcassonne, Lyon, Montpellier, Reims,
        Strasbourg, etc. (in Ornans, near Besançon, Musée
        Courbet)

Chapter 9

THE TWENTIETH CENTURY

World War I

While there were, in the last decades of the 19th and the first of the 20th centuries, considerable exchanges in all the cultural and technological domains between the leading European countries, a number of international conflicts among them arose quite regularly, but managed to be settled before the big confrontation took place. From the Franco-Prussian war in 1870 Germany emerged under the leadership of Bismarck as the strongest political power on the Continent. But France had not forgotten the wounds of the defeat and the loss of Alsace and Lorraine, and the wish to retaliate was kept alive by a strong nationalistic and patriotic movement, kindled by a number of first-class thinkers and writers (the "Action française" was founded in 1899). Bismarck succeeded in segregating republican France from the rest of royalist European states and was helped in his endeavors by England's policy of "splendid isolation". However, competition in the field of colonial expansion and conflicts of interest in various areas, among others in the Balkans, led to the formation of several alignments or coalitions such as the "Triple Alliance" be-

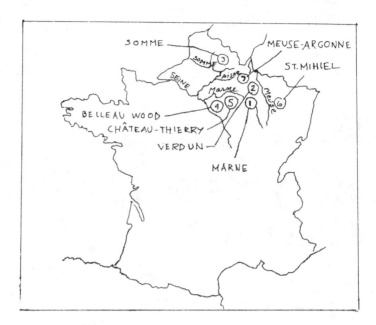

World War I

The "Lion de Belfort"

Nov. 11, 1918

1923 - 1953

tween Germany, Austria, and Italy: it was countered by the signing of the "Triple Entente" between France, Russia and England. The two hostile blocs maintained peace, while feverishly arming for a war which increasingly appeared unavoidable.

In June 1914, a seemingly trivial incident, the assassination in Sarajevo, Yugoslavia, of Archduke Ferdinand, heir to the Austrian throne, was seized by Austria as a pretext to crush the Serbians. Unexpectedly, the Russian tsar responded by ordering a general mobilization of his troops and Germany in turn reacted according to a preestablished strategic plan: it called for a lightning victory over France in order to face the Russians on the eastern front with overwhelming strength. Well aware of the French defense line in the east, the Germans crossed Belgium in a swift move and launched a fierce attack on the northern plains of France, whereupon England decided to declare war. As the Germans approached Paris and the French government left the capital to establish itself in Bordeaux, the army of General Joffre halted the invaders in a battle which is referred to as "the miracle of the Marne". It was followed by three years of practically total stalemate, as the opponents, "entrenched" along a line from Flanders to Belfort behind networks of barbed wire, pursued an exhausting murderous and extremely bloody "trench war". The French victory in defending Verdun was in terms of human lives the single most costly battle in French history. While Marshal Pétain and his "poilus"[1], whose motto was "Ils ne passeront pas" ("They will not get through") achieved unprecedented glory, close to half a million men perished in the fighting.[2]

The year 1917 brought a breakthrough. It had started with a series of setbacks both at home, where until Clémenceau's return to power the war was run inefficiently and where pacifist movements were steadily growing stronger, and abroad: in Russia the tsarist régime fell under the revolution led by the Bolsheviks. But in June

---

[1] "Poilu" means "hairy": it was the designation for the World War I French soldier, who had no time to shave in the midst of the trench war.

[2] Among others the brillant author Péguy. The father of modern poetry, Apollinaire, was wounded in the head.

the United States entered the war: 200,000 American soldiers disembarked by Christmas and a total of one million joined the allied armies before the end of hostilities.

In the fall of 1918, General Foch, in command of the joint French and British troops, forced the Germans under Ludendorff to retreat. On November 11, after the abdication of the Kaiser, all military operations ceased and the new German republic accepted an unconditional surrender. The treaty that followed was again signed in the Galerie des Glaces (Hall of Mirrors) at Versailles, in June, 1919.

WHAT TO SEE

- Paris: Musée de l'Armée at the Invalides
    Palais de Chaillot and Musée d'art moderne
    Statues of General Foch and General Joffre
    Replica of the "Lion de Belfort", Place Denfert-Rochereau
    Tomb of the unknown soldier under the Arc de Triomphe
- Lorraine: World War I defense lines; Belfort, Montfaucon, trenches
    American military cemeteries
    Ossuary of Douaumont
    Verdun: Museum
- Versailles: Galerie des Glaces
- Compiègne: Wagon where Germans signed surrender

The "Entre-deux-guerres"[3] and World War II

While France had won World War I, it can be said that she lost the peace which followed—at the Treaty of Versailles, Clémenceau was unable to get the English and American allies to agree to set the

---

[3] "Between-two-wars"

French eastern border so as to insure the future security of the country. Although it did recover Alsace and Lorraine, the territory of the Saar, which it was claiming, was put under the surveillance of the newly created League of Nations[4] for fifteen years, at the end of which time a plebiscite was supposed to be held. Germany was required to pay a huge indemnity, but no means were determined by which the peace terms could be enforced. More importantly, France was deeply scarred by the war: close to one and a half million soldiers had been killed and more than one million disabled. The vestiges of the devastating battles in Lorraine, such as the trenches covered with barbed wire, the numerous military cemeteries with rows of identical white crosses and the bloodchilling Ossuary of Douaumont, still visited by scores of tourists, bear witness to truly gruesome events. The idealistic American president, Woodrow Wilson, who resurrected Poland and Czechoslovakia and put three Baltic states, Estonia, Latvia and Lithuania on the map of Europe, was dreaming of a happy community of peacefully coexisting nations, but did not give the League of Nations the means of effectively enforcing its decisions or sanctions.

While France was struggling with a difficult economic situation, aggravated by debts contracted during the war, its allies wanted a speedy German recovery and made no effort to make the Germans pay the indemnity they owed to the victorious nations. The United States assumed once again its policy of isolation and noninterference, and France was alone in helping Poland to repel a new invasion from the east. The Bolsheviks, who were ruling Russia after the 1917 October Revolution, launched in 1920 a full-fledged offensive against Poland. They were stopped by the heroic troops of the newly resurrected Polish state, reinforced by a detachment of French soldiers under General Weygand, whose assistant was a certain captain Charles de Gaulle, in what was later called the "miracle of the Vistula River".[5]

At home, one political crisis followed another. Immediately after the war, the election went to the right and the workers were granted

---

[4] It sadly foreshadowed today's United Nations.
[5] Reminiscent of the "Miracle of the Marne."

an eight-hour work day. In 1920, the Communists, who followed the orders of Moscow, and the Socialists split. But in 1924 the left took over and the financial problems kept on worsening: the franc eventually collapsed entirely. When Poincaré was recalled to power in 1926, he managed to restore confidence and bring about an industrial expansion. At this time a new type of big business such as Renault and Citroën made its appearance. French colonies prospered and were honored in 1931 by a magnificent Colonial Exhibition. It took place shortly before the world crisis, which had begun in the United States earlier with the Wall Street crash, reached France.

In 1937, another glamorous "Expo" opened in Paris, at which time the Trocadéro was replaced by the beautiful Palais de Chaillot complex. It constitutes, together with the Eiffel Tower across the Seine, one of the most attractive modern ensembles in the capital.

In spite of political and economic crises, many French were enjoying a carefree and glamorous life. Even during the war years the arts had flourished and new fashion trends made their appearance, inspired by such designers as Coco Chanel (she was the one to free the female body from the constraints of corsets and give it its modern appearance) and the renowned Poiret (he had designed even infirmary clothes for those socialites who volunteered their help to the sick and wounded soldiers).

The theater, which had already been a craze during the "belle époque" attracted more and more enthusiastic audiences. Along with regular stage performances, crowds attended glittering shows at the Casino de Paris and the Moulin Rouge, immortalized by such names as Maurice Chevalier, Mistinguett and the American dancer and songstress Josephine Baker. Serge Diaghilev's "Ballets Russes" continued to exert their magic spell in Paris until they were moved to Monte Carlo.[6]

The so called "années folles" ("roaring twenties") which followed the end of the hostilities were rich in creative activity in all domains. Paris became once again the center of elegance, fun and inspiration,

---

[6] Diaghilev's last discovery, the dancer Balanchine, eventually became America's most famous contemporary choreographer.

a magnet for foreign artists and writers: Picasso, Modigliani, Hemingway, F. Scott Fitzgerald, Gertrude Stein (who held a salon and was a patroness to several great painters of the time), to name just a few. In literature, after the breakthrough in poetry brought about by Guillaume Apollinaire at the beginning of the century, new vistas were opened by the Dadaists and the Surrealists, and the period boasts such names as Proust, Gide, Cocteau, Giraudoux and Valéry. Emancipated women, cigarette in hand, attended all the events, festivities and shows on equal basis with men, although they did not yet have the right to vote.

In spite of the still visible wounds inflicted upon France during the war and a vague feeling of discomfort at the sight of a strong and speedily recovering Germany, no one wanted to think of the possibility of another international conflict. In the event one did erupt, France intended to safeguard only its own frontiers. For this reason, the French military undertook the construction of a powerful system of fortifications along its eastern border, the Maginot Line, which was thought of as unconquerable by the French chief of staff. One army captain happened to disagree, and strongly recommended the development of tanks and military aviation, but his advice went unheeded. His name was Charles de Gaulle.

In 1936, the leftists, Socialists and Communists, once again reunited, won the elections and the new "Front populaire" which voted a 40-hour work week and paid vacations, brought about a further devaluation of the franc and a considerable reduction of credits for military spending. At the same time, the German troops under the orders of Chancellor Hitler proceeded with the occupation of the demilitarized zone beween France and Germany and reached the French border. France and the rest of the world were stunned, but accepted this violation of the Versailles Treaty as a simple "fait accompli". There was no reaction, either, with the exception of some insignificant protest notes, for all the blatant violations that followed, although France did sign defensive alliances with Austria, Belgium, Czechoslovakia and Poland. Hitler, who had come to power in 1933, was making no secret of his intentions to conquer all of Europe. He had reinstated military conscription in 1935. Germany also withdrew from the League of Nations. At the same time, Mussolini attacked and conquered Ethiopia and eventually aligned Italy with Germany in a pact known as the Rome-Berlin Axis. And still no counteraction came from other European powers: they deluded themselves that, if there was a confrontation, it would take place between the Fascist states and Communist Russia. An indirect standoff between the two blocs had already taken place during the 1936 Civil War in Spain, during which the Soviets were helping the Republicans, while the Axis supported General Franco.

These delusions led further to a disastrous policy of appeasement[7] toward Germany in the face of new aggressions and violations of treaties. In 1938 Hitler annexed Austria and six months later prepared for the invasion of Czechoslovakia under the pretext that a part of that country, the Sudetenland, was largely inhabited by people of German extraction. In spite of their alliance with Czechoslovakia, France's and England's ministers Daladier and Chamberlain, seeking "peace at any price", settled with the Nazi dictator in the infamous Munich Agreement. Several months later, the Czech state was invaded in its entirety by the German troops, with still no opposition whatsoever from the Western powers.

Then Hitler, acting according to a well predetermined plan, made it clear that he was going to turn his attention to Poland. Finally awakened to the rude realities, France and England tried to negotiate with Russia. But the treacherous Stalin had already signed a pact of collaboration with Hitler. Germany attacked its eastern neighbor on September 1, 1939, with all the power it had accumulated during the years of feverish armaments, with all its superior artillery, armored divisions and sophisticated aviation. The Polish troops, though unprepared, gallantly resisted the invaders even though furious and relentless bombing of all the cities and countryside inflicted

---

[7] "Appeasement only invites aggression" state the authors of *A History of the Western World* by Lyon, Rowen & Hamerow (Rand McNally, 1972). The Romans had among their most often quoted proverbs the well known "Si vis pacem, para bellum" (If you want peace, prepare for war).

tremendous losses in materiel and human lives, both military and civilian. The Poles held out for about a month—longer than could have been expected under the circumstances (the "Blitz" in France, the following year, lasted only several weeks)—but were unexpectedly invaded on their eastern frontier by the Russians who advanced to a predetermined demarcation line, previously agreed upon with the Germans (Ribbentrop-Molotov pact). On September 3, 1939, France and England declared war on Germany.

The months that followed were a total stalemate and are known as the "drôle de guerre". They were marked by a deceptive inactivity on the part of the Germans who were reinforcing their position in Poland with the help of the odious Gestapo. But in April 1940, the powerful Wehrmacht invaded Denmark and Norway (while the Russian troops crossed into Finland) and, in May, triumphantly marched through Holland and Belgium to the French border. They also penetrated the French territory at Sedan, having taken the Maginot Line from the rear against little opposition. On May 11th, Winston Churchill replaced the "peacemaker" Chamberlain and vowed a bloody and difficult campaign while calling on other nations to help free Europe from the brutal assailant. The British managed to evacuate, under heavy German bombardment, some 300,000 French and English troops from the North Sea port of Dunkerque. The French defensive collapsed entirely, though the 1914 heroes Marshal Pétain and General Weygand were called once again to take command. They were helpless against the overwhelming German military superiority and the widespread lack of morale in the French ranks, from which the ardent patriotism of the 1914 "poilus" was markedly absent. On June 14th, the German troops entered Paris, and once again paraded down the Champs-Elysées. Pétain and Weygand, deeming that any further resistance was futile (an offer to accept a "Franco-British union" had been rejected by the French leaders, temporarily residing in Bordeaux), asked for an armistice, and the eighty-four year old Pétain established a collaborationist government in the "free", i.e. unoccupied zone of France, with headquarters in Vichy (this marks the end of the Third Republic). About the same time General de

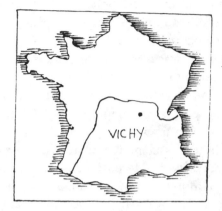

France during World War II

The Croix de Lorraine

Monument to the Martyrs
of Chateaubriant

Monument to Polish
Freedom Fighters

D-Day

Gen. de Gaulle

1944 Landing in Normandy

Gaulle, who had reached England, was calling on the French to continue their resistance and win the war side by side with the British. "France has lost a battle, but has not lost the war," he proclaimed as he started organizing the "Forces Françaises Libres."

Despite Pétain's ideas about collaboration, which brought shame upon himself and on France,[8] the Nazis' demands both in the occupied and unoccupied zones drained the country of its resources and did not prevent acts of cruelty and brutal retaliation, such as the burning of six hundred women and children in Oradour-sur-Glane. French "résistants" and members of the "maquis" who were captured were submitted to torture before being murdered and thousands were sent to forced labor and to concentration camps. Jews were rounded up and transferred in large numbers to deathcamps set up by the Gestapo in Germany and Poland (Auschwitz). Sadly enough, many French citizens, believing that Germany could not be defeated, took an attitude of "doing the best they could" under the circumstances and cooperated with the secret police. Although it may not have been as harsh as in some other countries (in Poland, for example, the hiding of a Jew was punished by death), the German occupation of France took its toll in all aspects of life. Pétain had to go from concession to concession and was eventually overshadowed by the entirely pro-German Laval. The two men, brought to trial after the end of hostilities, were sentenced to death. But Pétain's penalty, because of his meritorious past and his old age, was commuted to house imprisonment on the Ile d'Yeu. Fortunately, more and more patriotic Frenchmen had decided to save the honor of their country by joining the underground forces under the leadership of France's greatest hero of the century, Jean Moulin, who was denounced by a collaborator to the German chief of the Gestapo, Klaus Barbie, and tortured to death.

Meanwhile Britain was sustaining the war by its heroic defense in the Battle of Britain, in which it was helped by thousands of soldiers of different countries who had defected to the British Isles and were

---

[8]Though Germany tried to establish such collaborationist governments in all the occupied countries, Norway was the only other one to accept the offer.

204

A TOUS LES FRANÇAIS

La France a perdu une bataille!
Mais la France n'a pas perdu la guerre!

Des gouvernants de rencontre ont pu capituler, cedant à la panique, oubliant l'honneur, livrant le pays à la servitude. Cependant, rien n'est perdu!

Rien n'est perdu, parce que cette guerre est une guerre mondiale. Dans l'univers libre, des forces immenses n'ont pas encore donne. Un jour, ces forces ecraseront l'ennemi. Il faut que la France, ce jour-la, soit presente à la victoire. Alors, elle retrouvera sa liberte et sa grandeur. Tel est mon but, mon seul but!

Voila pourquoi je convie tous les Francais, ou qu'ils se trouvent, a s'unir à moi dans l'action, dans le sacrifice et dans l'esperance.

Notre patrie est en peril de mort. Luttons tous pour la sauver!

VIVE LA FRANCE !

GÉNÉRAL DE GAULLE

QUARTIER-GENERAL,
4, CARLTON GARDENS,
LONDON, S.W.1

Appeal of Gen. de Gaulle

1944

Marshal Leclerc

ready to fight for freedom. Although it was still superior at sea, England had only a hastily organized air force which had to sustain a full-fledged massive air offensive of the German Luftwaffe (air force). Fortunately, Hitler did not take the decisive step of invading England, and following in the footsteps of Napoleon, committed the error of attacking Russia in 1941. His troops became in turn victims of the vast Russian territory and the harsh winter climate.

Until 1942, however, the Axis countries were victorious on all fronts, which included the Balkans and Northern Africa.

While the United States had been from the very start sympathetic to the struggle of the Western powers, it did not want to get involved, but did extend limited military and intermittent economic aid to the British. It was drawn into war, however, after the December 7th, 1941, attack on Pearl Harbor by the Japanese, at which time Germany and Italy declared war on America.

The events that took place from then on are well known. In the Far East, General MacArthur contained the Japanese offensive, the Russians managed to repel the Germans in the east, and on June 6th, 1944, "D-Day", the allied troops landed on the coast of Normandy and subsequently drove the Germans out of France and Belgium. General de Gaulle and General Leclerc triumphantly entered Paris, which had been miraculously saved from the total destruction that had been ordered by Hitler.[9] In May 1945, the "Führer" committed suicide and shortly thereafter Germany accepted an unconditional surrender.

Because of the ambiguous role that the Vichy Government had played during the war, France was not invited to the Yalta, Teheran and Potsdam conferences in which Britain, Russia and the U.S.A. participated. Maybe the presence of the French would have prevented the signing of these disastrous agreements. President Roosevelt, well intentioned but in ill health and ill advised, gave in to the demands of the ruthless Soviet dictator Stalin and in effect agreed, over Churchill's opposition, to simply submit half of Europe to So-

---

[9] Such total destruction was carried out in other cities, in Stalingrad, Russia and in the Polish capital, Warsaw.

viet domination. Countries in central and eastern Europe which had gallantly fought as full-fledged allies for the cause of the world's freedom, such as Poland and Czechoslovakia, were simply sold out to Communism as were also other traditionally anti-communist countries: Hungary, Romania and Bulgaria. The three Baltic states, Latvia, Estonia and Lithuania were deprived of their independence to become Soviet republics. Albania and Yugoslavia were forced to be part of the Soviet "zone of influence", while nationalist forces were exterminated and communist regimes were set up. Germany was divided in two, and East Germany became a communist state. The Soviet Union, which had always acted treacherously and which would have been, without the help of the Allies, at the end of its resources, now reaped the benefits of its two-faced game. It soon started shaping itself into the strongest power in the world. While the Yalta agreements signalled the end of the real war, they opened the new excruciating era of cold war, which appears increasingly menacing as years go by. It is indirectly responsible for the tragedy of Vietnam, the many problems in Latin America, particularly Cuba and Nicaragua and the continuous repression and persecution in various countries (e.g., the bloody crushing of the Hungarian uprising in 1956, of the Czech attempt at freedom in 1968 and the ruthless suppression of the Polish labor movement Solidarity in 1981).

Since then the brutality of the Soviet regime has gone unchecked and uncountered. Such was the case with Afghanistan and the everyday blatant violations of human rights in communist controlled states. The rise of the Soviet power and its policy of expansion by aggression is reminiscent of Hitler's aggressive policy before World War II.

France was, however, included in the London conference of 1945, at which decisions were reached as to the occupation of Germany by allied troops. France was also honored with one of the five seats on the Security Council of the newly formed United Nations.[10]

---

[10] Unfortunately the abuse of the veto power by the Soviet Union prevents this organization from being effective.

WHAT TO SEE

- All over France: The "Croix de Lorraine", symbol of French resistance, and tombs of murdered "résistants"
- Brive-la-Gaillarde (Centre): Musée de la Résistance
- Paris: Monument to the Jewish victims of the war
- Normandy: Beaches where allied troops landed in 1944, museums and cemeteries, particularly Utah Beach, Omaha Beach and Arromanches.

War and Holocaust museums in various countries

Post-War France • The Fourth Republic

As could have been expected, De Gaulle took the reins of the French provisional government after the liberation. But the National Assembly, which replaced the Vichy government in the Fourth Republic, was again a prey to the struggles between several political parties, and the new constitution once more endowed the legislature with unlimited authority while leaving the executive practically powerless.

The General declined, under the circumstances, to actively participate in running the country. In 1945 women were at last granted the right to vote.

Aided by the American Marshall Plan and the internal modernization plan of Monnet, France eventually started recovering from the devastation and impoverishment caused by the war. It joined NATO, signed the Atlantic Pact in 1949 and was a co-founder of the European Common Market, which had originally comprised six countries: the Benelux (Belgium, the Netherlands, Luxembourg), France, West Germany and Italy and whose membership was more recently extended also to England, Ireland, Denmark, Greece and Spain.

The Fourth Republic had to face not only a continuation of internal instability (prime ministers had to submit their resignations one after another like in a kaleidoscope), but also increasingly difficult conflicts with its colonies. While they had shown total loyalty to France during the war, a vast majority of the members of the old "colonial empire" opted for independence.

France was ultimately forced to abandon Indochina (Cambodia, Laos, and Vietnam), after many heroic efforts of the French troops who fought the Soviety-supported Viet-Minh, but were virtually abandoned by the Parisian government (defeat at Dien-Bien-Phu, 1954).

Most painful of all was the Algerian crisis. Algeria had been considered by many Frenchmen as closest to their hearts, as part of the homeland: suddenly, it, too, wanted to break the bonds. The situation became so complicated that no satisfactory solution could be found, and at the height of the fever the French in Algeria and the army revolted against the government.

It appeared unavoidable to have recourse to someone with uncontested authority and the obvious choice was General de Gaulle. He accepted to lead the country on condition that the old constitution be replaced by a new one which would give the executive much broader powers. Thus France became in 1958 the Fifth Republic, and the new constitution was approved in a referendum by a vast majority.

The Fifth Republic: De Gaulle

When De Gaulle assumed control of the government, he had to face the formidable task of settling the Algerian crisis and after much wavering, eventually came to the conclusion that granting independence to Algeria was unavoidable. In spite of the "coup" staged by several higher officers and former companions of the General and the unrest that followed, Algeria was declared an independent state after a majority vote in favor of self-determination in 1962. The General also completed the task of "decolonization", while allowing former colonies to become members of "Communauté Française" (French Commonwealth) benefitting from French administrative and technical assistance.

In foreign policy, De Gaulle strived for total independence from France's allies, tightened bonds between France and West Germany, withdrew from NATO and established a French "force de frappe" (first-strike power). His anti-American and anti-British bias (he tried to prevent England from joining the Common Market) was not shared by many of the other French politicians. Among De Gaulle's closest collaborators were his premier, Georges Pompidou, and the famous author André Malraux, who became minister of culture and established the "Maisons de la culture" all over France. A leftist in his young years, Malraux was totally disenchanted with communism in the '30s and joined the "Résistance" during World War II. It was, however, still fashionable to be leftist during the "De Gaulle era" and the "gauche intellectuelle" (intellectual left) dominated the literary scene under the lingering influence of Sartre.

Some intellectuals and public figures, writers, actors, film-makers, eventually changed their attitudes toward Communism and the Soviets, especially after the bloody crushing of the Hungarian and Czech attempts at liberalization in 1956 and 1968. Others, such as Yves Montand, who is constantly seen wearing the "Solidarnosc" pin, did not make a turnabout until the Russian invasion of Afghanistan, the events in Poland and the behaviour of the French communist ministers in the Mitterrand government.

At the end of the first seven years of De Gaulle's presidency, the new elections of 1965 pitted him against Mitterrand, supported by Radicals, Socialists and Communists. The General, supported by the right and the center was reelected by 54.6% of the vote.

In spite of a marked economic progress, an improvement in housing and a number of reforms in the field of education which swelled French university enrollments to over 800,000 in the '70s, as compared to some 80,000 in 1939, a malaise persisted among the young (many of them leftist-oriented) who could not find jobs appropriate to their training and were protesting overcrowded facilities and an antiquated curriculum in higher education.

In May 1968, student unrest, which had started at the University of Nanterre several weeks earlier, ignited the violent rioting and famous crisis which eventually led to De Gaulle's downfall. The rioting, encouraged by sympathy strikes by ten million workers, spread to the Sorbonne, and the entire Latin Quarter became a battleground. At one time, seemingly overwhelmed by events, the General left Paris and fled with his family to Germany, allegedly to test the loyalty of the French army stationed in that country. Upon his return things went back to normal. But subsequently De Gaulle's referendum regarding a project of reform was defeated, and he stepped down in April 1969. He died in his rural retreat of Colombey-les-deux-Eglises in November 1970 at the age of 80.

The Fifth Republic after De Gaulle

In the presidential election that followed the General's resignation, the Gaullist candidate Georges Pompidou (who will be forever remembered by the controversial cultural "Centre" bearing his name and erected during his presidency on the former location of the old Parisian marketplace, "Les Halles") was elected with a comfortable majority. Gaullism continued and is still alive today although De Gaulle has been dead for a number of years. Pompidou basically kept the General's line in domestic and foreign policy, but attempted to innovate and modernize, and ended France's opposition to England's entry into the Common Market. By 1974 the new president, in increasingly failing health, appeared helpless and worried by the overwhelming, seemingly insoluble problems facing the nation, such as sky-rocketing oil prices, inflation and unemployment. He died suddenly in April of the same year.[11]

---

[11] President Pompidou's testament revealed that he wished a Gregorian mass at his funeral. Monks from the Benedictine abbey of Solesmes were brought to Paris, and the funeral mass was celebrated in his parish church on Ile St. Louis.

The elections of 1974 attracted a dozen candidates to the presidency. The Socialists and Communists formed a coalition or "common program" with some Radicals, while the right was divided between two Gaullist candidates and the Independent Republicans led by Valéry Giscard d'Estaing. Although the leftist candidate François Mitterrand won a majority in the "first Sunday voting", he was eventually defeated the following Sunday by Giscard, who had prevailed against Mitterrand in the first televised debate.

Giscard d'Estaing's seven years in power, essentially a continuation of Pompidou's policies, were marked by an attempt at revitalizing the economy by the development of high-technology industries and the construction of nuclear power plants. The President did not succeed, however, in reducing unemployment, and pursued a haphazard internal and foreign policy: at home, antisemitism, financial scandals, a haughty personal attitude; abroad, the refusal to penalize the USSR for the invasion of Afghanistan and to support the American anti-communist stand; the catering to the PLO at the expense of relations with Israel; the sending of French troops to Africa. By the time of the 1981 elections, Giscard had to face a powerful leftist coalition (Mitterrand promised four cabinet posts to the Communists), while he could not gain the unanimous support of the right.

If Mitterrand with his Socialists and Communists won both the presidential and the legislative elections, it was not only because the French were tired of Giscard and wanted a change, but also because Giscard antagonized the man who had so strongly supported him seven years before and had become his prime minister in 1974, Jacques Chirac. Chirac, head of the Gaullist party, the RPR, eventually became mayor of Paris. In 1981 he endorsed Giscard's candidacy with great reservations. François Mitterrand, who had made a swing from right to left in the midst of his political career and had lost two former election bids, became president of France with the help of his leftist coalition. He kept the promise made to the Communist Party at the time of the electoral campaign and appointed four Communists to head four ministries. With a comfortable majority in the National Assembly, he moved swiftly to carry out reforms that had been planned by the platform. The right and center became the new opposition. Soon after he took office, the abolition of the death penalty was enacted as well as a number of other laws unpopular with the majority of the population. Soon also, the French economy started to decline at a rapid pace. Whereas the SMIC (minimum wage) was raised by 10%, a still higher rate on inflation immediately eradicated the gains people had been looking forward to. In the summer of 1982, French citizens faced limitations on the amount of money they could take abroad, which made travel outside of France close to impossible. This rather insignificant measure was also a very unpopular one among a people for whom vacations are a right, not a privilege, and who consider the summer holidays as important as their daily "déjeuner". The President had to give in to the majority of the French in the emotional controversy with respect to the fate of the so-called "école libre": the socialist government had been steadily working toward the adoption of a law which called for the suppression of private and religious schools. After spectacular demonstrations by Frenchmen of all parties in various cities in the spring of '84, Mitterrand dismissed not only the minister of education, but also his prime minister Mauroy, as well as a number of other cabinet members. The four Communist ministers left the government at the same time, thus making a new split in the ranks of the left.

Ever since 1981 the rightist and centrist opposition, with such leaders as Chirac, Giscard d'Estaing and Barre, had been bracing for the 1986 parliamentary elections. In March 1986 the "législatives", which are held every 5 years, brought about, as had been expected, the defeat of the left. The new majority was faced by the issue of the so called "cohabitation" or collaboration with the socialist president Mitterrand, whose tenure was not to expire for another two years. While Barre was opposed to any such understanding, Jacques Chirac accepted to become Mitterrand's prime minister and formed a new cabinet. The rightist majority immediately passed a series of laws leading to "reprivatization" of most of the previously nationalized sectors and lifted a number of restrictions imposed on private enterprise.

Both the President and the Prime minister have continued to exercise their power individually, as described in the Constitution, although national defense and foreign policy issues have necessitated a degree of cooperation between the two men.

During the entire two years of this uneasy "power sharing", both sides were preparing for the 1988 April-May presidential elections. Chirac (55) was first to announce his candidacy (at the very beginning of the New Year),followed by Raymond Barre (64) on February 9th, while Mitterrand (71) kept the French in suspense until March 23, just about a month before the election, set for April 24th.

The first Sunday voting brought Mitterrand the expected largest percentage of votes: 34.11%; Chirac obtained 19.95%, Barre 16.53%, the Communist Party's candidate 6.76%—the poorest showing ever. The big surprise was the large number of people voting for the Front National candidate Le Pen, who received 14.38% of the votes while the polls' predictions had hovered only about 10.5%. The polls were, however, correct in predicting Mitterrand's final victory over Chirac on Sunday, May 8th.

Mitterrand scored 54.05% of the votes against Chirac's 45.95% in a heavy turnout (nearly 85% of eligible voters). Chirac conceded, while reiterating statements made before the elections that collaboration or "cohabitation" would no longer be possible, and promptly submitted his resignation. Mitterrand selected as his new prime minister the Socialist Michel Rocard, who had held earlier the post of Minister of Agriculture, Planning and Regional development. Rocard in turn proposed a cabinet made up predominantly of Socialists, many of whom had already been members of Mitterrand's former cabinets. On the Saturday following his reelection, Mitterrand signed a decree dissolving Parliament and called for general elections to be held in June, in a bid to win a left wing majority in the National Assembly.

President Mitterrand

Palais de l'Elysée

Palais Bourbon
(Assemblée Nationale)

Palais du Luxembourg
(the Sénat)

1988: new logo
of the French
franc

20th Century Arts and Letters

As has frequently been observed, the 20th century is, even more so than the 19th, a time of "isms" in ideologies, artistic movements and "schools", anxious to draft programs and manifestos and publish magazines. Many of them were short lived and interested above all in formulating their own rules, proposing their reforms and attracting attention and discussion. The interaction between literature and the other arts had also never before been as close, lively and complex. During the first years of the century the cinema was added to the visual arts.

In painting, the years 1900-1914 saw a continuation of 19th century trends and a number of artists can be considered as belonging to both centuries. A group of young innovators who called themselves *Nabis* ("prophets" in Hebrew) and were influenced by Gauguin and Cézanne, attempted to show in a more subjective way that form, color and pattern reveal the inner quality of objects. The two Nabis whose works are attracting much attention today are **Bonnard** and **Vuillard**. Bonnard eventually moved to the south of France and painted until his death in 1947 canvasses expressing his "joie de vivre" with increasingly bright and bold colors, almost as vibrant as those of the Fauvists.[12]

The *Fauvists*, among which Matisse, Rouault, Derain, Vlaminck and the Dutchman Van Dongen, displayed their new works at the Salon d'Automne in 1905. These were characterized by a vigorous touch and the clash of heightened, brilliant, "unreal" colors (purple, emerald, vermillion, cadmium, cobalt), "as violent and striking as a roar." A chance remark of critic Louis Vauxcelles, who compared the exhibition hall to a cage of "wild beasts" earned them the name of "Fauves".[13] They had all been more or less influenced by Van Gogh,

---

[12] Both Bonnard and Vuillard were associated with the *Revue Blanche* and Lugné-Poe's "Théâtre de l'oeuvre".

[13] "Fauve" means "wild beast." Vauxcelles also coined the word "Cubist": it had been suggested to him by Matisse's description of Braque's landscapes as being made up of "small cubes."

Matisse

Chagall: "Les Mariés
de la Tour Eiffel"

whom Vlaminck called "the real father of Fauvism" and whom he claimed to love "more than his own father or mother." Vlaminck used, with the possible exception of Derain, the most daring tones of the group and threatened to burn down the conservative Ecole des Beaux-Arts with his "vermillions and cobalts." Derain portrayed, in the sunny Provence where he had joined Matisse, intense Fauvist landscapes, until he came under the influence of Cézanne and parted ways with the movement.

Raoul Dufy was converted by Matisse's *Luxe, calme et volupté*,[14] displayed at the 1905 Salon: he described it as "a miracle of imagination transmuting drawing and colors." But Dufy is strikingly different from the other Fauvists because of his delightfully light touch, his precise and elegant "calligraphic" line and the utterly charming way with which he represents landscapes, seascapes, paddocks, regattas, races and other social events of his time. Dufy also designed decors and costumes for the ballet and fabrics for the renowned couturier Poiret.

Georges Rouault (1871-1958) was associated with Fauvism only very briefly and his very personal art, which he called "a burning confession", is actually closer to that of the *Expressionists*: these sought to exteriorize their inner life with intensity and violence and explored the world of the mind and the imagination. Rouault treated a broad range of themes of grave social importance and morbid subjects: buffoonery, debauchery, hypocrisy, the degrading of man's dignity, injustice and the indifference to human suffering in "series", such as *Judges* and *Prostitutes*, while using heavy black outlines similar to the medieval stained glass technique. He later concentrated on scenes from the Old and New Testaments and can be considered the foremost religious painter since the 17th century.

But the true giant who was born of Fauvism and spans three quarters of the century is **Matisse**. Master of color, he interpreted the world around him with serene exaltation, while discarding perspective and communicating the sensation of volume by the use of

---

[14] The title reiterates a famous line from Baudelaire's poem "Invitation au voyage."

Dufy: Chenonceaux

Dunoyer de Segonzac:
Proust on his deathbed

space, light, movement and arabesque. His dreamlike art, endowed with the quality of oriental splendor, combines vitality and subtlety and strives to express a love of life: he wanted it to bring "rest and comfort" to his "exhausted and harassed" fellow man. Thus, pure joy emanates from his whites, yellows, greens and blues as seen, for example, in the delightful Chapelle du Rosaire in Vence[15], of which he planned every single detail. The exhibition of his paper cutouts— graceful nudes, harmonious dancing figures, soaring birds and huge, tantalizing flowers-made a triumphant tour of the United States and endeared Matisse to many American art lovers.

Totally independent of schools and currents is the art of **Henri Rousseau**, called "Le Douanier". Although he was born in 1844, Rousseau did not get true recognition until the early 1900s, after having been "discovered" by Guillaume Apollinaire. This career toll-collector developed a unique style, while portraying the deceptively simple life around him and, more importantly so, a world totally unknown to him of exotic jungles, luxuriant vegetation, wild beasts, snake charmers and enchanting tropical flowers. Rousseau has often been simplistically categorized as a naive or primitive, while his "forests of desires" and most of his poetic, haunting scenes are highly sophisticated. His work has been linked to Freud's theories of the subconscious and interpreted as "touching upon the most forbidden primeval fantasies of Western man."

Two years after the Fauvist jolt, *Cubism* was inaugurated in 1907 by Picasso's landmark canvas *Les Demoiselles d'Avignon*, now at the Museum of Modern Art in New York.[16] Cubism, which radically transformed painting, is a current so well known that it, again, requires few comments or explanations. Its advent coincided with the programs of the literary avant-garde, headed by G. Apollinaire (who

---

[15] In Provence, between Grasse and Nice: a "must" for visitors of the area. Several other painters, Rouault, Léger and Cocteau, likewise decorated "their own" chapels. Picasso painted the murals of the chapel in Vallauris.

[16] This depiction of a brothel on Avignon street in Barcelona clearly shows Picasso's new style, freed from Western techniques and akin to the African and Oceanic tribal arts: the human figures are not representational, but recognizable and the faces are prototypes equating masks.

Picasso: Study for "Les Demoiselles d'Avignon"

Saint-Laurent 1988 fashions inspired by Braque

ALBERT GLEIZES

ANTOINE BOURDELLE 'LA DANSE'

authored a series of articles entitled "Les peintres cubistes"), the introduction of atonal music and the vogue of Negro masks and artifacts. Cubism's geometric handling of form was, as mentioned above, influenced by Cézanne (his works were displayed at a retrospective exhibition in 1907). Picasso became closely associated with **Braque**, Juan Gris and the theoretician of Cubism, Albert Gleizes, though each artist developed a highly individual style within analytical or synthetic Cubism. **Picasso** himself, who was born in 1881 in Spain and died in 1973 in France, where he chose to live all his adult life, is the very symbol of modern painting. This incomparably dynamic artist, who was linked with a variety of currents during his long lifetime, dabbled in all the genres, including theatre decoration. Several museums have sprung up to exclusively house his innumerable canvasses, sculptures, drawings and ceramics, the most important of which opened in the Marais section of Paris in September 1985.[17]

The contributions, in later years, of Fernand Léger, who was influenced by the Italian Futurists' manifesto *The Aesthetics of Machinery* and who incorporated mechanical elements, such as pistons and cylinders, into his vision of the world, are also considered Cubist paintings.

Cubism was a determining factor in the development of all the 20th century art that followed, such as Futurism and Abstract Painting. Its defiance of what had been traditionally accepted as man's perception of the universe led to Dadaism and Surrealism and their pursuit of the absurd.

Dadaism was born at the height of World War I, and, as the bloodshed increased, intellectuals came to question the fundamental values of their civilization, be it literature, architecture, music or painting. A small group of emigrés, meeting at the Café Voltaire in Zurich and representing an anti-art movement, took their name at random from a dictionary, and while "dada" means "hobby", it also implies nonsense or "baby-talk". The Dadaists were anarchistic

---

[17]This ultra-modern museum—its upper floors are even air-conditioned—is housed in the beautiful 17th century Hôtel Salé and contains over 3,000 pieces from the artist's collection of his own works.

and nihilistic and actively strove to shock—"épater le bourgeois" was the word—by ridiculing and desecrating all that had been hitherto considered as beautiful, lofty and sacred.[18] Most active in the group were the artists Hans Arp, Francis Picabia, Juan Miró and most importantly Marcel Duchamp, as well as writers Louis Aragon and André Breton.

Dadaism was quickly absorbed into *Surrealism*, which had been sparked to a large degree by Freud's theories of the subconscious and the metaphysical works of the 19th century Symbolist painters. The Marxist André Breton launched the famous *Surrealist Manifesto* in 1924 and dedicated it to Apollinaire. In it, he stressed the importance of the dictates of the mind without any control of the reason and of unconscious mental processes. The Surrealists believed that emotions and vital powers as reflected e.g., in dreams, should reach the paper and the canvas without being inhibited by the intellect. They advocated creating in a trance-like state a sort of "spontaneous" or "automatic" writing, painting and sculpting (this "automatism" is present to a certain degree also in Expressionism and Abstract Painting). The most influential Surrealist artists who worked in France are Yves Tanguy, Joan Miró and **Salvador Dali**.[19] The latter portrays everyday objects with shocking distortion, paradoxical juxtaposition and obscene connotations. His is a world of phobias, delusions and paranoia—our 20th century world gone crazy.

Marc Chagall is also considered a Surrealist—the term was coined by Apollinaire to describe Chagall's pictures exhibited in Paris in 1911—but there is nothing morbid or depressing about his art, which breathes at the same time joy, love and nostalgia. This prolific painter, sculptor and potter who died at 97 in Saint-Paul-de-Vence, had come from Russia to France before World War I and found himself at first under the influence of Cubism, Orphism and

---

[18] Thus, they painted the idolized face of Mona Lisa with a mustache and traced underneath several capital letters, starting with L H O..., which could be read with an obscene meaning.

[19] Also the Italian Chirico and the German Max Ernst, who is more often considered an Expressionist.

the literary and artistic avant-garde heralded by Apollinaire; in 1912 Chagall dedicated to the poet a large painting of biblical inspiration entitled "Hommage à Apollinaire". He later created a whole series of works based on the Old Testament, many of which are now housed in a special museum in Nice devoted to Chagall's "Message biblique" (others are displayed at the Fondation Maeght in Saint-Paul-de-Vence). Chagall, who was a great colorist, is particularly well known for his charming portrayal of Russian folk tales and Jewish folklore (fiddlers on the roof, peasants tending to blue and green cows, colorful villages and wandering Jews); he is also admired for the dream-like quality of his "weightless" floating figures and of his embracing couples.[20] Chagall made numerous contributions to historic and state monuments and buildings (stained glass windows at the cathedrals of Reims, Metz and the United Nations headquarters in New York, murals at Lincoln Center, ceiling at the Paris opera), as well as to stage decorations.

Two other "independent" foreign artists who created in France in the early part of the 19th century ought to be cited: the Russian Expressionist Soutine, whose statue was unveiled in Paris in 1987, and the Italian Amedeo Modigliani, who limited his art to the human face and figure: he gave them idealized proportions and a distorted, elongated, elegant shape, while using harmonious curves and clear, sharply delineated colors. "Modi" who could barely eke out a Bohemian existence in Paris, was an isolated figure, with no precursors or followers. Neither did he have admirers during his short life, except for the Polish poet Leopold Zborowski, who became an art dealer in order to help Modigliani sell his works. In spite of a romantic, seemingly happy love marriage and the birth of a daughter, the artist eventually drank and drugged himself to death at the age of 36.

As for *Abstract Painting*, which implies "analyzing, detaching, selecting, simplifying and geometrizing" before "distilling the essence from nature", its most widely acknowledged exponents are Piet Mon-

---

[20] "My painting," said Chagall, "strives to evoke the fantastic in nature. We ought to turn, since the world is turning. We ought to fly, but we are not flying."

F. LEGER

Giacometti: "The Dog"

*Le Corbusier:
the church
in Ronchamp*

drian, who used the rectangle as base for his two-dimensional spatial studies; Robert and Sonia Delaunay (Robert had been in earlier years linked with Cubism); Kandinsky and Vasarely. Jean Dubuffet, author of *L'Art brut préféré aux arts culturels*, is unrelated to any current or school.

From among the artists who devoted their talents almost exclusively to sculpture, three names deserve a special mention: two "Southerners", Bourdelle and Maillol, who shared the traditional Mediterranean cult of form and the Swiss born Alberto Giacometti. Bourdelle, an "emancipated" disciple of Rodin, has left a voluminous oeuvre of more than 900 sculptures, many of which can be viewed in the Paris museum bearing his name. **Maillol**'s works—a true hymn to the female body which he endows with solidity, power and serenity—adorn the Palais de Chaillot, the Jardin des Tuileries and innumerable museums throughout the world. **Giacometti** eventually broke away from the Surrealists with whom he had been associated in the 1920s and developed a unique and visionary art, at the same time endearing, moving and deeply disturbing . He portrays a "universal head", the head of man "the stranger" whose face, marked by anguish and suffering, Giacometti has attempted to "decipher." The artist's vision is contradictory: man is at the same time beautiful and ugly, fragile and durable, light and heavy: his huge feet weigh him down and bind him to the earth. But above all, man is mortal and therefore given by Giacometti the figure of a skeleton; his *City Square*, displayed at the Fondation Maeght in Saint-Paul-de-Vence, projects the image of the modern isolated and bereaved individual.

In architecture, **Le Corbusier** (also born in Switzerland) is the real innovator, particularly in the field of apartment buildings which were to combine aesthetic values with the utmost comfort and enjoyment of the inhabitants (e.g., his "Ville radieuse" in Marseille). Le Corbusier is particularly famous for his controversial ultra-modern cement church of Notre-Dame-du-Haut, erected on top of a hill in Ronchamp near Belfort.

French music was, at the beginning of the 20th century, still dominated by the generation of Dukas (*L'Apprenti sorcier*) and of **Ravel**, born in 1875, but whose best known works were composed in the 1900s (*La Valse, Boléro*, his Concerto for the left hand and his striking musical illustration of a text by Colette, the ballet score *L'Enfant et les sortilèges*). During the "iconoclastic" years of Dadaism and other revolutionary currents, art movements fermented in the numerous Parisian cafés and "boites de nuit." Erik Satie[21] wrote songs for the music halls and performed in some of the cabarets. At the "Boeuf-sur-le-toit" he gathered around him a group of young composers: Auric, Durey, Honegger, Darius Milhaud, Francis Poulenc and Germaine Tailleferre. They all had reacted against Impressionism and Symbolism and were baptized as "Les Six" by the incredibly versatile writer, artist and *animateur* Jean Cocteau, who played the cymbals with the "Group", publicized their music and enlisted their collaboration in his ballet *Les Mariés de la Tour Eiffel*.[22] Several members of "Les Six" became famous. Milhaud collaborated closely and successfully with the poet Claudel, whom he had joined in Rio de Janeiro where Claudel was ambassador. In 1940, Milhaud managed to reach the United States, thus avoiding the Nazi persecution of Jews and spent a number of years as a professor at Mills College in California. **Poulenc** is perhaps the best known of the group. His vast contribution to music consists of songs to the poems of such poets as Eluard, Max Jacob and Apollinaire, of piano pieces, religious works and musical scores for the theatre (among others, the already mentioned *Dialogues des Carmélites* and Apollinaire's *Mamelles de Tirésias*). The mystical composer Olivier Messiaen, who became in the 1930s a member of the group called "Jeune France"[23] and the towering figure of his pupil, Pierre **Boulez**, a follower of Schönberg

---

[21] Satie provided the musical score for Cocteau's *Parade*, which was performed in 1917 by Diaghilev's Ballets Russes with decors by Picasso.

[22] Chagall's favourite painting bears the same title: it was chosen by the French Post Office when it honored the artist by issuing a stamp with a replica of one of his works. The Eiffel Tower was a source of inspiration for all the artistic generation of Apollinaire.

[23] Messiaen loved birds and listened for hours to their singing and chirping, which he tried to incorporate into his music whenever he could; he devoted to it also entire pieces, such as the delightful "Exotic birds".

and recognized master of atonal music (the prestigious Collège de France opened its door to him and he was called to head, in 1977, the Institut de Recherche et de Coordination Acoustique/Musique—or IRCAM—at the Centre Pompidou), are the two foremost representatives of contemporary French music.

The name of Guillaume **Apollinaire**[24] came sharply into focus in connection with the arts discussed above, because of the pivotal role he played in all the revolutionary movements of his time. Apollinaire must again be mentioned in our consideration of modern poetry, because of what it owes to his visionary explorations of new poetic techniques, such as juxtaposition, simultaneity and discontinuity. The link between Apollinaire's poetics and Cubist painting is evident in his two collections of poems, *Alcools* and *Calligrammes*; the latter illustrates his daring venture into the figurative possibilities of verse. Apollinaire was the embodiment of 20th century man, and called "le prince de l'esprit moderne". In spite of the "classical" perfection of form and nostalgia of the past evident in some of his poems, Apollinaire wanted to live in the present. He celebrates the contemporary technological world and its Parisian symbol, the Eiffel Tower, "shepherdess of the herd of bridges over the river Seine".

A tentative list of other 20th century poets, forcibly incomplete and involving a difficult selection, cannot omit such names as the great intellectual **Valéry**; the inspired Catholic writer **Claudel**, who adopted a new form of expression, midway between verse and rhythmic prose, which he called "verset biblique" and whose outstanding contributions to the theatre are regularly featured on the Parisian stage (*L'Annonce faite à Marie*, *Le Soulier de satin*); Péguy, another poet of religious inspiration who wrote of Chartres and of Jeanne d'Arc and who was killed on the frontline in World War I;[25] Eluard, Supervielle, Reverdy and Michaux, all still very much present in the minds of French poetry lovers; the 1960 Nobel prize winner **Saint-John Perse**, a diplomat like Claudel, who lived in the United

---

[24] It actually is a pseudonym chosen by Wilhelm Apollinaris de Kostrowitzky, who was born out of wedlock in Rome to an adventurous Polish noblewoman.
[25] See above.

Calligrammes

DANS
FLETS   CE
RE   MI
LES   ROIR
SONT   JE
ME   SUIS
COM   EN
NON   CLOS
ET   **Guillaume**   VI
CES   **Apollinaire**   VANT
AN   ET
LES   VRAI
NE   COM
OI   ME
MA   ON
I

Mirror

MON CŒUR PAREIL A UNE FLAMME RENVERSÉE

Heart

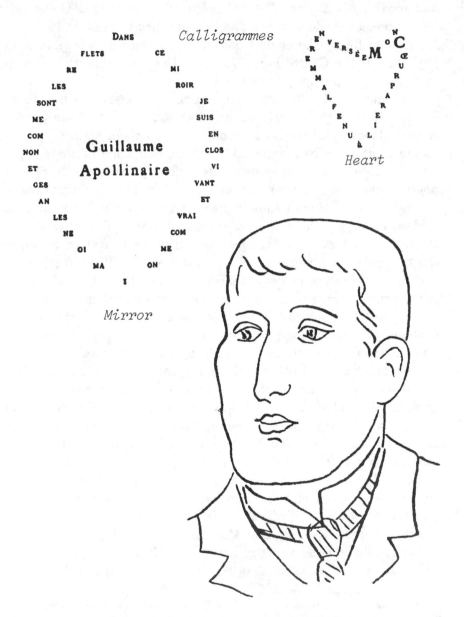

Apollinaire by Matisse

States since the Nazi occupation of France; René Char; Yves Bon-
nefoy; and, finally, **Francis Ponge**, who felt a very special affinity—
he called it "fraternité"—with the sculptor Giacometti and who fo-
cuses his attention on objects (*Le Parti pris des choses*) in an attempt
to "free himself from the old humanism with the help of things."[26]

Insofar as other literary forms are concerned, while some authors
advocated the startling innovations mentioned above and went into
all kinds of "verbal delirium", illustrative of what can be called our
"age of anxiety",[27] the novel in the traditional vein was, as already
stated above, despite the historical and sociological upheavals and the
ensuing nihilistic trends, alive and well and reached new heights of expression and psychological depths with such names as Alain-Fournier,
Radiguet, Romains, **Gide, Giraudoux**; the three Catholic writers **Mauriac** (*Thérèse Desqueyroux*), Bernanos[28] and Julien Green;
Saint-Exupéry, author of *Le Petit Prince*; the utterly charming
Colette; the nihilistic, antisemitic collaborationist Céline (*Voyage
au bout de la nuit—Journey to the End of the Night*), who became
an outcast, but whose style and use of violent and gross language
influenced an entire generation of writers; Montherlant and **Malraux** (*La Condition humaine*); and finally **Pagnol**, who portrayed
in such a vivid and delightful way his native Provence in fiction and
in plays.[29] Several of these novelists were also renowned dramatists,
but the prolific "master of the stage" **Anouilh** may very well be
considered the foremost playwright of the first two-thirds of our century. As for Marcel **Proust**, his monumental novel *A la recherche du
temps perdu*[30] (16 volumes in the earliest edition), featuring resur-

---

[26] Jacques Prévert was the beloved poet of post-war Paris. His humorous, witty
and often deeply sentimental poems ("Autumn leaves", "Barbara") were set to
music and immortalized by the most popular performers of our day.

[27] As seen in Jarry's crude farce *Ubu roi*.

[28] See chapter VIII above.

[29] Many splendid films based on Pagnol's works have been acclaimed both in
Europe and in America: *Marius, Fanny, César* and, in 1987, *Jean de Florette* followed by *Manon des Sources* (also *La Femme du boulanger—The Baker's Wife*—
adapted from Giono's short story).

[30] Literally "In Search of Lost Time". The widely accepted title *Remembrance*

gences of past experiences released by sensory associations that exist in our deepest subconscious,[31] has been called one of the greatest works of all modern literature.

The years preceding World War II saw, even more so than the earlier decades, an increasing political involvement on the part of authors along with a tendency to preach and prozelytize. Much of the literature of the *entre-deux-guerres* is socially conscious and international in spirit. While Gide and Malraux, totally disillusioned, eventually forsook, as seen above, the communist ideals which they had been advocating alongside with most of the Surrealists, **Sartre**, who became the leader of French intellectuals, carried the torch of leftist ideology until his death in 1980. Sartre's name is prominently associated with Existentialism, a philosophy and literary doctrine which he illustrated in his numerous essays, novels (*La Nausée*) and drama (*Huis-clos*, *Les Mouches*).[32] Sartre's life companion, Simone de Beauvoir, who has been called "historiographe de l'existentialisme" is a novelist of some stature in her own right, and best known for her autobiographical works.

Albert **Camus**, who shared with Sartre his sense of the absurd, his atheism and the notion of man's isolation in the face of the inevitability of death, rejected any classification linking his name to the Sartrian brand of Existentialism. Camus conceived the possibility of salvation through the fraternity of men, as illustrated in his novel *La Peste*. Camus' most widely read book is, however, *L'Etranger* (*The Stranger*), both for its philosophical implications and the beauty of its flawless, clear, concise, "classical" style. Camus' brilliant literary career—he also won recognition as a journalist, essayist and playwright and was awarded the Nobel prize of literature in 1957—came to an abrupt and premature end following a car accident in 1960.

The middle of the century saw the birth of what was called "anti-

---

of Things Past is not an exact translation.

[31] Such as the taste of a "madeleine" dipped in tea, the sound of a tune, the smell of a flower. Intellectual memory which permits recall, and involuntary memory which permits a total relived experience, are key factors.

[32] *No Exit*, *The Flies*.

roman" and "anti-théâtre" or "nouveau théâtre." The main exponents of this new kind of drama are Adamov (*Le Professeur Taranne, Ping-pong*); the talented, depressing Jean Genet (*Les Bonnes* ("The Maids"), *Le Balcon*) who tried to find answers to the problems of humanity in Evil;[33] Samuel Beckett, whose depressing tragic farces illustrate "the absurd" by means of a language and plots which are in themselves manifestations of irrationality (*En attendant Godot, Fin de partie*);[34] and the inexhaustible Ionesco, particularly popular with the American college audiences. Ionesco's sense of absurdity is reflected in a humorous, exhilarating theatrical world of verbal fantasy and "fantastic situations": *La Cantatrice chauve* (*The Bald Soprano*) *La Leçon, Jacques ou la soumission, Les Chaises* (*The Chairs*). His *Rhinocéros*, which had a brilliant run in the United States, tackles in a more serious vein preoccupations, such as the evils of conformism and totalitarianism, which had already surfaced in some of his humorous plays.

The term "anti-roman", "nouveau roman" or "chosisme" ("thingism", preoccupation with objects) has been applied to the literary output of a variety of writers after the middle 1900s. What these authors have all in common is the conscious break with the traditional novel, its plot, omniscient narrator, chronology, character development and psychological analyses. This mistrust of the ways fiction had been conceived up to that time is expressed in Nathalie Sarraute's *L'Ere du soupçon* (*Age of Suspicion*, 1956). Another woman author indirectly linked with the "new wave" is Marguerite Duras, who was already world famous (novel *Le Square* and film *Hiroshima mon amour*), before her autobiographical novel *L'Amant* (*The Lover*) created a sensation on both sides of the Atlantic in 1984. Nobel prize winner Claude Simon is best known for his lengthy and baffling *Route des Flandres*, in which he suppressed most of the punctuation.[35]

---

[33] Genet started his literary career in prison, where he was serving time for thievery, prostitution and other infractions of the law.

[34] Instead of talking about absurdity, the very concept of the play illustrates it, plunges the spectator/reader into it, so that it is experienced—often viscerally—as a result.

[35] Apollinaire had already suppressed all punctuation from his poems (the most

Michel Butor, whose novel *La Modification* is not only more accessible, but constitutes fascinating reading, innovates by having the narrator use the second person "vous" in lieu of the traditional "je"; this is an "interior monologue" at an interesting remove: the narrator attempts to distance himself, think objectively, but engages in "interior monologue" nonetheless. Robbe-Grillet's *La Jalousie* (as well as *Le Voyeur* and *Dans le labirynthe*) are frequent choices of texts in university level literature courses.

A number of these university courses have, since the late 1960s, increasingly focused not so much on the reading of literature as on theory and a new brand of criticism, called "nouvelle critique". The "nouvelle critique", stemming both from Saussurian Structuralism and Semiotics (the study of the system of signs), has pursued the exploration of fundamental and determining structures common to all men of all times as evident in e.g., myths, and has served as an umbrella for scholars from such divergent disciplines as literary criticism (Barthes), philosophy (Michel Foucault, Derrida), psychoanalysis (Lacan), linguistics (Chomsky), anthropology (Lévi-Strauss) and theories of Marxism (Althusser).[36] The literary magazine *Tel Quel*, founded by Phlippe Sollers in 1960, has been an outlet for a number of authors focusing on the so-called "écriture textuelle". These writers who are extremely intolerant of the traditional criticism have been involved in violent controversies; thus, Raymond Picard attacked Barthes in an incisive pamphlet, *Nouvelle critique ou nouvelle imposture?* But the new vistas and avenues opened by these novel, original insights and ingenious, though often contradictory approaches, constitute a fascinating step forward, which makes turning back the clock impossible.[37]

---

famous is "Le Pont Mirabeau"), but he felt, and justly so, that the rhythm of the verse would itself dictate the necessary pauses.

[36] The authors of *La Littérature en France depuis 1945* (Bersani et al., Bordas, 1970) have divided these writers for the purpose of simplification into three groups: "the children of Saussure", "the children of Freud" and "the children of Marx."

[37] Many scholars of this new generation lecture every year at American institutions of higher learning. Columbia University regularly invites as visiting pro-

Some observers seem to detect in the later 1980s what they call "a return to the plot in the land of literary theory", while citing the unprecedented success of the biographical novels of both Duras (see above) and Robbe-Grillet (*Le Miroir qui revient*).[38] In fact, traditional fiction writing has never stopped having its adepts, since there are in France many audiences with a variety of tastes and many classes of readers outside the intellectural elite. Memoirs or journals, however, which often focus not so much on the lives of the authors, but on their work, the events that shaped it, and the very process of writing, are a particularly important 20th century genre.[39]

The last two decades have witnessed a tremendous vogue of the historical novel: Maurice Druon's *Les Rois maudits*, which retells the story of Philippe-le-Bel's accursed posterity (see ch. IV), has been made into a film and beaten all previous records of best selling books. Every year brings fame and fortune to authors who tackle the lives of such figures as Aliénor d'Aquitaine, Anne d'Autriche and Mme de Maintenon. In fact the selection of titles available each new season on French bookstands defies any attempt of doing justice to this diversified market. Let us just add that the vast body of "littérature francophone" (literary contribution of non-French writers of French expression),[40] of which the great Senegalese statesman and poet Léopold Senghor and the rich spectrum of "littérature québecoise" are prime examples, generates, both in France and abroad, much interest and enthusiasm.

---

fessors, among other celebrities, Kristeva, Todorov and Genette, while Derrida is the "éminence grise" at Yale.

[38] An article in the *New York Times Literary Supplement*, cited by *France Magazine* (Fall 1987), talks about "younger French writers bringing back the old furniture that the New Novel had thrown out".

[39] Malraux: *Antimémoires*; Sartre: *Les Mots* (*The Words*); Genet: *Journal du voleur* (*The Thief's Journal*); Ionesco: *Journal en miettes* (*Fragments of a Journal*), as well as the already mentioned authors of biographies.

[40] Some 270 million people worldwide speak French. Twenty-seven nations have adopted French as their official language.

WHAT TO SEE

- Paris: Centre Pompidou
      Musée d'art moderne
      Musée Picasso
      Musée des arts décoratifs
      Musée du costume
      Musée Bourdelle, and Bourdelle's statue of Polish poet
            Mickiewicz on Place de l'Alma
      Maillol's sculptures in the Jardins des Tuileries and in front
            of the Palais de Chaillot
      Paris Opera: ceiling painted by Chagall
- Near Paris, Pontoise: Musée d'art moderne
- Pont-Aven (Brittany): Museum (19th and 20th century art)
- Assy (Haute Savoie): church decorated by Rouault
- Metz and Reims cathedrals: stained glass windows by Chagall
- Ronchamp, near Belfort: Le Corbusier's church
- In Provence:
      Antibes: Musée Picasso
      Biot: Musée Fernand Léger
      Menton: Musée Cocteau (on the beach)
      Nice: Musée Chagall ("Le Message biblique")
      Saint-Tropez: Musée de l'Annonciade
      Saint-Paul-de-Vence: Fondation Maeght
      Vallauris: Musée Picasso, chapel decorated by Picasso
      Vence: Chapelle du Rosaire, decorated by Matisse
      Villefranche: chapel decorated by Cocteau

Part III

FRANCE TODAY

The French Institutions: The Executive and the Legislative • The "Administration" • The Political Parties • Ethnicity

The Executive: While maintaining the separation of powers, the 1958 Constitution established a strong, independent executive, consisting of a President and a Premier (prime minister). Under this Constitution, the President has far reaching powers. As Head of State, he accredits ambassadors and negotiates and ratifies treaties. On the national level, he is Commander-in-Chief of the Armed Forces. He appoints the Premier and, on the latter's proposals, the other members of the Cabinet. He presides over the Council of Ministers and promulgates laws.

He has the right to dissolve the National Assembly (Assemblée Nationale), to call for a referendum by the people and to assume extaordinary powers in case of crisis. The President resides at the Palais de l'Elysée.

The French President is elected for seven years (since 1962 the popular vote has replaced a system of electoral colleges set up in 1958), by direct universal suffrage. Frenchmen vote in presidential elections on two Sundays, two weeks apart.[1] In the first round of

---

[1] Election of the new president must fall 20 days at the least, and 35 days at the most, before the expiration of the term of the incumbent. The official campaign begins on the day of the publication of the list of candidates (that is, at least 15 days before the first day of voting), and ends on the Friday before the elections. Advertising facilities and financial aid are provided by the state, and candidates have access to official billboards displayed in front of public buildings. They may affix two posters upon them, one to announce their platform, and the other to post schedules of electoral meetings and radio and T.V. appearances. After the election, the state reimburses 250,000 francs of the campaign cost for each candidate who has received at least 5% of the total vote. Those who receive less than 5% are reimbursed for 20% of their expenses. Political advertising on radio or television is not permitted in France. According to the electoral law, however, candidates are granted a maximum of two cost-free hours of publicity during the period of the campaign. Regulations also provide for media coverage of the presidential campaign in news programs. Stations and networks are required to give equal coverage to every candidate's declarations. It is forbidden by law to

elections, which can be considered as a "super primary", there are usually many candidates, representing the various political parties. If no candidate obtains absolute majority, the two candidates who win the most votes on the first Sunday then compete in the second round of elections. Between the first and second rounds, all sorts of alliances, agreements and vote transfers are possible.

The Premier directs the actions of the Government. He sees that laws are executed and he is responsible for national defense.

The Cabinet drafts statutory texts (ordinances and decrees) as well as Government bills. It is responsible to the National Assembly.

Several mechanisms govern relations between the executive and the legislative:

On the initiative of at least one tenth of the Deputies, a motion of censure may be deposited against the Government. The National Assembly then rules by absolute majority.

In the event of a conflict between the executive and the legislative, the President of the Republic may dissolve the National Assembly. If this happens, a new Assembly is elected and it cannot be dissolved for one year after the new elections.

The Legislative: The Parliament, composed of the National Assembly and the Senate, wields the legislative power.

The National Assembly, elected by direct universal suffrage for five years by citizens of both sexes having reached 18 years of age, is composed of 491 Deputies, 473 of whom represent Metropolitan France, 10 the Overseas Departments (or DOM: Guadeloupe, Martinique, French Guyana, Réunion, St. Pierre et Miquelon) and 7 the Overseas Territories (or TOM: such as French Polynesia and New Caledonia).

The Senate, elected for nine years by indirect universal suffrage, is composed of 322 members, renewable by thirds every 3 years and meets at the Palais du Luxembourg.

The Parliament has the right to initiate laws in the same way as the Government does. Relations between the National Assembly and

publish or otherwise communicate any public opinion poll regarding the election in the week preceding it.

the Senate are governed by a system of conciliation, involving the creation of joint committees. In the event of a persistent disagreement, the National Assembly has the last word.

Various specialized councils or advisory boards assist the executive and the legislative in their actions. The most important are:

The Conseil Constitutionnel (Constitutional Council), made up of nine members, three appointed by the President of the Republic, three by the President of the National Assembly and the Senate respectively, and of former Presidents of the Republic, sees to it that the Constitution is upheld.

The Conseil Economique et Social (Economic and Social Council) is a body of 200 members appointed for five years from among the representatives of the main economic and social fields.

The Conseil d'Etat (Council of State), which is the supreme court in administrative matters, also advises the Government on drafting bills and decrees.

The "Administration": France is, as was discussed above, divided into 22 "régions", each comprising from 2 to 7 departments (96 in the mainland with Corsica, and 5 overseas). The smallest territorial entities are the "communes" (townships), ranging from 300 to 1350 inhabitants. The "commune" can be described as the basic unit of local democracy. Each "département", which has since the Revolution been the essential administrative entity in France, is run by a "préfet" appointed by the government. Measures concerning economic planning and regional development are vested in the "régions" run by regional "préfets", who serve as focal points for the channeling of government funds to the different departments.

The political parties: France is a democracy and all political parties are entitled to be represented in the Parliament. These parties range from far right to far left (the terms "right" and "left" were first used in France at the time of the 1789 Revolution). The National Assembly sits in a semi-circle with conservatives to the right, "liberals" (Socialists and Communists) to the left, and members of "middle of the way" orientations in the center. There is still a multiplicity of small political parties: within the "left", Maoists, Trotskyists, "Lutte ouvrière", "Ligue communiste révolutionnaire" "Radicaux de gauche", Ecologists,[2] etc.; within the right, although many of the formerly independent parties have united under the banner of Lecanuet's Centre Démocrate, a number still exist independently: such are the CNIP (Centre National des Indépendants et Paysans): the PFN ("law and order" Parti des Forces Nouvelles); two royalist organizations and, most importantly, the FN or Front National. The historic system of a large number of weak, undisciplined parties has increasingly been turning into a system with fewer, more powerful and more disciplined parties, united in two large coalitions ("bipolarization"). After the 1981 elections, these coalitions consisted of four major parties in the Parliament, two on the left, the "Parti Socialiste" (PS) and the Parti Communiste (PC); and two on the right, the "Union pour la Démocratie Française" or UDF (mainly "Republicans" and "Democrats") and the Gaullist "Rassemblement pour la République" or RPR. But later developments, brought about by the sharp decline at the polls of the Parti Communiste and an upsurge of votes mainly in urban areas in favor of the ultraconservative Front National,[3] eventually led in the mid 80 s to a five party system, con-

---

[2] The Ecologists—"les Verts"—, an amalgam of several heterogeneous factions, grew out of campaigns of pressure groups advocating the "protection of nature" and fighting against pollution. They never managed to play a role similar to that of the "Greens" in Germany and their poor performance in local elections after 1981 has further shown the weakness of their organization.

[3] Le Pen is the leader of that movement and his slogan "Les Français d'abord (Frenchment first)!" has been acclaimed by xenophobic Frenchmen, tired of unemployment, economic insecurity and increase in crime, and wishing to go back to "traditional values." The FN's platform is both racist and anti-immigration, calling for the expulsion of foreign workers, while blaming them for the lack of jobs, the delinquency, and the economic problems of the country. The FN's main target are the immigrant workers from Algeria: "They have no job qualifications, says an FN spokesman, and they bring six, seven or eight children and several wives with them. Then they all go on welfare, driving the system into the red, and it's the French taxpayers who end up footing the bill." France has, in fact, taken in during the 20th century more refugees and foreigners than any other European country. Since 1975, families have been entitled to join immigrant workers in France in order to facilitate their social integration. But, because of the unemployment figures, the government is now offering sizeable sums of money to

sisting of these two medium-sized "extreme parties" and the three major parties discussed above.

Ethnicity: Some of the nationalistic trends present in France have translated into a different kind of attitude on the part of ethnic cultural groups which had been forcibly integrated into the French political, economic and social life in the 19th century. Since World War II, however, there has been an effort to revitalize the so-called sub-cultures of different regions, mainly Brittany, the "Pays Basque" and the Occitanie. Though deprived of its language under the educational system of the Third Republic, Brittany counted at the beginning of the 20th century over a million Breton speakers, a figure which today has shrunk to half a million. The tongue is now being taught from kindergarten to university in Brittany, and the universities of Rennes and Brest deliver Bachelor and Master of Arts degrees in Breton. In and around Paris, the Breton language is taught in 11 high schools and at the Paris VIII University. While few Bretons now oppose Brittany's union with France—separatist tendencies are limited to a few scattered groups—their feeling of being a different people with their own culture and specific characteristics and customs has remained very strong. As for the "Basque Country", it has not given up its aspiration to reunite under one banner its former "seven provinces". In the Occitanie, where several million people still speak a "langue d'oc" and where a conscious effort to create a contemporary Provençal literature has failed, in spite of the revival kindled by poet Mistral in the second half of the 19th century, a certain dislike and distrust of the "North" has persisted since the Middle Ages.[4] The strongest separatist feelings exist in Corsica which, as it will be recalled, did not become part of France until 1768. Numerous terrorist attacks on the French police and administration are a constant reminder of the wish, on the part of some Corsicans, to break their relatively recent ties with the "mainland."

---

unemployed foreigners who agree to go back to their country.

[4] See above, Part II, ch. 2.

The Judiciary • The Military

The Judiciary: Public order in France is enforced by the Department of Justice (Ministère de la Justice). As seen above, at the beginning of the 19th century Napoleon ordered the codification of French laws and the Civil Code was enacted in 1804. The judicial system comprises civil jurisdictions, which judge disputes between private parties and criminal jurisdictions which punish violations of the law. These consist of the following courts:

- the "tribunaux d'instance", which hear cases of minor importance;
- the "tribunaux de grande instance" which take care of more important cases and at times act as appellate courts;
- the police courts which deal with petty offenses and may impose sentences of imprisonment;
- the "tribunaux correctionnels" or courts of petty session which hear more serious offenses;
- the "cours d'assises", made up of three magistrates and nine jurors, and which are courts of criminal jurisdiction (the only possible recourse against the decisions of this jurisdiction is an appeal to the Cour de Cassation and an appeal for mercy to the President of the Republic);
- the "cours d'appel" which deliver judgments on appeals brought from lower courts;
- the "Cour de Cassation", which is the Supreme Court. It decides whether the application and interpretation of laws by the lower courts was correct.

Besides courts of regular jurisdiction, France has established a system of courts for the administrative jurisdictions, headed by the Council of State (Conseil d'Etat); and a Supreme Court of Justice (Haute Cour de Justice) for exceptional events, such as the judging of the President of the Republic for acts of treason and other members of the government for crimes and misdemeanors.

In 1981, the Parliament did away with capital punishment and the guillotine was stored in museums, albeit the majority of the French population favors the death penalty.

The Military: The President of the Republic is Chief Commander of the French Armies. Military service is compulsory for young men at the age of 18 and lasts for 12 months; deferment can be granted until the age of 25 (27 for doctors). As an alternative to service in the Armed Forces a conscript may elect one of two 16 month programs in defense or in technical aid service in French overseas Departments and Territories, or in programs of cooperation with other countries.

The French Military consists of four branches:

- Nuclear Strategic Organization (Force Nucléaire Stratégique), encompasses the deterrent capabilities of Mirages jets, missiles, nuclear submarines.
- Tactical Nuclear Weapons Force (Arme Nucléaire Tactique) is conceived for the battlefield use of nuclear weapons in all army corps.
- Conventional Weapons Force (land, air, and naval).
- Overseas Force for the defense of overseas lands and territories.

Compared to the heated and often divisive defense debates of most Western democracies, the stability of France's domestic consensus on nuclear deterrence and the resilience of its nuclear strategy is in sharp contrast with the rest of Europe's attitudes and protests regarding the deployment of Euromissiles. De Gaulle's legacy of an independent nuclear deterrent appears as the cornerstone of the country's ultimate security, to the extent that nuclear weapons are not a subject of public debate: the debate is about how to increase, rather than cut, defense expenditures and where to focus modernization priorities in the military programs. The Socialist president Mitterand reiterated, in a statement made on October 24, 1987, his belief that the nuclear strategy is the "most powerful deterrent" and "the best way to avoid war."

Industry and Commerce • Transportation • Nuclear Power • "Commercial Services" • Agriculture • The Work Force

Industry and commerce: France is the world's fifth industrial power after the United States, the Soviet Union, Japan, and West Germany. Lacking in natural resources and particularly energy, France has to compensate by creating an outstanding technology. Advances and innovations are evident in many fields, including engineering, computer services, electromechanics, electrical equipment, carbon and graphite products, telecommunications and electronic components. The top products exported by France to the United States are airplanes, helicopters, aircraft engines, uranium, automobile parts and equipment (including tires), organic chemicals and refined petroleum products, as well as missiles, bombs and components for rockets. Wine and natural spirits (Cognac) hold, naturally, an important place on the export list, as do foods (Dannon for example is a subsidiary of the French Gervais-Danone group), crafts, perfume and clothing. It may surprise readers to learn that the ball point pen business was developed by the French BIC Corporation; that the French Ada language system has become the universal language programming chosen by the United States Army; that American hospitals use the polio vaccine developed in France, considered the best in the world, and that when people board the New York city subway, they are most likely riding in a French made car.

Transportation: The transportation sector dominates the major contracts won by France, whether in the field of aeronautics, automobiles, subways or trains, and the means of transportation in France are both sophisticated and efficient. French automobiles have done very well in Europe and outside of Europe and shown a superior performance on difficult terrain as well as on expressways: France is finally just about to get an adequate network of "autoroutes" (tourists must beware, however, since the vast majority of expressways are toll-roads, extremely expensive by American standards). The French airline and "Airbus" industries have major contracts with European and United States airline companies, and, while France does not export trains across the Atlantic, its domestic railway system (SNCF), which covers the entire territory like a spiderweb, is indeed superior: the streamlined trains (80% run on electricity) are renowned for their unfailing punctuality, their modern appearance and the comfort they offer to the passenger. The projected construction of several new "railway express routes", will allow the TGV ("trains à grande vitesse") to travel the 415 kilometers between Paris and Lyon in 2 hours; and the 31 mile long Eurotunnel between France and Great Britian scheduled for completion in 1993 (a ten billion dollar project financed by private funds) will make it possible to cross the channel in 28 minutes and to get from London to Paris in 3 hours—the same time it takes to fly.

Nuclear power: As is well known, France stands among world leaders in the field of nuclear research.[5] The French government's goal is to provide 20% of the country's energy needs and all the electricity through nuclear power plants. This daring program, launched after the 1973 oil crisis, has been in full operation ever since that time.

"Commercial services" account for about 50% of France's domestic production. These services have been, as can be expected, undergoing vast changes. The "grande surface", a replica of the American big supermarket or K-Mart store, has attracted a wide clientele and contributed to a drop in the number of small retail stores in the last two decades. The French hotel trade has also evolved in order to keep up with booming tourism and several new hotel chains have sprung up to provide the necessary number of accommodations (Méridien, Novotel, Sofitel, PLM).

Agriculture: France has traditionally been, because of its geography and climate, a major agricultural country, but the nature of farming has changed radically in recent decades due in part to

---

[5] Electricité de France has joined Thomson in developing simulators for use in nuclear power plants, and is thus involved in training programs for the security teams monitoring plants in the United States.

exigencies of the European Agricultural Common Market. Several factors have contributed to the modernization of farming methods in France, such as mechanization and the increased use of chemical products. The "biological revolution" is responsible for new practices of hybridization and perfected methods of breeding. France produces and exports superior quality meats, cereals, fruits and vegetables. The so-called "agro-alimentaire" or "green petroleum" is flourishing, particularly in the field of milk products: France is the second largest producer of cheese after the United States, and has more varieties (about 400) than any other country in the world.

The modernization of French agriculture means a lessening in the number of individual farms and, consequently of people working in agriculture: larger farms and an increase in yield has led manpower to desert agriculture for industry and services.

The work force: Wage earners constitute the bulk of the labor force (over 80%). The work week, which has been set at 40 hours in 1936, has been reduced to 39 hours after the Socialists came to power in 1981 and will eventually be further reduced to 35 hours. Since February 1982, the length of paid vacations has been increased from 4 to 5 weeks.[6] Several laws adopted as early as 1973 offer job security to wage earners, who can no longer be discharged at will by the employer.

Another keystone in France's social policy was the adoption of a law on continued vocational training. The State pays trainees who are not employed, laid off workers who are being trained for a new job and mothers who wish to find employment. Such pay can vary from one to five times the going SMIC rate.[7] Young people between the ages of 16 and 18 who do not work are entitled to assistance amounting to one-third of the SMIC rate.

The number of unionized workers in France is far below that in

---

[6]There are, besides, numerous holidays paid by tradition or statute (many of which are religious holidays), notably New Year's Day, Easter Monday, May 1st, Ascension Day, Whit Monday, July 14th (the national holiday, called in America "Bastille Day"), August 15th (Assumption), All Saints Day, November 11th and Christmas Day.

[7]The SMIC, as explained in ch. 9, Part II, is the minimum wage.

other European countries (less than 30%). Wage earners belong to five major labor organizations: the General Confederation of Labor, (Confédération Génerale du Travail or CGT), linked to the Communist party; the CGT-Workers Force (CGT-FO), originating out of a split with the CGT; the French Democratic Labor Confederation (CFDT), with socialist leanings; the Catholic oriented French Confederation of Christian Workers (CFTC), and the General Confederation of Supervisory and Management Personnel (CGC). The right to strike is set forth in the Constitution, and every worker is free to join whatever union he pleases or to refuse to belong to a union. The management of enterprises is grouped within the National Council of French Employers (CNPF). Unemployment is still the single most important problem facing France, and candidates to the presidency rank it as first, before "peace" and "liberty". Early retirement in government-controlled companies is not only encouraged but enforced: the "retraite anticipée" or "pré-retraite" is a frequent phenomenon for employees between ages 54 and 58.

The Educational System

There are three levels of education in France: primary, secondary and higher education. It is controlled by a highly centralized administrative infra-structure created under Napoleon I. School attendance is mandatory from ages 6 to 16. Private schools enroll about 14% of the student population. The centralization of public education in France provides, in theory at least, a uniformity and standardization of the curricula. The country is divided into regional "Académies" headed by "Recteurs" who are representatives of the Ministère de l'Education Nationale.

Children on the elementary level are enrolled, under the age of 6, in pre-elementary schools, "écoles maternelles" or kindergarten. Nearly three quarters of all children aged three attend school in France; tots can under certain circumstances enroll at the age of two.

Children between the ages of 6 and 11 attend grade schools ("écoles élémentaires") which are coeducational; tuition is free, as well as books and school supplies. While concentrating on basic skills, the curriculum now stresses imagination, creativity and development of eye-hand coordination.

Classes are numbered from 12 to 1, "1" is the highest and last grade in the "lycée", before the so-called "terminale". Marks range from 0 to 20, and the score of 10 is considered passing.

From ages 11 to 15 students attend a secondary educational institution of one type or another, which is also tuition-free and which is basically divided into two levels or "cycles". The first (short term),[8] which lasts 4 years, is dispensed either in the Collèges, or CES, where classes stop at the "classe de 3e", or else in the "lycées"; but only the lycées offer the "second cycle" or "long term" secondary education. The last three years of the "lycée" (2e, 1re and "terminale") lead to the famous "baccalauréat" ("bac" or "bachot") in a variety of disciplines (such as philosophy/letters, economics/social studies, mathematics/physics, etc.; there is even a technical "bac" with different fields of specialization). The "bac", which opens doors to higher education is an important examination; it requires months of preparation and assiduous work on the part of the student and strong nerves on the part of the entire family (unsuccessful candidates are given more than one chance at passing this dreaded examination). The holder of a "bac" can enroll either at a university or in one of the institutions of higher learning, called "grandes écoles".

After the 1968 student riots, a series of reforms and specifically the "Loi d'Orientation" passed in November of the same year brought drastic changes to the entire system of university education. The one hundred faculties, Law, Science, Medicine and Letters (further subdivided into sections, such as English, History, French Literature, etc.), which formerly constituted 23 universities, have been replaced by some 780 Teaching and Research Units (UER), grouped in a larger number of universities and university centers. These units are now

---

[8]It can lead to a certificate of vocational aptitude (CAP) or to a vocational studies certificate (BEP).

the basic elements of the new university structure.

The goal of the "Orientation law" was to encourage the universities to "bring themselves in line with the democratic evolution and the industrial and technical revolution" and to stress self-government, participation by staff and students, and pluridisciplinarity. The University of Paris (often erroneously referred to as the "Sorbonne")[9] which before the new law enrolled over 150,000 students, was divided into 13 autonomous universities.

Another landmark innovation was, following the American pattern of "credits", the establishment of the so-called "unités de valeur" or UV. The acquisition of a determined number of UVs leads to a degree called DEUG (Diplôme d'Etudes Universitaires Générales) and is obtained after two years of general "multi-curriculum" studies in the first "cycle". After one or two more years of studies (2nd "cycle") with a concentration on one major field, successful candidates can earn a "Licence" and the next higher degree called "Maîtrise". Potential scholars can go on to a "Doctorat" during the 3rd "cycle", provided they can find a professor willing to supervise and sponsor their research, or else they work toward a "Diplôme d'Etudes Spécialisées" or DESS.[10] "The Doctorat d'état" is conferred upon candidates whose research is recognized by a jury to be an original and important contribution to the field, and after an oral presentation of a thesis or a series of works which usually require long years of preparation.[11] As mentioned earlier, any student holding the baccalauréat can attend the university but this "free access" policy has resulted in high failure and dropout rates during the first

---

[9] Actually the "Sorbonne" was the Faculty of Letters at the Paris University with an enrollment of some 40,000 students. It is now the name of University Paris IV. The French students' current designation for the "university" is simply "la fac".

[10] The "doctorat d'université" is a lower-level degree, which does not give the right in France to exercise professions for which a state degree is required.

[11] There is, in France, a highly esteemed title of "Agrégé", which is bestowed upon candidates who have successfully passed an extremely difficult special examination in a given discipline. The "Agrégation" opens the doors of the most coveted teaching careers.

year of studies. Such is not the case with the prestigious "grandes écoles", where the number of admissions is limited to several hundred and where students are accepted only if they rank among the highest achievers on an extremely difficult entrance examination. The competition is so fierce, that preparation for these exams can last several years in special preparatory schools. Some of the best known "grandes écoles" are the Conservatoires, the Ecole des Beaux-Arts, the Ecole des Ponts et Chaussées, the Ecole Centrale, the Ecole Nationale d'Etudes Politiques, the Ecole des Hautes Etudes Commerciales (HEC), the highly respected Ecole Normale on rue d'Ulm in Paris,[12] the Ecole Polytechnique (or X) and the Ecole Nationale d'Administration or ENA, created after World War II in 1945. The ENA is already "venerated" in spite of its young age: it is said to symbolize "a certain form of power" and all its alumni have held or now hold high-level political or economic posts. Giscard d'Estaing is a graduate both of the ENA and the Polytechnique, which still seems to be the most prestigious.[13]

Most students do not have and do not need much money (some depend on small government scholarships): they have health insurance and special "vouchers" allow them to get very adequate meals at university cafeterias literally for a pittance. Tuition at French universities is minimal, thus students need not work and can devote all their time to studying. There is also, especially in large cities, no "campus life" to speak of, and no athletics in which students can get involved; they do spend, however, much time in the cafés and parks surrounding the universities, such as, in Paris, the Jardin du Luxembourg and the Boulevard St. Michel ("Boul Mich", a block away from the Sorbonne, in the very heart of the Quartier Latin); the street is lined with bookstores and innumerable eateries, and is the center of student life.

It would be impossible to give an idea of all the learning possibil-

---

[12] Many prominent writers (Péguy, Romains, Giraudoux, Sartre to name a few) were graduates of this institution.

[13] As discussed in *La Mafia polytechnicienne*, a bestseller written by the son of a former French ambassador to the United States, Jacques Kosciusko-Morizet.

ities offered in France by government sponsored and private institutions. Some of these are highly specialized in practical fields, characteristic of the French way of life: culinary schools (in Paris such as La Varenne, Cordon Bleu, Maxim's Academy and Le Pot-au-feu) initiate their numerous adepts of all ages into the art of gastronomy ("haute cuisine"), while schools of oenology admit students wishing to become experts in wine-tasting and buying.

The People and Their Lifestyles • The Family; Religion; Food • Leisure, Sports and Vacations

As can be expected, the French have by now completely recovered from the effects of World War II and are enjoying an ever higher standard of living. While there are marked differences in the way of life of various social classes—a cross-over from a lower to an upper one is less common and more difficult in France than in most other countries—there are signs of prosperity and what is called "a good life" in all strata of the population. First on the list of desiderata after a house or a condo[14] is the possession of a car, though the French are used to walking and really enjoy it,[15] and though they have at their disposal, as we have seen, a superior network of public transportation: the Paris "métro" (subway) for example, is not only punctual and efficient, but often aesthetically satisfying (the Louvre subway station, e.g., is adorned with replicas of famous art works, displayed in showcases).

---

[14] Less fortunate families are, naturally, renters. Since, after World War II, there was a shortage of housing, the government has provided the working class with "cités ouvrières" and HLM's ("habitation à loyer modéré). These inexpensive, but modern and well equipped apartment buildings cover large areas in the outskirts of big cities.

[15] This may be one reason why the French generally keep slim: most French visitors to the United States are amazed and shocked at the number of overfed and oversized Americans.

Next in importance as a status symbol is what the French call a "résidence secondaire" or country house.[16]. Owning a second home is considered a priority especially for Parisians and people living in large cities, not only because of the pleasures connected with the spending of week-ends in the lovely French "campagne", but also for the health benefits derived from leaving the noisy, congested and polluted city streets. The French are prepared to spend long hours in traffic jams as long as they can "get away".[17] Weekends, which are not a French invention, but have become a sort of cherished institution in France,[18] are often extended in that country to several days: as mentioned earlier, there are numerous religious and other national holidays, and it is customary to take extra vacation days between the actual holiday and Saturday: this is called a "pont" or bridge. It is essential for people going to France on business to carefully check the calendar before making travel plans: some months, e.g. December and May are almost entirely "out" for business purposes.

Weekends are spent on rest, sports, gardening, entertaining, reading, walking and visiting historic sites and monuments. There is no Sunday school, since religious education is now dispensed on Wednesdays, which have replaced the traditional Thursdays as the students' day off, but many Catholics attend mass on Sundays. About 90% of the French population are Catholic, and about 80% are baptized, married in church and buried in a religious ceremony; however, only between 20 and 25% actively practice their religion.[19]

---

[16] France has been called a "world champion" in this field: 20% of all families are two-property-owners.

[17] There are all kinds of sophisticated "strategies" of beating the others to the road, such as leaving on Saturday at dawn rather than on Friday night and returning at daybreak on Monday. Schools are in session for a half-a-day on Saturdays, but this does not appear to have much bearing on the weekly "exodus".

[18] The Frenchman's love affair with the week-end has an adverse effect on the number of people voting in elections which are held on Sundays.

[19] There seems to be, though, a great spiritual revival among the believers, and monks belonging to several religious orders have re-established themselves in abandoned medieval abbeys (such is the case with the Benedictines at the Mont-Saint-Michel). An interdenominational religious community has been founded in Taizé near Mâcon where thousands of young people gather and join in ecumenical

The Protestants—about 800,000—constitute 1.5% of the population and the Jewish minority counts around 500,000. After World War II France has opened its doors to the greatest number of Jewish refugees in the world after Israel, in spite of a latent anti-semitism,[20] reinforced in the last decades by new bonds of friendship and commercial ties between France and various Arabic nations. The number of Moslems in France has steadily increased since the mass immigration of manual workers from North Africa; a number of mosques and innumerable Arab groceries and eateries have sprung up all over France.

These week-ends of togetherness tend to reinforce the close family bonds for which the French are known, and which have undergone no basic change, despite rebellious and violent attitudes on the part of some young people and the number of children alienated from their parents and defying their authority. As in all countries, there is an ever increasing number of single parent families: the divorce rate—divorce proceedings have been simplified to the utmost—has doubled between the mid '70s and the mid '80s.[21] Women have made tremendous strides since World War II—they have finally acquired the right to vote and can now manage their money and personal property; but the MLF (Mouvement de Libération de la Femme) and other feminist movements in France are incomparably less vociferous and influential than those in the United States (according to author and journalist Françoise Giroud, the French woman is glad to be a "sex object" and finds the idea of confrontation with men repugnant). While they have never been socially segregated by men and have always been the dominant force at home, many women

---

prayer. The Pope visited Taizé during his last stay in France.

[20] Dating back to the late 1800s and the French collaboration with the Germans during World War II. There has fortunately been of late no recurrence of acts of violence against the Jews, such as the bombing in Paris of a popular Jewish restaurant on rue des Rosiers and of the rue Copernic Synagogue in the early 1980s.

[21] 59% of people divorcing are between 20 and 34 years of age (the average duration of a marriage—12 years—tends to decrease). The projection for the 1990s is that one marriage out of 4 will end in divorce.

have now also acceded to the highest echelons both in industry and in government.[22] 90% of all French women consider themselves, however, primarily mothers and homemakers and do not seem to resent their numerous household chores, which are more time consuming in France than in the United States.[23]

Inspired largely by the long standing desire to boost the birth rate (France has for centuries been threatened by depopulation), the government offers a whole range of advantages to families through substantial tax rebates, aid to large families, vacation camps and health-related sojourns in the mountains or spas for children, advice to households and collective services to families.

Another factor strengthening the family bond in the French household is the meal taken in common, especially on Sundays and holidays and which continues to be a ritual, despite the simplifications imposed by an ever more stressful and rapid pace of life. "Together at dinner" is still the accepted rule, while lunch is increasingly eaten separately, especially if both parents are working. The "déjeuner" or lunch remains, however, the principal meal of the day. Many husbands do return home to share it with their family[24] and most stores close for lunch in order to give their owners and employees an opportunity to truly relish this sacrosanct ceremony.[25]

---

[22] During the presidency of Pompidou, Simone Weil was minister of health; Giscard d'Estaing entrusted Alice Saunier-Séité with the Ministry of University Education, and during Mitterrand's term several women were secretaries of state. One of them, ex-minister of Social Affairs Georgina Dufoix, stated in an interview that "it is a good time to be a woman in France, because she is recognized both as a career woman and a mother."

[23] Not only because of a less well developed technology, but also by choice: the French dislike paper napkins, and clothes dryers are unpopular because they allegedly damage the nap of the fabrics. Many men, although their number may be dwindling, never do any cleaning or work in the kitchen.

[24] "Ladies lunches" are practically unknown in France—and social clubs for women still a rarity.

[25] This can be very inconvenient to tourists, not only because in the provinces there is strictly nothing to do from 12 to 2 p.m. (even museums and banks are closed), but because the time of the "break" varies considerably from place to place and from store to store: thus all open air "marchés" in Paris fold up for good at 1 p.m. sharp, while the all important bakeries and other food stores

Although the many recent changes in the French eating habits are universally known—lighter, leaner "nouvelle cuisine", less fat, less sugar, less wine (but more champagne)—food is still the Frenchman's major preoccupation and source of enjoyment: 70% of the population believes that no other country can match the quality of French fare. Whereas the figure of 25% of the Frenchman's budget spent on food and drink in 1970 (it was almost 38% in 1959) has still substantially decreased in the 1980s, cooking is universally considered an art requiring careful preparation and a discriminating choice. The supermarket shelves are loaded with frozen meats and vegetables, but the vast majority of shoppers, even the young ones, prefer to buy fresh:[26] hence the tremendous popularity of open air markets which come to both commercial and residential streets of all cities including Paris, usually twice a week, in rotation.

In spite of the Americanization of numerous aspects of their lives, of which the "franglais" is the most striking manifestation,[27] the French stick most of the time to their traditional eating habits: a light breakfast, consisting of a "bol"—larger than any cup, smaller than a bowl—of cocoa, coffee or milk and a croissant or "brioche"; a substantial lunch (except, maybe, for the college population "on the run") and a slightly less substantial dinner, unless company is expected.[28] Dinner is late by American standards: because of the

---

reopen at 4; only department stores in Paris and supermarkets in large cities do not close during the day, but buyer traffic at lunch time is extremely light.

[26] The French like quality in everything they buy including, naturally, clothes: they prefer to purchase less but it must be elegant and well made.

[27] In spite of all the futile efforts—some with the help of a law passed in 1975—to curb the influx of American words into the French vocabulary, their number is steadily growing: "living", "marketing", "shopping", "grand standing", "escalator", "stress" and so on; even "computeur" is often replacing the French "ordinateur".

[28] If company is present, and in the upper strata of society, whether at lunch or at dinner, a rather inflexible menu is served, according to long established patterns and the dictates of etiquette: a rather short "cocktail hour", which should not last more than 30 minutes, and during which such "apéritifs" as portwine, sherry, but most often champagne, will be served rather than hard alcohol (though scotch is also always available), and with a minimum of tidbits: guests must have

extended lunch break, offices and businesses don't close until 7 or
even later and the people who work must still beat the traffic before
sitting down to the table, often only by 8:30 pm.

While home cooking is highly appreciated, French restaurants
do enjoy, as has always been the case, a well-deserved reputation.
Everything touching upon the restaurant business is devised to simplify the client's choice: menus must, by law, be displayed in the
window or at the door of the establishment and service is often included in the price of the meal. The French, even more so than
tourists, avail themselves of "guides" to good eating places, such as
publications by Michelin and Gault & Millau, and will happily make
the recommended detour to sample the world renowned gastronomy
of a Bocuse near Lyon or a Verger in Mougins.[29] When it comes
to food, the sky is the limit for the otherwise parsimonious Frenchmen, known for his "hoarding" habits and his stocking filled with
gold and cash. This Frenchman, who has always preferred cash deals
("liquide", "espèces" or "comptant"), has been turning more into a
spender than a saver, since the American way of paying with credit
cards was adopted and is now widespread. The French also often pay
with personal checks.[30]

---

a sufficient appetite for the upcoming meal. The latter usually consists of an hors-
d'oeuvre ("foie gras" is one of the most highly appreciated), an "entrée" (such as
fish or a "terrine"), a meat course with vegetables, followed by salad, an assortment of cheeses, dessert and fruits—if these include grapes, scissors and a bowl of
water for rinsing are provided. Assorted wines naturally accompany each course.
As in other countries, coffee—as well as after-dinner drinks ("digestifs")—are usually served in the living room, but at night many Frenchmen will refrain: they
value their sleep and will often drink instead an herb tea ("tisane" or "infusion")
after returning home, if it is not offered at the party. The French never "eat and
run", but linger politely after the meal even on weekdays. It is customary for
hosts to serve some time after the dinner freshly squeezed orange or grapefruit
juice, after which the guests feel free to leave.

[29] It is customary for Frenchmen to indulge, once in a while in a "gueleton"
or gastronomic feast, whether at home or in a restaurant; it is often followed by
a "crise de foie" or liver trouble on the part of the participants. The medicine
cabinets of the French are filled with drugs to relieve the discomfort. There is
also always a good supply of system cleansing mineral waters on hand.

[30] The universally accepted credit card is the VISA, called "carte bleue". It

If many French opt, in everyday life, for a lighter diet ("cuisine minceur"), it is because they have become increasingly health minded: health food stores are doing a thriving business and "gym clubs" have proliferated: even the TV offers regularly a "Gym-tonic" workout program. There is superior health care—and also a welfare system—in France: practically all Frenchmen are covered by insurance for expenses connected with sickness and treatment, hospitals and medication. The insurance pays for all costs of childbirth: if the mother is a wage earner, she is entitled in most cases to the equivalent of 90% of her salary during the six weeks preceding and eight weeks following birth. Old age pensions, help, and advice for senior citizens ensure the well being of an ever growing number of people over 60: they constitute some 20% of the population.

Health considerations may also play a role in the Frenchmen's wish for more leisure and a further reduction of working hours.[31] The French already increased their leisure time by about 10% between the mid 1970s and the mid 1980s, according to the French Statistics Bureau INSEE. Much of this time was allocated to television watching, though a sizeable portion went to sports, which the French enjoy tremendously, both as spectators and active participants. Among the most popular sports are football (soccer), jogging, tennis, skiing, hiking, rugby, as well as "boules" and "pétanque" (a southern version of bowling). Swimming has become much more widespread, since a number of municipalities through France have built public swimming pools and made them available to people of all ages. Golf is undergoing what is called a "démocratisation" and is

---

may surprise a foreign resident of France or a tourist possessing a French checking account to see how readily his checks are accepted everywhere, mostly without a request for identification: the reason is that the penalties for bad checks are extremely stiff: a single check that has bounced may deprive the person who has issued it of all his bank accounts and all his credit to the end of his days!

[31] In his "essai" on "lazy France", *La France paresseuse* (Seuil, 1987), Victor Scherrer wonders how France can hope to be competitive on international markets, while working less and less: with 1500 or 1600 hours of "effective" work per year per person, the country is far behind the United States, Japan, Germany and other countries of the Common Market.

accessible to a growing number of Frenchmen in all strata of society (mountain climbing attracts a small, but skilled elite). Practically the entire French population is passively participating in sports by watching championships and matches either in person or on TV. The "Tour de France" bicycle race or "big loop", which ends on the Champs Elysées in Paris each July, has kept several generations of French breathless and has been compared to "an epic", "a myth", and "a Cornelian drama". Its popularity seems to have undergone a slight decline lately, but it is still considered one of the most important events of the summer and has fired the imaginations of foreign sports fans: to everybody's surprise, an American won the race in 1986. Throngs line up along the roads on the Tour's itinerary; others watch it on what the French call "le petit écran" (small screen). The bicycle race and soccer matches unleash manifestations of unbridled enthusiasm, as well as horse races on which many French bet money. A sizeable part of the population likes to gamble. According to a Paris-Match poll in the mid eighties, more than 50% of the French play the lotto, 30% the National lottery, 32 and 21% respectively the "tiercé" and the "quarté" horse races.

Leisure obviously also means vacations which have become a "sacred" institution. Some 54% of the French travel during their holidays, but only 1 out of 6 chooses to go abroad: France itself, with its long, excellent coastline, numerous beaches and variety of mountain resorts offers a plethora of vacation spots. In recent years, some segments of the French society have turned to inland and rural France, still largely unexplored. The modestly priced "gîtes ruraux" country lodgings and "American plan" on farms are more and more frequently included on lists of accommodations, along with "châteaux-relais", top class hotels, large hotel chains, more moderate hotels, "pensions de famille" and "auberges". Camping grounds and trailer parks are also plentiful and usually filled to capacity.[32]

---

[32] Many French choose to go to spas, as they strongly believe in the beneficial qualities of spring water, virtually for all the existing diseases. Extended stays ("cures") are prescribed by doctors, and covered in full by health insurance and Social Security.

Whereas the French have traditionally taken off for their summer holidays in July, and primarily in August, the month of the huge exodus" and horrendous traffic jams on all the main arteries,[33] the fifth week of vacation, added after the 1981 elections, has prompted particularly the more affluent families to divide their vacations between summer and winter; one of the factors contributing to this development is the great vogue of skiing. The French have many excellent slopes, many ski champions and are very excited that France was chosen to host the 1992 Winter Olympics in Albertville (French Alps).

Culture • The "Patrimoine" • Museums, Art, Books, Music • The Performing Arts and Festivals • The Mass Media: Television, Radio and Press

The cutback in working and increase in leisure hours gives the French an opportunity to spend more time also on "culture". France has always been a great foyer of arts and letters and has through the ages attracted prominent intellectuals and artists from various countries. But until recently only a minority elite of Frenchmen took advantage of the privileged cultural ambiance France had to offer. The middle of the 20th century has brought culture to the masses, while giving them the possibility of attending, by means of television, theatrical performances, opera, travelogues, historic films, concerts and art exhibitions.

While not every Frenchman avails himself of this opportunity to broaden his horizons (only 1% of museum visitors come from the working class), the government has taken further measures to spread culture even in the most remote regions of the country. One of the important steps was, on the one hand, the creation, following the

---

[33] The authorities' relentless effort to stagger the departures has proved to be successful in recent years.

initiative of De Gaulle's Minister of Culture André Malraux, of a number of "Maisons de la culture" in the provinces and, on the other, a concerted effort to bolster the safeguarding of the French national heritage or "patrimoine". A special committee created in 1964 has systematically drawn up a list of all the artistic treasures of the past. From the Versailles palace to the smallest rural churches in Brittany, France has a wealth of monuments of historical or architectural interest in need of protection: these have been catalogued in two different categories, either as "classified" or "listed". While laws are less strict for "listed" buildings, the owner of a classified monument can undertake improvements or changes only with the government's permission; but he is entitled to subsidies and loans if the work is authorized.

The safeguarding of natural sites is entrusted to departmental commissions which establish a list of areas worthy of protection in the general interest. In urban areas, the protection of old neighborhoods against the deterioration brought about by time and the assaults of modern urbanization has been a great concern. In some instances the restoration of an entire neighborhood takes place once a "perimeter" of renovation has been established. A recent increase in funds allocated to archeological digs also contributes to the enrichment of the French "patrimony".

The State owns and operates a large number of museums[34] and oversees some 850 privately owned museums nation wide. It also acts as a patron of the arts by helping young artists survive, by backing creative initiatives with public commissions, by financing artistic training and education, and by upholding the long-established French Academy of Art in Rome (Villa Médicis), where young Frenchmen can perfect their talents.

France is a beehive of literary creativity and over 700 literary

---

[34] 15 in Paris alone. The Centre Pompidou stands out as the symbol of success of mass culture, with some 8 million visitors yearly. But the 33 French national museums have a very limited combined annual budget of just over $10 million for new acquisitions. In 1988 a nationwide drive was launched to raise the 5.7 million dollars necessary to purchase, from the Order of Malta, Georges de La Tour's painting "Saint Thomas."

prizes are awarded to successful authors each year. The awarding of the Goncourt, Femina, Renaudot, Interallié and Médicis, and of the French Academy's Grand Prix de Littérature always constitutes an important event in the nation's cultural life. The State extends help to writers in the form of scholarships, loans or subsidies.

Loans and subsidies are also available to publishers. France stands among the countries publishing the most books, particularly literary works which constitute 35% of the total output. The French are avid readers: according to a Fall 1987 poll published by *Le Point*, 74% have included the reading of books on the list of things "that make them happy".[35] Frenchmen mostly buy the books they read, although they also have at their disposal a number of libraries; these are, however, not as numerous and as accessible as in the United States. While the most renowned French libraries' principal aim is to safeguard the country's intellectual heritage—the Bibliothèque Nationale in Paris houses over 7 million volumes, a rich collection of periodicals, prints, engravings, coins, and medals, and by virtue of a 16th century law obtains a copy of every book published in France—the role of many others is to encourage the public to read: the Centre Beaubourg is visited yearly by over 4 million readers. The Archives Nationales in Paris (Hôtel de Soubise and Hôtel de Rohan) preserve documents pertaining to France's long history.

The Frenchman's love for music—listening to it tops the list of "what makes him happy" compiled by *Le Point*—is reflected in the number of songs that were hits abroad, the number of singers who have become world famous and in the figure of over 250 million records and cassettes sold yearly in France in the 1980s (many French call themselves "mélomanes" or music addicts). The young generation in particular considers music an essential part of their lives: 80% of the young people own and regularly listen to the radio, a sizeable percentage are equipped with a walkman and 3 million play a musical instrument. While most list "rock" and "folk" as their preference, classical music attracts a good number of listeners. The

---

[35] The French are great enthusiasts of polls and statistics: there are figures and percentages for just about every aspect of French life.

government's programs called "Jeunesses Musicales" enable young people to attend concerts featuring great artists for a minimal fee.[36] Concert halls are invariably sold out, as are most performances in the moderately priced state owned theatres.

The French have always had a passion for the theatre, dating back, as discussed above, to the medieval miracle plays and farces: it has reached an apogee in the 17th century, when the Comédie Française was created under royal patronage, and maintained this interest ever since. Today's government is also actively promoting this art form by offering subsidies, not only to government sponsored Parisian theatres, but also to newly established troupes in the Parisian suburbs and in other French cities, and to itinerant companies which perform in the four corners of the hexagon. This effort at decentralization is particularly evident in the proliferation of festivals—drama, music, folklore, dance and poetry-all over France. Among some 100 well established festivals[37] which attract tourists from distant parts, those of Avignon, Orange, Cannes, Antibes and Nice, Aix-en-Provence, Bordeaux, Royan and La Rochelle, Strasbourg, Brittany, the Abbeys of Royaumont and of Noirlac and the "Nights" of Flanders and of Burgundy require special mention, as well as the Marais festival in Paris. A number of châteaux and historic monuments (e.g., the Invalides and the Louvre's Cour Carrée) feature, on hot summer evenings, a "spectacle son et lumière", which uses the interplay of light and sound (music and voices of prominent actors in dialogue), to recreate the important historic events which took place at the site. Some, like the château du Lude near Le Mans, include a "total audio-visual feast", with dancing, duelling and horseback riding amidst breathtaking pageantry.

If the attendance at the movies has somewhat dwindled due to the competition of TV and the other performing arts just discussed, it does not mean in the least that the Frenchman's taste for film has

---

[36] Some churches, such as the Ste Chapelle offer free recitals. The magnificent Sunday afternoon concerts at Notre-Dame in Paris, famous for the sound of its organs, are a not to be missed opportunity.

[37] Not counting the small regional and village festivals.

decreased: in fact he is just as much a "cinéphile" as a "mélomane". Cinema, developed thanks to the inventiveness of Louis Lumière in 1895, has always held an important place in the cultural lives of the French. The discriminating fans belong to "ciné-clubs", and read not only the numerous film reviews which appear in the daily papers, but also specialized publications such as *Cahiers du cinéma*.

As mentioned earlier, the Frenchman is an assiduous radio listener and television watcher who can avail himself of a constantly growing number of channels in addition to the original TF 1, Antenne 2 and France-Régionale 3. The programs on French TV as well as on the radio are superior: many are devoted to art, history and literature, and are often rebroadcast by the Canadian network (such is the case with "Apostrophes", the weekly panel discussion of new books presented by Bernard Pivot). A program on French television is never interrupted by commercials which appear at certain times of the day under separate listings. Clearly, they must be both aesthetically satisfying and entertaining in order to hold the attention of the viewers and are not only in good taste, but also artistic, and often thoroughly charming.

One out of two Frenchmen only reads a daily newspaper (the papers are substantially more expensive than their American counterparts: a single copy can cost up to a dollar). While an unprecedented interest in magazines can be noted—*Paris-Match, L'Express, Le Nouvel Observateur, Elle, Jours de France* are the leaders, although they follow in popularity publications such as *Télé-7-jours, Télé-poche* and their likes (*Sélection du Readers Digest* is also a favourite)—the sale of some Parisian newspapers seems to be on the decline. The most widely read are *France-Soir, Le Monde, Le Figaro, Le Parisien libéré, Le Matin*, the communist-oriented *L'Humanité* and the Catholic publication *La Croix*.

Paris

In front of the Sorbonne, on the little square which separates this venerable building from the still more venerable Hôtel or Musée de Cluny, stands a statue of Montaigne in a pensive pose, with the following inscription: "My heart belongs to Paris ever since my childhood. I am French solely because of this great city, great and incomparable in its variety—the glory of France and one of the noblest ornaments of the world." These lines were written by Montaigne four hundred years ago. He knew the Ile de la Cité, the Sainte-Chapelle, Notre-Dame, the "rive gauche", the church of St. Germain-des-Prés and the Louvre as it was then, still unconnected with Catherine de Médicis' Palais des Tuileries. But he never saw the Panthéon, the Concorde, the Madeleine, the Champs-Elysées with its Arc de Triomphe; why even this very Sorbonne owes its present shape, as do the Institut de France, the Palais Royal, the Invalides and the Place des Vosges, to the genius of 17th century architects. Montaigne could not have imagined the splendor of today's Paris, with its large, elegant boulevards conceived by Haussmann and its modern architectural complexes such as the Palais de Chaillot; nor could he have foreseen four hundred years ago the erection of an Eiffel Tower. But he did sense that Paris was destined to remain unique and would never have an equal.

The "rive gauche" (left bank) is the one that has changed least: this is where the village of Lutetia (inhabited by the Parisii who eventually gave its name to the capital) spilled out from its original boundaries on Ile de la Cité to the "hills", which were not victims of the floodings of the Seine: those turned regularly parts of the right bank into marshes ("marais" in French: they were gradually drained by monks). The Ile de la Cité remained for a long time the "cité royale", the heart and center of power not only of the city, but of the entire country of France after the Capetians definitively chose it as their capital. This tiny "island" is crowded with historic monuments and vestiges of the past, such as the Palais de Justice, former residence of the kings, its awesome Conciergerie and Gothic gem "La

Sainte Chapelle" which was erected on the orders of Saint-Louis, and where mass is still celebrated every day of the week. While a relatively recent Hôtel-Dieu or hospital has replaced its medieval counterparts,[38] Notre-Dame, restored by Viollet-le-Duc in the 19th century, stands in its original 12th and 13th century splendor. In front of the cathedral, an underground museum or "archaeological crypt" now offers to visitors the sight of various layers of structures which have accumulated during long centuries and have been discovered by recent excavations.

The "rive gauche", already inhabited by Gallo-Romans (ruins of Roman baths can be seen along the Boulevard St. Michel[39]),is still today, as it was in the Middle Ages, the center of learning, artistic and intellectual activity and is known to have a different character and mentality than the "other side" of the city across the Seine. The "rive droite", while it also possesses famous "art districts", such as the Montmartre, is more modern and mainly known as the "affluent" part of the capital, where banks and luxury boutiques have settled and where elegant apartment buildings were erected in the 19th century. As we know, Haussmann endowed Paris with an entirely new appearance and he is responsible for the division of the city into 20 "arrondissements". These vary greatly in size, shape and character.[40]

The Paris of today is at the same time Paris of yesterday—offering a visual summary of the entire French history—and Paris of tomorrow: this novel aspect of their beloved city is not without causing great concern to its inhabitants. The skyscrapers of la Défense had

---

[38] The first of a series of hospitals erected on that location dates back to 650 A.D.

[39] An amphitheatre existed near today's Musée de Cluny and the remnants of a forum were unearthed under the rue Soufflot.

[40] The most elegant used to be the 16e (between the Seine and the Arc de Triomphe), the 8e (around the Champs-Elysées), the 7e (on the left bank, including parts of St. Germain) and the 17e (north of the Arc de Triomphe); recently the Marais section with the Place des Vosges (Paris 3e) is returning to its 17th century elegance and prestige. The "arrondissements" are included in the Parisian postal zipcode: e.g., 75015 is Paris 15e. While modernizing the capital, Haussmann unwittingly razed invaluable vestiges of medieval Paris, such as the city wall erected by Philippe-Auguste at the beginning of the 13th century.

already ruined for them the elegant perspective from Place de la
Concorde through the Champs-Elysées and beyond the Arc de Triomphe. Then came the Centre Pompidou (sarcastically nicknamed
"la Raffinerie" by Parisian cab drivers): popular and functional as
it may have proven in its role of "disseminator" of culture to the
masses, it still is to many, and not without good reason, an intoler-
able eye sore. Next, during the presidency of Mitterrand, black and
white columns of unequal height, the "colonnes Buren", sprang up
in a seemingly haphazard fashion in the harmonious courtyard of the
17th century Palais-Royal and brought about angry reactions of the
Parisians. Now, the idea of placing a huge plastic pyramid within
the walls of the Louvre is meeting with a storm of protests.[41]

Meanwhile, Paris is getting "taller" and cleaner: more and more
buildings have been sanded and freed from layers of grime accumulated during their long existence. And more and more books and
articles are added daily to the already extremely voluminous literature devoted to this "city of lights": it almost seems that "all has
been said" and nothing new or original could be added. But Paris
is an unending source of inspiration and keeps on being glorified in
prose, poetry and song. It has been compared to a beautiful woman,
to a queen, to a goddess, and called a "paradise": paradise of artists
and art lovers, theatre lovers, history buffs, music fans, intellectuals
of all disciplines and...gourmets. In order to get an idea of how much
there is to do and see in Paris, one needs only glance at one of several
weekly publications (such as *Pariscope* or *L'Officiel des spectacles*),
listing the innumerable activities, sport events, films, plays, concerts,
exhibitions and lectures available every day of the year, as well as
restaurants, night clubs and cafés. Many such cafés have played an
important role in the launching of the various intellectual art and
literary movements born in France: the Café Procope, for example,

---

[41] Many Parisians also object to the interior design of the Musée d'Orsay which
opened in December 1986 to house treasures of 19th century art. The advocates of
these modern additions to Paris argue that when the Eiffel Tower was first erected,
it was considered a monstrosity, but has since become the beloved landmark of
the capital. The Tower, however, does not stand within the perimeter of any
historic building, nor does it block any view or perspective.

brings back the memories of the 18th century *philosophes*, while "Le Flore" and "Les Deux Magots" still seem to resound with the discussions of Sartre and the members of his Existentialist group.[42]

Eateries are listed by specialty, by "arrondissement" and by business hours (approximate prices are also detailed). "H.C." or "hors catégorie" is the designation for restaurants that have become synonymous with the finest in French gastronomy (La Tour d'Argent, Maxim's, Lasserre, Ledoyen, Le Grand Véfour, Laurent, Crillon, Taillevent, Archestrate, Pré Catalan in the Bois de Boulogne, to name a few) and that are known to local people as well as to tourists. Less well known to those who do not live in Paris is the magnificent choice of delicacies available not from restaurants, but from highly specialized food merchants: the incomparable ice cream from Berthillon on Ile de la Cité; the "bread as an art" from the ovens of master-baker Poilâne; Lenôtre's unsurpassed pastries; the superb selection of caviars, foies-gras and truffles from Petrossian; and the wide range of "palate pleasers" sold by "épiceries fines" and de luxe caterers such as Hédiard and Fauchon, both behind the church of La Madeleine.[43]

These establishments, like all the other food stores and eateries in Paris, from the corner "bistrot" or "brasserie" to the five star hotel restaurant, send out their buyers at the crack of dawn to Rungis (between Paris and Orly), where the former Halles have moved to make place for the Centre Beaubourg. This enormous complex of wholesalers supplies perishables not only to the capital, but, indirectly, to all of France: decentralization has somehow not affected

---

[42] Paris has 120 churches, 80 theatres, 300 art galleries, 465 cinemas, 333 monuments regularly visited by tourists, 340 kiosks, 1000 restaurants, 8000 cafés, and 331,000 small artisan workshops (according to *Paris-Larousse*, 1983).

[43] Fauchon is the most renowned caterer in the world: the quality of the product, elegance of presentation, originality, imagination (over 4,500 specialties imported from 50 different countries, a daily choice of 150 dishes) and...astronomic prices are the characteristics of this enterprise, which supplies some 800 stores in France and over 100 clients worldwide. Fauchon was a victim of two terrorist attacks: an earlier explosion destroyed a large part of the building and an arson in the early 1980s claimed the life of the owner.

the field of food. Thus, if you buy or order fresh fish or shellfish on any French coast, be it in Brittany or in Provence, you may be sure that what you eat does not come straight from the sea, but has been channelled through the central distribution in Rungis.

Yes, in many respects Paris and its metropolitan area still remain the big center, the foyer, the privileged spot where everything originates and all things converge. A thorough visit of the city will confirm what you already know of its place in France of yesterday and of today. But the itinerary routinely recommended to tourists will not unveil some of the most intriguing aspects of the capital, which is called "Paris aux cent villages" and which could also be called "Paris aux cent visages". These hundred "faces" that usually elude the eyes of strangers are the faces of old villages such as Montmartre, Auteuil, Montparnasse, Contrescarpe, Mouffetard and Clignancourt (the latter is least unknown because of its well publicized "marché aux puces" or flea market), Ménilmontant and Charonne, where the old Père Lachaise cemetery is located[44]: each has its characteristics, its specialized trades and crafts, its own way of life. These hidden, secluded places, not to be found on plans or in tourist guides, can be discovered through much reading, some inquiring and above all, through exploration. Only innumerable walks along the streets of this multifaceted City, at the same time old and modern, lofty and down to earth, distant and intimate, luxurious and unpretentious, frivolous, yet deeply spiritual, will reveal the real Paris, incredibly complex and always fascinating, where one can truly enjoy both unparalleled excitement and the proverbial French "douceur de vivre."

---

[44] The Père-Lachaise is well worth an artistic and literary pilgrimage and a visit to the tombs of such celebrities as Abélard and Héloïse, Molière and La Fontaine, Musset, Chopin and Balzac.

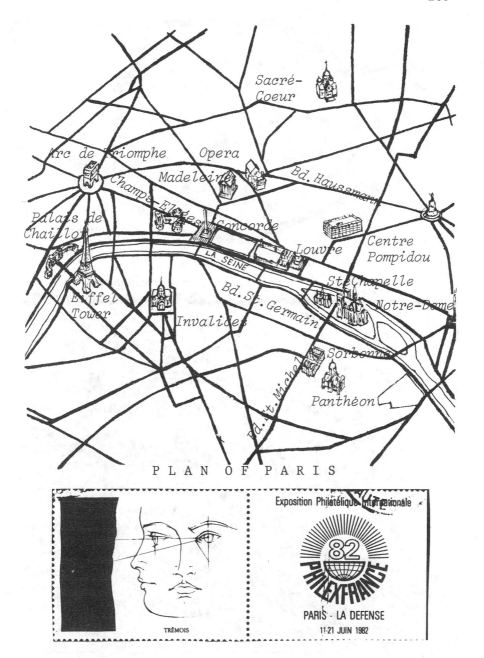

Sacré-Coeur

Arc de Triomphe   Opera

Madeleine

Champs-Elysées   Concorde   Bd. Haussmann

Palais de Chaillot

Louvre   Centre Pompidou

LA SEINE

Ste Chapelle

Eiffel Tower   Bd. St. Germain   Notre-Dame

Invalides

Bd. St. Michel

Sorbonne

Panthéon

P L A N   O F   P A R I S

TRÉMOIS

Exposition Philatélique Internationale

82 PHILEXFRANCE

PARIS - LA DEFENSE

11-21 JUIN 1982

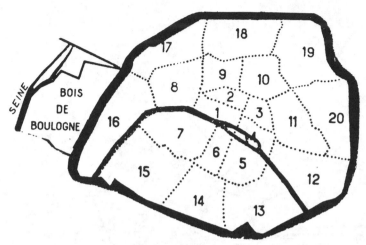

The 20 "arrondissements"

THINGS TO REMEMBER

PART ONE
GEOGRAPHY AND DEMOGRAPHY

Administrative divisions: (95) départements, grouped into (22) "régions"

The land; the "hexagon"

Seas: the Mer du Nord or North Sea, La Manche or English Channel, the Atlantic Ocean, La Méditerranée (or Mediterranean Sea)

Seaports: Le Havre, Marseille, Bordeaux, St. Nazaire (shipyards), Brest, Toulon

Mountains:
The Pyrénées
The Alpes (Alps) (highest peak in Europe: Mont-Blanc)
The Jura
The Vosges, the Ardennes
The Massif Central
(The Massif Armoricain)

Rivers:
The Seine (estuary at Le Havre)
The Loire
The Garonne (mouth: La Gironde)
The Rhône (delta)
The Rhine (Le Rhin)

Cities:
Paris, Bordeaux, Le Havre, Lille, Lyon, Marseille, Nantes, Nice, St. Etienne, Strasbourg, Toulon, Toulouse

Most important former provinces:
Brittany * (Bretagne), Normandy* (Normandie), Ile-de-France*, Champagne*, Burgundy* (Bourgogne), Alsace*, Lorraine*, Provence*, Languedoc*, Guyenne, Gascogne, Touraine*, (Anjou, Vendée, Poitou)

PART TWO

I. THE BEGINNINGS

Prehistory
Terra Amata settlement (Nice)
The Dorgogne
Grottos, Les Eyzies, Lascaux
Brittany: menhirs, dolmens (Carnac)
The Celts: Celtic tribes, lifestyle, art (Treasure of Vix)
Greek colonization: Marseille (Massilia, 600 B.C.), Nice,
Arles, Antibes
Roman "Provincia" (120 B.C.)
Caesar's conquest of Gaul: Vercingétorix surrenders
at Alésia 52 B.C.
The Roman Colonization and Heritage:
"Pax romana", legal system, urbanization
roads, aqueducts (Pont du Gard)
language
Roman vestiges: Arles, Nîmes, Orange, St. Rémy,
Vaison-la-Romaine
Eze (La Turbie)
Religion: Christianity: martyrs (Ste. Blandine, St. De-
nis)
Emperor Constantine ends persecution (312 A.D.)
The Barbarian invasions and the birth of France
Barbarians invade the West of Europe (5th Century
A.D.)
Germanic tribes:
Vandals (destroy Autun—Augustudunum—in 3rd c.
A.D.)
Goths, Visigoths, Ostrogoths
Franks
Burgundians
Alamans (Lombards)
Invasion of the Huns under Attila, repelled (451 A.D.)

by Mérovée (role of Ste. Geneviève)

The Merovingian Dynasty

Clovis, chief of Franks, baptized and crowned king
in Reims (496 A.D.)
wife: Ste. Clotilde
Other Merovingians (slow decadence, Moorish invasion,
victory of Charles Martel at Poitiers, 732 A.D.)

The Carolingians

Charlemagne (son of Pepin)
crowned emperor in Rome in 800 A.D.
capital in Aix-la-Chapelle (Aachen)
wars with "infidels" (*The Song of Roland*)
administration, arts, the Carolingian Renaissance
Division of Charlemagne's empire among his grandsons
Charles, Louis and Lothaire (Lotharingia—Lorraine)
"The Strasburg Oaths"—1st document in Old French
(842 A.D.)

II. THE MIDDLE AGES: FRANCE FROM THE Xth TO THE XIIIth CENTURY

The Norman Invasions. The Capetian Dynasty
Rollo marries Gisèle and settles in Normandy (beg.
10th c.)
Decline of the Carolingians—the Capetian dynasty
Hugues Capet crowned in 987 A.D.
William the Conqueror's conquest of England
Battle of Hastings 1066
The Bayeux Tapestry
Consequences of William's conquest:
Louis VII and Aliénor of Aquitaine (2 daughters)
Henry II Plantagenet and Aliénor. Sons:
Richard-the-Lionhearted
John Lackland

Wars with Louis VII's son Philippe-Auguste

North and South
"Langue d'oil" and "langue d'oc"
Albigensian crusade (beg. 13th c.)

Society in the Middle Ages
The feudal system:
The Nobility or warring class:
lord (suzerain)
vassal (liege)
homage
knighthood (dubbing, accolade)
chivalry
lifestyle
the medieval "château-fort"
The Commons or working class:
the peasants—the seignorial system
serfs—villains
"corvées" (free labor), taxes, bans
the burghers (bourgeois), cities—Paris
The Clergy: secular and regular
Cluny—Benedictine monks—revival, way of life,
influence
Cistercians: St. Bernard—monastic reform
Dominicans and Franciscans

The Crusades
Attempt to liberate the Holy Sepulchre from Turks
preached by Pope Urban II at Clermont-Ferrand
1st (1095)—Conquest of Jerusalem: Christian Kingdom
of Jerusalem
2nd—preached by St. Bernard at Vézelay: Louis VII,
Aliénor
3rd—Philippe-Auguste, Richard-the-Lionhearted
4th—Sack of Constantinople

7th—St. Louis (+ 1270)
The Templars, the Hospitalers (Knights of Malta)
Consequences of the Crusades

12th and 13th Century Capetians
Louis VII's son: Philippe-Auguste (1180-1223)
Wars and territorial acquisitions from: the Count of Flanders
  the Plantagenets
  the "South" (part of Languedoc)
Louis VII's grandson: Louis IX or St. Louis
  great king, great administrator, warrior,
  holy life, dies during the 7th Crusade

III. THE MIDDLE AGES: ARCHITECTURE, ARTS, AND LETTERS

The Romanesque–half-cylindrical vault (voûte en plein-cintre)
Church Plan: Nave (nef)
  Aisles
  Transept
  Choir
  Chevet, apse (apsidial chapels) (ambulatory)
  Porches
  Towers
  Buttresses (counterforts)
  Portal, tympanun, lintels
  Pillars, capitals
Romanesque sculpture (ex. Chartres); Romanesque painting
  (ex. St. Savin)
Churches: Vézelay, Poitiers, Cluny, Moissac, Autun
  Arles, Toulouse (St. Sernin)

The Gothic (three styles of Gothic)
pointed arch (ogive)
flying buttresses
stained glass windows (roses)
Gothic sculpture (ex. Reims, Amiens)
Churches: Paris: Notre-Dame, Ste. Chapelle; Amiens (the
"Beau Dieu" and "Vierge dorée"); Chartres; Beauvais;
(Bayeux); Reims (the "Smiling Angel"); (Sens, Senlis);
Rouen; Laon; (Le Mans)

Education
The universities
University of Paris on Ile de la Cité
Abélard. Latin Quarter (left bank). Royal charter (1200 A.D.)
and papal charters
Sorbonne: 1257 A.D.; student life
4 "facultés" or "colleges": Arts, Law, Medicine, Theology
7 Liberal Arts: trivium: grammar, rhethoric, logic
quadrivium: arithmetic, geometry, astronomy, music

Literature
Hagiography: lives of saints
"Chansons de geste" (songs of deeds): *Chanson de Roland*
Breton cycle (Celtic tradition): Marie de France ("lais")
Tristan & Yseult
Arthurian romances and courtly romances.
Chrétien de Troyes (*Yvain, Lancelot, Perceval*)
Drama: liturgical drama, mystery plays, miracle plays,
farces

IV. THE LAST TWO CENTURIES OF THE MIDDLE AGES

France in the 14th and 15th centuries:
Philip-the-Fair (Philippe-le-Bel), governs with "légistes"
    shrewd and cruel
Convocation of the Estates General
Papal See in Avignon
The Extermination of the Templars
The "Hundred-Years' War":
    Causes of the war—no direct Capetian heir to throne
    The Valois-Capetians. Disastrous defeats (Crécy, fall of
        Calais, Poitiers, Azincourt)
    French throne offered to English King
    Joan of Arc—finds Charles at Chinon; Charles VII (the
        Dauphin) crowned king in Reims
    Joan's victory at Orléans
    captured at Compiègne; burned at the stake in Rouen in
        1431
    The role of Burgundy; Charles VII (mistress Agnès Sorel)
        and Jacques Coeur
Louis XI—victory over Charles-the-Rash:
    return of Burgundy to France

Life, arts and letters in the 14th and 15th centuries:
Literature: poetry: Villon (Charles d'Orléans)
    theatre: *La Farce de Maître Pathelin*
Music: polyphony
Architecture: "Gothique flamboyant"
Painting: Fouquet. Miniature painting "Les très riches
    heures du Duc de Berry."
Tapestries: Angers, The Unicorn tapestries

V. THE SIXTEENTH CENTURY

The Renaissance
Reasons: Fall of Constantinople
Discovery of pagan antiquity
Copernicus, heliocentric theory
Invention of printing press
Charles VIII invades north of Italy
Discoveries of new lands

The Italian Wars:
Charles VIII and Louis XII both married to Anne de Bretagne
French kings' claim to Kingdom of Naples
François I (1515) great Renaissance king—wars with Hapsburg Charles V, defeat of the French, peace signed under reign of son of François I, Henri II: Calais returns to France (1558)
Consequences: Italian Renaissance penetrates France: architecture, palaces and gardens, churches, sculpture, nude statues, furniture, decorative arts. Italian artists: Del Sarto, Cellini, Leonardo da Vinci ("Mona Lisa")

Three Great Kings:
François I—love of art, "joie de vivre", festivities and hunting, interest in letters: founds Collège de France; great builder (Chambord, Fontainebleau)
Henri II—married to Catherine de Médicis (mistress Diane de Poitiers)
Henri IV—best of French kings

Reformation and Wars of Religion
Influence of Catherine de Médicis. The Guises and the Huguenots
The massacre of St. Bartholomew (1572). Assassination of Henri de Guise and of Henri III.
Henri IV converts to Catholicism in order to get the crown

(Bourbon-Capetian)
Signs Edict of Nantes (1598), brings prosperity to France

Humanism and Letters
"Rebirth": Characteristics:
1) Respect for classical antiquity
2) Respect for man
3) quest for learning (encyclopedic knowledge)
4) delight in life, enthusiasm, curiosity, science
5) cult of beauty
6) adventurousness
7) presumptuousness, optimism
8) quest for exploration, invention
9) quest for freedom from all constraints

Education: study of Greek and Hebrew texts ("Collège de France")
Philosophies: Neoplatonism, stoicism, epicurism, skepticism
Writers: Rabelais*, La Pléiade (Ronsard), Montaigne*

Architecture and Arts
Châteaux: Amboise
Blois,* Chambord,* Fontainebleau*
Azay-le-Rideau, Chenonceaux,* Chaumont
(Anet)
Architects: Philibert Delorme (Chenonceaux gallery, Tuileries, Anet)
Lescot: Louvre
Sculpture: Jean Goujon, Germain Pilon (kings' tombs at St. Denis)
Painting: Italian masters at Fontainebleau (Il Primaticcio, Rosso)
Portraits: Clouet

VI. THE SEVENTEENTH CENTURY

Reign of Louis XIII (son of Henri IV, murdered in 1610),
married to Spanish princess Anne of Austria
Regency of his mother Marie de Médicis during his minority
Richelieu comes to power (1624) and paves the way for abso-
lute monarchy
Deploys strategy against: Austria (Spain)
the Huguenots
the powerful nobility (forbids duelling)
Shows interest in arts and letters (French Academy, 1635)
Regency of Queen Anne of Austria, after Louis XIII's death
(1643)
Mazarin: minister after Richelieu's death (1642)
Revolt and civil war called the Fronde

Reign of Louis XIV (1638-1715), married to Spanish princess
Marie-Thérèse of Austria
Personal rule starts in 1661 (the trial of superintendent Fouc-
quet)
Bourgeois ministers (Colbert)
Wars with neighboring states
Administration, commerce, colonial expansion
Court life and etiquette
The court at Versailles
Religious intolerance
Jansenists: (Port-Royal)
Protestants: Revocation of the Edict of Nantes in 1685

Literature, Architecture and Arts
Currents: Baroque, "préciosité", ("burlesque"), Classicism
(the tenets of Classicism), Academicism.
Literature: Corneille,* Racine,* Molière,* La Rochefoucauld,*
La Bruyère, La Fontaine,* Descartes,* Pascal,* Mme
de la Fayette, Mme de Sévigné*
Architecture: Mansart, Le Vau*, Hardouin-Mansart*

Landscaper: Le Nôtre*
Buildings: Vaux-le-Vicomte. In Paris: the Luxembourg,
    the Louvre, the Invalides, Place Vendôme, Place des
    Vosges
Sculpture: Coysevox, Girardon
Painting: (Philippe de Champaigne), Poussin,* Le Lorrain,
    Georges de La Tour,* Le Nain, Le Brun*
    Portraits: Mignard, Largillière, (Rigaud)
Music: Lully, (Charpentier), Couperin-le-Grand

VII. THE EIGHTEENTH CENTURY

The Regency and the Reign of Louis XV (1715-1774)
Louis XV 5 years old at death of his great grandfather Louis
    XIV in 1715: regency of his great-uncle Philippe
    d'Orléans
Louis married at 15 to Polish princess Marie Leszczynska
Not interested in governing. Wars with Austria and Prussia
Loss of Canada and India
Gain of Lorraine ("kingdom" of Marie's father Stanislas)
Purchase of Corsica
Role of Mme de Pompadour
Economic recovery, commerce, enrichment of the bourgeoisie
Gracious life, intimate interiors; furniture "Rococo" style; gas-
    tronomy, new foods

Louis XVI
Grandson of Louis XV, good natured and full of good will,
    but weak
Married to Austrian princess Marie-Antoinette whose ways
    alienate the French people
Problems with internal and foreign policy; help to the Ameri-
    can War of Independence
New style and taste: Roman antiquity

Arts in the 18th century
Painting: Watteau*
  Boucher,* Fragonard,* Chardin* (Greuze). Neoclassicism:
    David
  Portraits: Quentin de La Tour,* Mme Vigée-Lebrun*
Sculpture: Houdon
Architecture: Gabriel
Music: Rameau, (Gluck)
Literature: the Enlightenment
  Fiction: abbé Prévost
  Theatre: Marivaux (poetry: Chénier)
  The *philosophes*: Montesquieu (*The Spirit of Laws*)
    Voltaire (*Candide*)
    Diderot (*Encyclopédie*)
    Rousseau: powerful influence in many domains (the two
      Discours, Emile, Le Contrat social)
    Beaumarchais: *The Barber of Séville*
      The Marriage of Figaro

The Revolution & the "Directoire"
Convocation of Estates General (1200 deputies of the 3 "or-
  ders")
1789 (May): The Third Estate becomes the National Assem-
    bly then the "Assemblée Constituante" with the mis-
    sion of voting a new constitution
  July 14 (Bastille Day): revolution starts in the provinces,
    exodus of the aristocracy; the King "cooperates"
  August: suppression of privileges of the clergy and the
    nobility
  "Declaration of the rights of man and the citizen"
    The Declaration dismantles the ancien régime and its
    system of hierarchy and privileges; citizens are free
    and equal: "liberté, égalité, fraternité;" law is the ex-
    pression of a "general will". Private property assured
    by law

October: The people of Paris rush to Versailles and force the royal family to take residence at the Tuileries

1790: New Constitution divides the former 35 provinces into 83 departments, declares freedom of religion. France becomes a constitutional monarchy with the

1) executive power in the hands of a hereditary king, "delegated" by the nation

2) legislative power in the hands of the Assemblée Législative (born of the Assemblée Constituante)

3) judiciary power in the hands of elected judges (free justice)

1791 (June): Louis XVI and family try to flee abroad; they are recognized in Varennes and brought back to Paris

1792: war with Austria; after first French defeat, King and family imprisoned at the Temple (August). Declaration of "Fatherland in danger." After the victory of French troops at Valmy the Assemblée Législative becomes the "Convention." Abolition of monarchy and proclamation of the 1st Republic. The Convention becomes a tribunal

1793: King judged (role of St. Just) and guillotined in January on Place de la Concorde. Rouget de Lisle composes the *Marseillaise*. Reign of Terror and of the Montagnards: Danton, Marat and Robespierre (the "Incorruptible"). Execution of the Girondins (Mme Roland) and of Marie-Antoinette

1794: Execution of Danton and of Desmoulins (Spring) "Thermidor" (July): Execution of Robespierre (and of St. Just)

1795-99: The Directoire—period of transition

Achievements of the Convention: 1795 treatise (France gets West bank of the Rhine and Belgium); abolition of slavery; creation of the Louvre museum and of the "grandes écoles": (Polytechnique, St. Cyr, Ecole Normale, Conservatoire,

etc.); unification of measure and weight systems
("metric system")

VIII. THE NINETEENTH CENTURY

Napoleon Bonaparte (1769-1821)

Born in Corsica—father lawyer: 8 children

Victories over the English (1793) and Austria (1796 Arcole, Rivoli in Italy). Victory over England in Egypt, but his fleet destroyed by Nelson. 1799—overthrows the powerless "Directoire", establishes the Consulate and becomes First Consul. Puts order in the administration, encourages agriculture and industry, maintains and consolidates the achievements of the Revolution in the fields of social relations, economic institutions and government.

Institutes secondary schools (lycées)—free education (French elite)

Banque de France (the "franc"), "préfets" in "départements", Legion of honor

"Code Civil," Conseils d'Etat, courts of appeal, Supreme Court

Amnesty for royalists and priests who had refused the "oath of allegiance"

Treatise with Pope. Sells Louisiana to the U.S.

1802 - Bonaparte becomes Consul for life; wife Joséphine, château de Malmaison

1804 - Napoleon crowned emperor at Notre-Dame by the Pope Court life

10 years of wars of the "Grande armée": many great victories (Iéna, Austerlitz, Wagram); defeat at Trafalgar (fleet destroyed by Nelson)

Brothers: Louis - king of Holland

Jerome - king of Westphalia

Joseph - king of Spain (disastrous guerrilla war)

1810- divorces Joséphine and marries Austrian Princess Marie-Louise. Son "Roi de Rome"

1812 - disastrous Russian campaign

1814 - enemies (Prussia and Austria) invade France and enter Paris, Napoleon is exiled to the Island of Elba

Restoration of the Capetians:

Louis XVIII, brother of Louis XVI returns from exile

1815 - The Hundred Days: Napoleon comes back, is defeated at Waterloo and exiled to St. Helena, where he dies

Louis XVIII, liberal king, followed in 1824 by younger brother Charles X, conservative king

1830 - Revolution; Charles X flees, Louis-Philippe (d'Orléans) becomes king: "July Monarchy"

The July Monarchy, The Second Republic and Second Empire

Louis Philippe (1830-1848), "bourgeois king"

Motto of his government "get rich"

Economic growth; railroads

Opposition from republicans, Bonapartists and "legitimists"

Overthrown by 1848 revolution, proclamation of Second Republic

Louis-Napoleon Bonaparte (nephew of Napoleon I, son of king of Holland) elected president. After coup d'état of December 1851 becomes Napoleon III

The Second Empire

Napoleon III married to Eugénie de Montijo

Brilliant court, additions to Louvre

Revamping of Paris (Haussmann)

Dictatorship at home. Disastrous foreign policy (Maximilian in Mexico)

War with Germany (1870); defeat at Sedan

Napoleon III overthrown

The Third Republic to 1914

1871: Surrender of Paris to Germans. Treaty signed in Versailles

Loss of Alsace and Lorraine and payment of huge indemnity

National Assembly in Versailles headed by Thiers, dominated by monarchists

Revolt of the Commune in Paris and bloody repression

Constitution of 1875: president elected for 7 years, 2 legislative assemblies, endowed with more power than the executive; ministerial instability

After resignation of MacMahon, victory of anticlerical republicans

The Dreyfus affair splits the country into two opposing factions (Zola)

Nationalists vs. socialists and communists

Separation of Church and State

Public lay education

The working class, the CGT, "social Catholicism"

World exhibitions: "Expo 1889" (Eiffel Tower), & 1900

New inventions and technology. The "belle époque "

Colonial expansion: Tunisia, Indochina, Congo, French West and East Africa

Letters, arts and sciences

Literature: Romanticism: Chateaubriand,* Lamartine, Musset, Vigny

Victor Hugo* (fiction: Dumas)

Romantic realists: Stendhal, Balzac,* Mérimée* (*Carmen*)

Realism: Flaubert*

"L'Art pour l'art"

Symbolism: Baudelaire* Verlaine,* Rimbaud, Mallarmé, Maeterlinck

Painting: Neoclassicism: David,* Ingres*

Romanticism: Géricault,* Delacroix*

Realism: Daumier,* Courbet*

Landscape painting: Corot, The Barbizon School: Théo-
dore Rousseau, Millet
Impressionism: Manet,* Monet,* Renoir,* Degas,* Pis-
sarro, Sisley, Berthe Morisot, Cézanne,* Toulouse-
Lautrec*
Symbolism: (Moreau, Redon, Puvis de Chavannes)
Post-impressionism: Van Gogh,* Gauguin*
Pointillism: Seurat (Signac)
Sculpture: Rude, (Arc de Triomphe), Carpeaux, Rodin*
Music: Romanticist Berlioz*
Bizet,* Gounod,* Massenet (operas), Offenbach* (light
opera), César Franck, Gabriel Fauré, Saint-Saëns*
Symbolist Debussy*
Science: Pasteur, Marie Sklodowska-Curie

IX. THE TWENTIETH CENTURY

World War I

Two coalitions: Prussia, Austria, Italy
France, Russia, England
Incident in Sarajevo
Invasion of Belgium and France by the Germans. March on
Paris
French counterattack, the "Miracle of the Marne"
Trench war, Verdun (1916)
American intervention, Russian revolution
Victory of Allies under Marshal Foch
Armistice; November 11, 1918: Treaty of Versailles (peace
terms)

The "entre-deux guerres" and World War II

France in shambles. 1,500,000 men million killed and wounded
Germany remains strong. American isolationism
Political crises in France; 1936: "Front populaire"

Two ideologies: fascism and communism (Spanish civil war, 1936)

Hitler comes to power 1933—leaves League of Nations

1938 - Annexation of Austria

Invasion of Czechoslovakia (Munich agreements)

1939 - Pact between Germany and Russia

Invasion of Poland (September)

Declaration of war by France and England

1940 - Germans invade Holland, Belgium and France, by-pass Maginot line (Dunkirk)

Vichy government ("unoccupied zone"); Pétain, Laval

De Gaulle's appeal

1941 - Germany attacks Russia;

December: Pearl Harbor, America joins war

1941-1943 German occupation in France: collaborationists and "résistants"

The Gestapo; extermination of Jews

Fighting in North Africa

1944 - June D-Day: landing in Normandy

August: Generals de Gaulle and Leclerc enter Paris

1945 - Yalta agreements, division of Europe

The Fourth Republic:

Gen. de Gaulle takes over briefly, but withdraws because of weakness of executive

1945 - vote given to women, NATO

Common Market

Loss of colonies (Defeat in Indochina)

The Fifth Republic: De Gaulle

1958 - De Gaulle returns to power. New Constitution (strong executive).

Settles Algerian crisis. France leaves NATO

1968 - student rioting brings about crisis

1969 - De Gaulle steps down

After De Gaulle:

Gaullist Pompidou becomes president. Continues De Gaulle's
policies. Dies sudenly in 1974

Giscard d'Estaing (Independent Republican) elected president
against leftist coalition of socialists (Mitterrand) and
communists (Marchais)

1981 - Elections won by Mitterrand—Leftist coalition (New
opposition main figures: Chirac, Barre, and Giscard)

1986 - Parliamentary elections won by the rightist opposition.
"Cohabitation": Socialist President Mitterrand and Gaullist Prime Minister Chirac

1988 - Mitterrand reelected president
Nominates Socialist Rocard as prime minister
Dissolves National Assembly

Arts and letters

Currents: Fauvism, Cubism, Dadaism, Surrealism, Expressionism, Abstract Painting

Painting: The Nabis: Bonnard* (Vuillard)
Fauvists: Dufy, Rouault,* Matisse* (Derain, Vlaminck)
Cubists: Picasso,* Braque,* Juan Gris, Léger
Dadaists: Joan Miró
Surrealists: Salvador Dali,* Tanguy, Chagall*
Abstract Painting: (Mondrian, Delaunay)
Independents: Henri Rousseau,* Modigliani, Dubuffet

Sculpture: Bourdelle,* Maillol,* Giacometti*

Architecture: Le Corbusier*

Music: Ravel,* Milhaud, Poulenc,* Boulez*, (Messiaen)

Poetry: Apollinaire,* Claudel,* Ponge,* Saint-John Perse*

Fiction: Proust,* Gide, Giraudoux, Mauriac,* St. Exupéry,*
Malraux,* Sartre*, Camus* Butor, Duras,* Robbe-
Grillet,* Claude Simon (Sarraute)

Theatre: Anouilh*
Beckett,* Ionesco*

"Nouvelle critique"

PART THREE

The French Institutions:
   The Executive: the President, the Premier, the Cabinet
   The Legislative: The Assemblée Nationale (National Assembly)
   The Sénat (Senate)
The political parties
   Leftist: Socialists (PS), Communists (PC)
   Rightist: Gaullists (RPR), Republicans (UDF) and Front National (FN)
Industry & commerce: Production and exportations. Transportation
   Importance of nuclear power
The work force: work week, vacations, labor unions, SMIC
The educational system: elementary education
   secondary education (2 cycles: collèges and lycées)
   higher education: UER & universities
      UVs and diplomas (3 cycles)
      "grandes écoles"
Paris:
   History (Lutetia, "rive gauche", "rive droite")
   General plan of the city and most important monuments

* of particular importance

APPENDIX

The Dordogne-Périgord and Prehistory

Known interchangeably as "Dordogne"[1] or "Périgord" (its capital city is Périgueux), this south-west region has a mild climate and striking natural beauty. It is also, as seen in ch 1 of Part II, the best source of information about the Paleolithic homo sapiens. People come from the four corners of the world to visit the prehistoric caves, but they linger on in the area for the "confit" of goose, for "foie gras", for the wild "cèpes"-mushrooms and, generally speaking, for the superb gastronomy which, in this part of the country, has become a true art.

There are, in the region, some 1,200 grottos, 25 of which were decorated by the Cro-Magnon man who inhabited the Dordogne Valley for more than 40,000 years. He left not only paintings and carvings, but burial places[2] containing weapons, tools, jewelry and pottery. The most famous and probably also the most exciting prehistoric cave in France is Lascaux, which was discovered accidentally by hiking schoolboys in 1940. The underground atmosphere and darkness had preserved the paintings in pristine shape and colors: the paint looked as fresh as if it had just been applied. Over 200 yards of walls and arches were covered by frescoes and engravings of galloping horses, reindeers, cows, fighting bulls and other animals which inhabited the south-west of France some 15,000 years ago. An enigmatic scene portrays a wounded bison, losing his entrails and looking down on a pitiful human figure with a totem-head, flat on the ground, arms stretched out, having lost his grip on the totem he had been holding. Evidently, man was not always pictured as a victor in his struggle for survival. The absence of tools suggests that the cave was not used as a dwelling, but a place of worship and rituals.

To loess, ochre and charcoal used as a base, the prehistoric artist added egg whites, juices from plants and animal fat to obtain some twenty four colors ranging from yellow to red, and from blue to black. The paint was blown through hollow bones onto the wall, rather like modern spray painting. The artist also painted with fingers, sticks, pads of fur, reeds and pieces of moss. A lamp, equipped with moss to act as a wick, was found

---

[1] The region surrounding the fertile valleys of the Dordogne (a tributary of the Garonne) and of the Vézère rivers.

[2] The Cro-Magnon man was quite sophisticated, and capable of abstract thinking. It seems that he believed in afterlife; he buried his dead and spread flowers on their graves.

on the floor, showing how the work could have been done in the darkness of the grotto.

Lascaux was opened to marvelling visitors for about 20 years until deterioration of colors forced the closing of the cave in 1963. Only a handful of VIPs are allowed into that "sanctuary" nowadays, but throngs of tourists, who must during the peak season carefully plan to get entrance tickets in advance, can visit Lascaux II. Twentieth century artists have, with the same materials and techniques as those used by their prehistoric counterparts, created an exact replica of the original grotto.

While Lascaux richly deserves its name of "Sistine Chapel of the prehistoric era", Les Eyzies-de-Tayac, located in the Valley of the Vézère, has been called "the cradle of history" after the significant discovery, in the 2nd part of the 19th century, of a Cro-Magnon skeleton and of the remarkable grotto of Font-de-Gaume. Some 200 paintings (mammoths, deer, rhinoceros, a wolf, a bear and a man) are pictured on the undulating, uneven walls. The bodies of the animals were made to espouse the contours of the rock and are endowed with a lifelike reality. Other richly decorated caves in the vicinity of Les Eyzies are Cro-Magnon, Laugerie, La Mouthe, Combarelles, La Madeleine, Cougnac and Villars. At Rouffignac, drawings of mammoths stretch over a kilometer-long gallery, which visitors can view from a small electric train running alongside of the decorated walls.

For devotees of more recent history, the Dordogne offers vestiges of the Gallo-Roman civilization, medieval châteaux-forts and innumerable treasures of Romanesque, Gothic, and Renaissance art. And all over the region stores and open-air marchés tempt the traveller with famous delicacies produced and exported by the Périgord: top quality strawberries, dried and canned "cèpes"-mushrooms, the renowned "prunes d'Agen" and walnut oil (which has also become very fashionable in New York in the past decade). But there is a particular demand for the highly appreciated duck and goose liver and for the most expensive of all the gourmets' fantasies: truffles, the "black diamonds" which sell for as much as 2000 francs a kilo. They grow underground among the roots of trees and can be discovered only with the help of dogs and pigs especially trained for the job.

As is well known, the wines of the Dordogne which are part of the vast family of "vins de Bordeaux", are excellent and beautifully compliment the regional delicacies discussed above (e.g., the red Bergerac and white Monbazillac, particularly recommended to accompany the "foie gras").

The Gauls

The Gauls or Celts (Keltoi in Greek) were a vigorous people widely distributed throughout continental Europe and the British Isles. They were fearless warriors and great hunters. They also bred cattle, pigs and especially horses: their "cavalry" was often decisive in the winning of battles in which they also made use of chariots. They mined copper and iron and were skilled craftsmen, who left behind lovely artifacts and beautiful jewelry (see ch. 1, Part I).

The Gauls were tall, blond, blue-eyed and fair-complected. Men usually sported a mustache, and occasionally a beard. While women wore a tunic, the garb of the Gallic men was in sharp contrast with that of their Roman conquerors: it included long trousers or "breeches" and a sort of woolen cape called "saie" (Latin: "saga"). They also loved to adorn themselves with bracelets and collars of precious metal. The Gauls who settled on the territory which was later to become France—there were about 15 million of them—constituted an agricultural society, divided into a number of tribes. Some of the tribal names have survived until this day in the French toponymy.[3] In spite of their diversity, these tribes shared the same language, social structure, customs and religion. Family bonds were very close, the father being the supreme master and having the right of life and death over his wife and children. Women took an active part in the community and often went to war at their husbands' sides.

The tribes were ruled by a landed "noble" class called "equites" by the Romans, but the supreme power was wielded by priests, called "druids", who gathered for yearly meetings in the territory occupied by the Carnutes: these gave their name to Chartres, which seems to have been the most important Celtic shrine.[4] The druids imposed strict rules of secrecy concerning religious matters, which may be one of the reasons why the Gauls left no written testimony (tradition was transmitted orally by bards, who were held in high esteem). We must therefore rely almost entirely on Roman

---

[3] E.g., Andegavi - Anjou, Bituriges - Bourges, Namnetes - Nantes, Pictavi - Poitou, Turones - Tours.

[4] The Cathedral of Chartres was erected on a spot venerated since time immemorial as possessing a "sacred stone". The "Carnutes" were "guardians of the stone". This stone was allegedly incorporated into the floor of the church by medieval master builders (cf. Louis Charpentier's breathtaking account, *Les Mystères de la Cathédrale de Chartres*, Laffont, 1966). A modern revival of Celtic rituals is now once again taking place in the Cathedral. Permission for the performing of pagan ceremonies was granted by local church authorities and met with violent protests on the part of some Catholics, who complain of the "shameful misuse" of a Christian place of worship.

sources for information about the Gallic theocracy. Druids were knowledge-able in medicine and astronomy and were both judges and teachers—the only ones in the Europe of that time to stress ethics. Their basic teaching may be summarized in the following three commandments: honor the gods, be brave and do no evil. The Gauls believed in metempsychosis and the migration of souls after death into the "paradise of the setting sun" (which may explain the unusual number of menhirs and dolmens in the most ex-treme western part of the territory, the Bretagne). They had a number of deities,[5] representing mostly forces of nature and the elements. Thus, there was a divinity of the earth, of the night, and of the moon (she was later assimilated with Diana). The goddess Sequana gave her name to the Seine River; the god of hot springs Borvo or Borbo (present in the French word "bourbe" or mud) to a number of spas (such as La Bourboule), as well as to the House of Bourbon; Nîmes comes from the name of the god of the healing fountains Nemausus. Taran or Tarainis was the god of light, air, clouds and storms, and Teutates, which means "national" in Celtic, was the principal god, protector of travellers and patron of the arts and of commerce (he was "equated" with Mercury). The Gauls practiced a sort of animism and believed also in the existence of a number of "genies" in fountains, springs, trees, forests, etc.

Mistletoe was the object of particular worship and considered a panacea against all ills. The cutting of this sacred plant with a golden sickle by druids clad in white robes was vividly described by the Roman author Pliny the Elder. White bulls were sacrificed during the ceremony which took place at the time of the June solstice. Human sacrifice was also widespread (it was thought at one time that dolmens were used as sac-rificial tables), and the ritual was confirmed by the recent unearthing from peat bogs near Manchester in England of the body of a young Celt, who met with a violent death 2,200 years ago, presumably to honor the Celtic gods Tarainis, Teutates and Esus. A *New York Times* article of January 26, 1988, entitled "Bog Man Reveals Story of Brutal Ritual" describes in detail this fascinating discovery.

---

[5] They were, after Ceasar's conquest, only gradually incorporated into the Roman "Pantheon" and received then their "antropomorphic" representations.

The *Chanson de Roland*

Charlemagne has conquered all of Spain from the hands of the Saracens, except for the lands belonging to Marsile, who signs with the Emperor a peace agreement he does not intend to keep. As Charlemagne crosses the Pyrénées on his way back to France, Marsile surrepticiously attacks at the cap of Roncevaux, with a force of 100,000 men, Charlemagne's rear guard under the command of the Emperor's nephew Roland, assisted by Olivier, his friend and "companion" (which, in the Middle Ages meant more than a friend). Olivier, who is "sage" (wise), exhorts Roland, who is "preux", to call back the French troops by sounding his "olifant" (horn made of an elephant tusk). But Roland is too proud to follow this advice and does not summon help until it is too late to save the French: they are all killed. The sounding of Roland's horn is however, not a futile gesture: Charlemagne returns in time to punish the treacherous attackers and ensure a proper burial for the heroic French knights. The "Song of Roland" is composed of 291 assonanced decasyllabic "laisses" or stanzas of unequal length. The oldest manuscript dates back to the end of the 11th century.

83.

Oliver says: - Of Pagans I see throngs
And our force is far from being strong,
Companion Roland, pray, do sound your horn
Charles will hear: his army will return.
Roland retorts: - A fool I'd be; in shame
I would lose in fair France my renown and my fame!
With Durendal, you'll see, I will strike mighty strokes,
So that its precious blade will drip with Pagan blood.
Woe to foul Pagans! Surely, death will be their lot!
Not a one will be spared, I swear, so help me God!

171.

Now Roland feels that his eye-sight is gone,
Yet he succeeds in standing up alone;
The color also from his cheeks has gone,
He sees in front of him a huge grey stone.
He strikes ten strokes, knowing what is at stake,
The steel grates, but, alas, will neither chip nor break.
The Count invokes the Virgin's holy name.

- Good Durendal! what pity and what shame!
I die: thy lot can no more garantee;
How many battles did I win with thee!
So many fiefs, and those enormous lands
White-bearded Charles now holds in his hands!
May no man ever have a claim on thee
Who would in battle from another flee!
A worthy vassal had thee; and when he is gone
In blessed France there'll never be an equal one.

175.

Roland now feels few moments but remain,
Prone on the hill he turns his head t'ward Spain.
He beats his breast, contrite with grief and pain:
- Mea culpa! Have mercy, God, and pardon all
The sins I have committed, both the big and the small
From the day I was born, until this very day
When I'm struck down with death; have mercy, God, I pray.
To God, his Lord, he then extends his right-hand glove:
Angels to Roland's side now descend from above.

268.

Emperor Charles has returned from Spain
To his capital Aix, where he will now remain.
He goes to his palace; as he enters the hall
He is forthwith approached by the fair maiden Alde.
And she asks him: - Where is "Roland le Capitaine"?
To take me for his wife, as you know, he did swear.
Charles is overcome by grief he cannot bear.
He weeps; at his white beard he's seen to pull and tear.
- Sister, dear friend, alas, Roland is a dead man;
But I promise to make the best exchange I can:
Louis' my choice; no doubt, you clearly understand,
He is my son, the one who will get all my land.
But to this Alde responds: - What a strange thing to say!
God, his angels and saints will not have it this way!
For when Roland is dead, alive I cannot stay.
She pales; at Charles' feet she is then seen to fall

And dies forthwith. Oh God! Have mercy on her soul!
The French barons shed tears, as Alde is mourned by all.

(Translated by M. Wagner)

The Mont Saint-Michel

The Mt. St. Michel is at the same time a monument and a landmark, built with cold stone, but which played in French history the role of a flame, a torch and a symbol. The rock, on which the most famous European fortress of all was erected, was at one time an island, and the island was the residence of Archangel St. Michael, the saint who, unlike most other saints, was never a human being, but is pure spirit, the Conqueror of Satan and, in Paradise, according to the beliefs of medieval man, the most important Being after God. To medieval man, prayer was closely associated with action: "St. Michel" was both a saint and a soldier, a mystic and a realist.

According to legend, St. Michel appeared in a dream to Aubert, the bishop of Avranches, in 709 A.D., and ordered him to build a chapel in his honor atop Mont-Tombe, which was at the time a granite rock rising in the midst of an ancient forest, a short distance from the sea. Within the space of a year, the sea which had once submerged the forest, filled up the bay after a tremendous tidal wave and the rock became, except at low tide, an island cut off from the coast of Normandy.

The cult of St. Michel spread rapidly: at the time of his baptism, Rollon, 1st Duke of Normandy, endowed the Abbey equally with the other principal Norman monasteries; and it was taken over by Benedictine monks, whose ideal was both religious and military. In 1058 a spectacular Romanesque church was built on top of the island; according to Henry Adams, "this 11th century abbey was to architecture what the *Chanson de Roland* was to literature". In 1203, the Mont passed from the Anglo-Norman to the French crown, and in the same year Philippe-Auguste ordered the erection of a new Gothic monastery which was completed in the record time of twenty-five years. The result is a magnificent church perched on a summit one fourth of its size and clinging to the cliff. It has, for good reason, been called "La Merveille" (the Marvel) and considered by some the "eighth wonder of the world." A masterpiece of harmony and true expression of the French Gothic's architectural genius, the "Marvel" covers the Mont's northern flank with a tier of buildings, made to provide everything necessary for both monastic life and hospitality. Through the ages throngs, not thousands but millions, seeking St. Michel's blessing came to this renowned shrine, from the most powerful crowned heads to the humblest pilgrims, who had to be steered to the abbey by guides around numerous pockets of treacherous quicksand. The Mont, for centuries a foyer of relentless activity, comprised an Almonry, a huge store-room filled with provisions necessary to feed the large crowds, a Guest Room and a Knights Hall, where important personalities feasted, while the monks ate separately and frugally in their upper level Refectory. They also worked assiduously at the copying of manuscripts in the monastery's Library or Scriptorium, and meditated in the seclusion and serenity of the Cloister, adjacent to the church on the very top of the rock.

The Mont eventually took on the dual role of both a shrine and a standard-bearer of the French dynasty, and became a national fortress which never fell into the hands of the enemy, even under such violent attacks as those that were launched by the English during the Hundred Years' War. And this heroic resistance doubtlessly inspired Jeanne d'Arc's mission: according to the heroine's own account, one of the "voices" which prompted her to come to the rescue of France was that of "Messire St. Michel".

After years of glory came years of decline, and at one time, following the French Revolution, the Mont served (as did many other venerable buildings, such the Abbey of Fontevraud) as a state prison.

In 1965, a thousand years after the Benedictine monks settled at Mt. St. Michel, they were permitted to return, "temporarily", but had to depart after several months. Then two of them came back and were allowed to stay, on condition that they confine themselves to limited quarters and not interfere with tourism. And now, the walls which were built hundreds of years ago in order to glorify God resound again with the voices of brothers celebrating daily mass.

Today, the Mont St. Michel is very much alive once more. Such multitudes come to visit this incredible landmark from the four corners of the world—over 2 million yearly—that on holidays, and especially at times when the famous high tide rushes in to surround the Mont and cut it off from the coast of Normandy, it is impossible to circulate in the one and only "street" of the former fortress. Tourists must wait in line to buy souvenirs or be accommodated in one of the famous restaurants and auberges, such as "La Mère Poulard," renowned for its unparalleled omlet, but which will also serve customers fresh seafood from the bay and an "agneau des prés salés", this lamb with a unique flavor, which grazes on the salty grass of surrounding lands.

These grasslands are evidence of the new peril that looms over Mont
St. Michel: dikes that were built in order to reclaim the bay from the
sea and the causeway erected to link the Mont with the mainland have
contributed, among other factors, to the filling with silt of the shallows
surrounding the islet. If drastic steps are not taken immediately, the Mont
could within a few years become a "dry dock." An all-out campaign has
been launched in order to save Mont St. Michel through the costliest works
ever envisaged for the sake of a historic monument in France. The plans
call for the reestablishing of the environmental equilibrium disrupted by
man. They also include the eliminating of the jetty and replacing it by
either an underwater tunnel or an overpass. The grassland surrounding
the Mont will then disappear and the Wonder will become, once again, as
author Henri Queffélec put it, "a battered sea-going vessel."

The Templars

The religious military order called "Templiers", or Poor Knights of
Christ and of the Temple of Solomon, was established in 1118 at the time of
the Crusades during the early years of the Frankish Kingdom of Jerusalem
(in 1118) by Hugues de Pains (or Payens) and eight other knights who had
followed Godefroi de Bouillon to the Holy Land. They vowed to insure the
security of pilgrims travelling to the Holy Sepulchre and to defend the Christian religion. King Baudouin II put at their disposal quarters adjoining the
former Jewish Temple, which is at the origin of the Order's name. Hugues
de Pains travelled all over Western Europe and brought back from France,
England, Italy and Spain immense donations and important numbers of
proselytes. The knights, who wore over their armor a white cloak with a
large red Latin cross, enjoyed from the very outstart a tremendous prestige,
due in part to the endorsement of St. Bernard de Clairvaux who drew up
their rule. Outside of their military duties, the knights had such obligations
as attending mass three times a week, observing abstinence three times a
week (Friday, Monday and Wednesday) and solemnly adoring the Cross at
three different times of the year. The Order on its part distributed alms
three times a week, since its members themselves possessed no money: they
were held to vows of poverty, chastity and obedience. St. Bernard had high
praise for the simplicity, faith and unmatched bravery of these "sunburnt
soldiers of Christ" who unflinchingly sought "complete victory or a saintly
and glorious death". The Order heroically defended the Holy Land until the
very last, and when it definitively fell into Moslem hands, they withdrew

to the island of Cyprus.

Gradually, the Templars diversified their activities and became a superbly organized army in itself. They enjoyed the highest prestige and were showered with privileges: the Grand Master was equal to monarchs and responsible directly to the Holy See; members of the Order could be judged only by the pope. At the beginning of the 14th century the Templars possessed immense riches—they even functioned as bankers to kings and princes—and were masters of some 9000 landed properties in the Christian world. They had fortified headquarters in Paris, known as "Le Temple", which occupied about one third of the city's area. Their power, wealth, haughtiness, the absolute secrecy with which they surrounded themselves, as well as their rivalry with other orders, notably the Hospitalers, created a climate of jealousy, hostility and suspicion. These feelings were kindled by the calculating and unscrupulous Philippe-le-Bel, who spared no effort and no trickery to achieve his goal of appropriating the Templars' riches and settling with them some old accounts. He had been humiliated by the Order's refusal to admit him as a member and to advance him further loans. By 1307, the King was truly desperate for money. For fear of a revolt, he had to give up the idea of levying more taxes and he no longer could victimize the Jews, whom he had expulsed from France after having confiscated all their possessions.

Well assured of the backing and collaboration of the puppet pope Clément V he had installed at Avignon, Philippe struck like lightning by having all the knights surreptitiously arrested throughout France on the same day (October 5, 1307). A lengthy, ignominious trial followed: two years later 56 knights were burned at the stake, while refusing to admit to any guilt. The Templars had been accused of all kinds of horrible crimes, among which connivance with the infidels, heresy, blasphemy and idolatry: they were supposed to adore an idol designated as "Baphomet", the identity of which was veiled in the deepest mystery. With the help of the Pope, Philippe eventually succeeded in having the Order abolished and the Grand Master, Jacques de Molay, who had rotted in prison for 7 years, sentenced to death. Before his martyrdom at the stake, the Commander recanted the statements he had made earlier under torture, and which were, as he was duplicitously told, to help other knights recover their freedom. He then summoned the Pope and the King to appear before the tribunal of God within a year: both, in effect died suddenly and without apparent cause in a matter of several months.[6]

---

[6] In spite of Clément V's efforts—it seems to historians that he attempted to "wash

The members of the abolished order who had not been persecuted dispersed and went into hiding, but a persistent legend maintains that they were absorbed by other secret societies, notably by the Freemasons. The search for the secrets and the lost or buried treasures of both the Templars and the Cathars (whom some researchers have attempted to link with the Templars) continues to this day.[7]

A new hypothesis has recently been advanced in connection with the investigation of the Turin shroud. The facts that have been established so far are that 1) the shroud was originally folded, so that only the face of the as yet unidentified victim of crucifixion (but believed to be Jesus Christ) was visible, and not unlike a portrait; 2) that before it came into the possession of the House of Savoy, its authenticated history dates back to the 14th century, when it was made public by the family of a French knight, Geoffroy de Charney. Charney was a next of kin of the Templars' Grand Master, Jacques de Molay. Thence the conjecture: the image of Christ on the shroud, brought back by the Templars from the East and of which the identity was so jealously guarded, could be this mysterious "Baphomet", adored by the Templars, who, even under torture, refused to divulge the holy secret.

François Villon

Villon was a thief, a drunkard, a pimp and a murderer, and we owe most of the information we have about his life to his criminal record. But he is also one of the greatest French poets.

He was born in 1431, the year of Jeanne d'Arc's martyrdom, and lived through the last dark phase of the Hundred Years' War. He earned a Bachelor's and then a Master's degree from the University of Paris, but preferred to the company of scholars that of prostitutes, burglars and members of the dreaded Paris underworld, called "La Coquille." He was imprisoned on various occasions was sentenced to the gallows more than once, and then was each time pardoned (in 1461, in Meung-sur-Loire, he was saved by an amnesty granted to all prisoners by the new king, Louis XI, during his first visit to that town). After 1463, year in which he was again

---

his sins in floods of blood"—the Templars in Spain and Portugal were acquitted. Their possessions, however, were distrubuted by the pope to kings and other religious orders.

[7]It has fired the imaginations, among others, of the authors of the best seller *Holy Blood, Holy Grail* (Michael Baigent et al., Delacote Press, NY, 1982), who have managed—though they arrive at farfetched, and fantastic conclusions—to discuss some aspects of the question in an interesting manner, especially in the first part of the book.

*involved in a serious crime—the death sentence was eventualy commuted
to banishment—Villon disappeared without a trace, while leaving behind
a slim, but very significant œuvre. It consists mostly of "ballades", which
are "poèmes à forme fixe." In them, we find both realism—they are not
devoid of either humour or sarcasm and are full of crude expressions and
descriptions—and lyricism: the poet reflects on the evanescent quality of
things, the inevitability of death and ponders the ephemeral existence of
man, whose body, glorified, admired and pampered in life, disappears like
melting "snows" and turns to "ashes and dust."*

*Villon's preoccupation with the theme of "vanitas vanitatum", which
was taken up in the 17th century by Bossuet in his striking* Oraisons
funèbres, *is particularly evident in three consecutive poems of his* Testament: *the "Ballad of the Ladies of By-Gone Times", the "Ballad of the
Lords of By-Gone Times" and "Another Ballad": their refrains "Mais où
sont les neiges d'antan?", "Mais où est le preux Charlemagne?" and "Au-
tant en emporte le vent" are famous and frequently quoted. The last one
became the French title of both the novel and the film* Gone with the Wind.

Ballad of the Ladies of By-Gone Times

("Ballade des dames du temps jadis")

Tell me where, in what land can be
Flora, the beauty from Rome?
And Archipiades, and Thaïs
Her cousin and kin from home?
And where is Echo, whose choice
Was to carry o'er waters one's voice,
And whose beauty was more than sublime?
But, where are the snows of by-gone times?

Where is wise Heloïse, for whom
Pierre Abélard was gelded and doomed
To withdraw as a monk to Saint-Denis?
For her love all his suffering has been.
And where is also the Queen
Who ordered Buridan to be sewn
In a sack in the Seine to be thrown?
But, where are the snows of years gone?

Queen Blanche with lily-white skin,
Whose song was to a mermaid's akin,
Big-footed Berthe, Beatrice, Alis,

And Harembourgis who held Maine,
And Jehanne, the good maid from Lorraine,
In Rouen burnt by the English for shame?
Where are they? Where? Virgin Sovereign!
But, snows of by-gone years don't remain.

Prince, do not ask in a week
Or a year where they are, do not seek
A reply, and ponder these lines:
But, where are the snows of by-gone times?

(*Translated by M. Wagner*)

Perhaps even more famous is, however, Villon's "Epitaphe" known also as "Ballade des pendus" (Ballad of the Hanged), which he undoubtedly wrote while awaiting his own execution. It is a stirring poem, unique in its realistic representation of death, the poignant note of despair, and the moving appeal for forgiveness, pity and understanding, as exemplified in the ballad's first stanza:

Brother men who live on, when we're already gone,
Do not show toward us that you have hearts of stone,
For, if your pity for us wretches you show,
The Almighty his mercy upon you will bestow.
You see how - five or six - to the gallows we're tied,
Our flesh which in life to feed too well we tried
Is already devoured and rotting, as it must,
And we, the bones, we turn to ashes and to dust.
No man today our lot should mock or laugh away,
But for God's absolution of all of us must pray.

(*Translated by M. Wagner*)

Rabelais

The Abbey of Thélème

For Brother Jean, Gargantua erects the Abbey of Thélème (which in Greek means "free will") on the beautiful banks of the River Loire. The structure is a magnificent Renaissance château, six stories high, built in the shape

of a hexagon, with a great round tower at each of the six corners. It
is more sumptuous than Bonnivet, Chambord or Chantilly, has alabaster
fountains, baths, a hippodrome and lists, but no outer wall, no clock and
no church: each of the 9332 rooms is, however, equipped with a private
chapel. Entrance to the Abbey is forbidden to undesirable people such as
bigots, hypocrites, men of law and usurers.

How the Thélémites were governed and what was their manner of living.

Their entire life was spent not according to laws, rules or statutes, but
according to their free will and judgment. They got up from bed as they
pleased: they drank, ate, worked, slept when they felt like it. Nobody woke
them up, no one forced them either to drink or to eat or to do any other
thing. This is the way Gargantua had set it up. And the Order's rule
consisted in one single clause: DO WHAT THOU WILT.

Because men of free condition and who are well-born, well-bred and
used to refined company, have a natural instinct and goad that prompts
them to virtuous deeds and restrains them from vice; it is called honor.
When the same men are, by vile subjection and constraint repressed and
enslaved, they divert the noble inclination which made them naturally turn
to virtue, in order to shake off and break this yoke of servitude. For we
always long after forbidden things and desire what is denied to us.

Because of this, they [the Thélémites] entered into laudable emulation to
do, all of them, what was they saw was pleasing to just one of them... They
were so nobly educated, that there was not one among them who could not
read, write, sing, play musical instruments, speak five or six languages, and
compose in them both poetry and prose.

Gargantua, Ch. LVII
(Translated by M. Wagner)

Montaigne: *Essais*

Of the Education of Children

For a child of noble family who seeks learning ...to enrich and furnish
himself inwardly, I would rather make of him an able man than a learned
man, I would also urge that care be taken to choose a guide with a well-
made rather than a well-filled head ...

Let the tutor make his charge pass everything through a sieve and lodge nothing in his head on mere authority and trust: let not Aristotle's principles be principles to him any more than those of the Stoics or Epicureans. Let this variety of ideas be set before him; he will choose if he can; if not, he will remain in doubt. Only the fools are certain and assured. (I.26)

Of Cannibals

Now, to return to my subject, I think there is nothing barbarous and savage in that nation, from what I have been told, except that each man calls barbarism whatever is not his own practice; for indeed it seems we have no other test of truth and reason than the example and pattern of the opinions and customs of the country we live in. *There* is always the perfect religion, the perfect government, the perfect and accomplished manners in all things. Those people are wild, just as we call wild the fruits that Nature has produced by herself and in her normal course; whereas really it is those that we have changed artificially and led astray from the common order, that we should rather call wild. The former retain alive and vigorous their genuine, their most useful and natural virtues and properties, which we have debased in the latter in adapting them to gratify our corrupted taste . . .

. . . I am not sorry that we notice the barbarous horror of such acts, but I am heartily sorry that, judging their faults rightly, we should be so blind to our own. I think there is more barbarity in eating a man alive than in eating him dead; and in tearing by tortures and the rack a body still full of feeling . . .

They said that in the first place they thought it very strange that there were among us men full and gorged with all sorts of good things, and that their other halves were beggars at their doors, emaciated with hunger and poverty and they thought it strange that these needy halves could endure such an injustice, and did not take the others by the throat, or set fire to their houses. (I.31)

(Translated by Donald Frame)
Reprinted from *Montaigne's Essays and Selected Writings* 1963, courtesy of St. Martin's Press, NY

Versailles

Versailles is not only the embodiment of French Classicism, the epitome of French quality, the apotheosis of French arts and crafts, the dazzling incarnation of a glorious and absolute reign and the symbol of an era, it is also the most frequently imitated and most widely known royal residence ever built for a monarch in the Western world.

This splendid palace started as a mere "hunting lodge" of Louis XIII, who ordered in 1624 the erection of a small château west of Paris, in an area rich in game. Louis XIV may, indeed, have fallen in love at first sight with his father's modest residence: he enjoyed the seclusion of Versailles both for hunting during the day and romantic adventures at night. But the decision to move the Court, and therefore the "French capital", to a "safe place" away from Paris was dictated by wisdom and foresight, and proved to be an effective means of avoiding the turmoil and civil unrest that had plagued the Kingdom during the first half of the century. This move forced the heads of the proudest and most powerful French families to leave their strongholds in the provinces and come to live as the King's personal domestics in Versailles, "the only place under the sun" fit for living for anybody who wanted to be somebody during the "grand règne." For this is where the Sun-King himself resided, in the midst of unprecedented splendor: the château's orientation, construction and decoration were consciously inspired by the myth of the Sun and Apollo. No effort or cost was spared to make Versailles not only magnificent, but truly fabulous; and, as mentioned earlier, this cost was staggering. One of the major expenditures was the draining of marshes around the château and bringing in the water necessary for the gardens and the numerous fountains, which are still today perhaps the most beautiful sight of Versailles.[8]

The gardens were considered as important a part of the royal residence as the château itself and came alive with a vast population of mythological gods and divinities, created by the most talented master sculptors of the time (mainly Girardon and Coysevox). The gardens of Versailles mark the triumph of the so-called "jardins à la française", with rigorously ordered parterres, shrubs and flowerbeds. But even if man's dominant role in arranging, disposing, ordering and imposing logic and symmetry is obvious,

---

[8] Over one million gallons of water are required for the Fountain of Apollo alone to play for just one hour. Until our own day the water needed for the Versailles fountains was drawn from nearby pools and the more distant Seine by a gigantic pump built at Marly in 1675. Today the "great waterworks" play on the 1st and 3rd Sunday of each month from May to September.

the gardens are in perfect harmony both with the buildings and the surrounding nature; the pools reflect the sun and the sky, the statues and the vases, just like the mirrors of the Galerie des Glaces and other halls reflect the nature outside while extending it and "inviting" it to live within the walls of the palace.

The King's preoccupation with plants is evident in the colossal Orangerie, conceived by Hardouin-Mansart in the purest "style Louis XIV."[9] It once sheltered thousands of oleanders, pomegranates and palm and orange trees. The first plants to come to Versailles were the 1,000 orange trees confiscated by Louis from Vaux-le-Vicomte after Fouquet's arrest.

And the Superintendent's superb team of architects and artists Le Vau, Le Nôtre and Le Brun, started on the construction of the new Versailles the very year of Fouquet's downfall, in 1661. Around Louis XIII's brick and stone structure, Le Vau, Dorbay and finally Hardouin-Mansart erected the Versailles which still stands today, and to which the Court moved definitively in 1682. The general plan of the building was, however, conceived by the King himself. The grounds were inaugurated as early as 1664, with the three-day long festivities called "Plaisirs de l'Ile enchantée", given by Louis in honor of his first official mistress, Mlle de La Vallière. Two plays of Molière were premiered in the sumptuously illuminated gardens. The King himself took part in the performances and danced in the ballets.

Once the château was completed, it became only one element of an extremely vast complex. The central section served as quarters for the King, whereas the south and north wings were reserved for royal princes and persons running the court. Ministerial wings housed the government and, behind the south wing, the "Grand Commun" accommodated thousands of personal attendants to His Majesty. In front of the palace, beyond the Place d'Armes, buildings were erected for the King's horses and carriages.

With leisure in mind, Louis eventually added to Versailles the Grand Trianon, a one-floor marble and stone building designed by Hardouin-Mansart and surrounded by a simple garden. In this pavillion the King gave intimate suppers for a privileged few, but used it especially for quiet dalliance with the great love of his life, Mme de Montespan.

There was little room for privacy in the Sun-King's life: Versailles is also, among many other things, a symbol of the strictest etiquette that ever regulated the days of both the ruler and his entourage. Louis, who worked exceptionally hard at his "métier de roi" imposed an inflexible discipline

---

[9]The Orangerie housed the press during the Conference of industrialized nations which was held at Versailles in June of 1982.

not only on his subjects, but on himself as well.

He usually started his day as early as 8 A.M. Series of ceremonials began with the "Sun's rising" and continued till night: such were the various "Entrées", "Levers", "Couverts" and "Couchers"—"petits", "très petits" and "grands"—during which every single gesture was performed according to a pre-determined protocol. Thus, when the King dressed, one fortunate courtier was allowed to help him with the right sleeve of his shirt while another's privilege was to help him put on the left one. The King ate almost always alone, though he was attended and watched by many. His younger brother, Monsieur, was often present and handed the King his napkin, but was only rarely invited to participate in the meal. Louis had a Gargantuan appetite and could devour during one sitting several soups, numerous eggs, a whole bird, (partridge, chicken, duck or goose), salad, a roast, a goodly portion of ham, of which the King was particularly fond, and a variety of desserts, such as fruit, candied fruit, pastry and jams.

After a strenuous day, the dynamic King still had enough energy for fun at night and thoroughly enjoyed the numerous festivities organized for his pleasure by entire teams of authors and entertainers. Attendance at daily as well as at exceptional functions at the Court was mandatory for anybody who wanted any kind of "standing" and the indispensable royal favor. Absence was not tolerated, was scrupulously noted and could result in dire consequences.

The Duke of Saint-Simon left us in his voluminous *Mémoires* many vivid descriptions of the court life at Versailles. He relates, among others, the following incident, which reveals Louis' selfishness, insensitivity and total lack of understanding. After his marriage to Mme de Maintenon and when austerity had become the rule of the day, the aging and bored King found particular solace in the company of the Duchesse de Bourgogne, his grandson's young wife. At one time, the Duchesse, who was pregnant with her third child and felt sick, requested permission not to accompany the King at an outing that had been planned: the permission was not granted. When, the following day, Louis was told that the Duchesse had miscarried, his only comment was that "the succession to the throne was already well assured." Little did the King know, that within a short time his own son, the Grand Dauphin, as well the Duc and Duchesse de Bourgogne and their older son would die, (as mentioned in ch. 7 of Part II), while leaving his younger grandson as sole heir to the French crown.

This grandson became Louis XV and made (as did all the other descendants of the Sun-King) important changes and additions to Versailles, such as the Opera and the Petit Trianon, designed by Gabriel: it was enjoyed in turn by Mme de Pompadour and Marie-Antoinette. This fun-loving young queen added also to the Trianon Gardens, as will be remembered, a Temple of Love, a "Belvédère" and her farmhouse, the "Hameau" or hamlet.

Versailles continued to be the "French capital" until the Revolution, which played havoc with the palace; in 1792, the sale of royal furniture was ordered by the Convention. Louis XVIII decreed Versailles' reconstruction, but it was Louis-Philippe who enacted it, while bringing about some disastrous changes such as stripping the north and south wings of their irreplaceable decorations. Fortunately, the Chapel, the Opera and the royal apartments were spared. Louis-Philippe eventually transformed Versailles into a Museum of French History, which was inaugurated in 1837.

Since World War II big strides have been made toward the bringing back of the palace to its original look and splendor. Substantial donations, many from Americans, the returning of furnishings and minute restoration work, such as was performed on the royal bedchambers, have given the palace not only an authentic look, but authentic detail as well; so much so, that Versailles resembles now the Sun-King's palace more closely than at any time since the 17th century.

Rousseau and Voltaire

His first Discours (1750), in which Rousseau tries to show how civilization, arts, letters and luxury have corrupted the unspoiled primitive man was followed by a second Discours (1755) on the origins of inequality between men. In this truly revolutionary work, Rousseau examines the concept of property and the evils of wealth, as he tries to retrace the history of the development of primitive man. He concludes that the only recourse of the poor is the use of force.

Discourse on the Origin of Inequality (2nd part)

The first man, who, having enclosed a piece of land, had the idea of saying: "this belongs to me" and found people simple enough to believe him, was the true founder of society. How many crimes, wars, murders, how many misfortunes and horrors could have been spared to mankind, if someone had pulled out the stakes or filled the ditch and shouted to his neighbors: "Don't you listen to this impostor; you will be doomed if you forget that the fruits of the earth belong to all, and that earth belongs to no one!"...

So long as men were satisfied with their rustic huts, their clothes made of animal skins and fastened with thorns and fishbones....so long as they could keep happy with arts and crafts that could be produced by the hands of a single person...they lived free and healthy, in honesty and happiness to the extent made possible by their very nature....but from the moment when man felt the need to be helped by another and realized that it was to his advantage to have to himself provisions sufficient for two, equality disappeared, property was introduced, work became a necessity and vast forests turned into radiant fields which had to be watered with the sweat of men, and where soon slavery and wretchedness were seen to germinate and grow with the crops.

Rousseau sent a copy of his work to Voltaire, who answered with an impertinent and sarcastic letter, while refuting and deriding the arguments advanced by Rousseau in both of his Discours. The first paragraph reads as follows:

Letter to Rousseau

August 30, 1755

I have received, Monsieur, your new book denouncing mankind. I thank you for it. You will be appreciated by men to whom you squarely tell the truth, but you will not improve them. No one could have depicted with more vivid colors the horrors of civilized society, in which, ignorant and weak as we are, we invest so much hope. No one has ever put to work more wit than you in the attempt to equate us with animals;[10] the reading of your work makes one feel like walking on all fours. However, since I have lost that habit over sixty years ago and could not possibly revert to it, I am leaving this posture to those more worthy of assuming it than you or myself.

(Translated by M. Wagner)

---

[10] Or: "make us look stupid." Voltaire purposely uses the expression "bête", which has the double meaning of "animal" and "stupid".

Impressionism

Impressionism is an art movement which was born in France in the latter part of the 19th century and has radically changed the concept of painting. It is linked with Realism because of its concern with the way things really look and the depicting of the commonplace. While Boudin and Jongkind must be acknowledged as influential precursors, the two painters most instrumental in the bringing about of this revolutionary artistic breakthrough are Manet and Monet. In spite of Monet's quip "We paint as birds sing; paintings are not made with doctrines", a group of adherents and followers eventually gave Impressionism a system with its own aesthetic principles.

Manet (1833-83) had been a true inspiration to the Impressionists. His rejection of all constraints (The *Déjeuner sur l'herbe*, for which Manet took as models his mistress Victorine and his fellow-Impressionist Bazille, created, as will be remembered, a resounding scandal) attracted the necessary public attention to the budding new current. But the spontaneity of his vision, his choice of everyday subjects and his faithful rendition of the effects of light and air can be considered the very basis of Impressionism. The Impressionists did away with everything that had been dear to the Academicians, such as didactic, mythological, historical, religious, sentimental—and even exotic—subjects, and forsook all moral and social preoccupations. They painted what they saw around them and centered on a purely visual experience, divorced from any intellectual connotations. Their motto was: "Paint not what you know, but what you see, what strikes you at the precise time when you paint." Thus they depicted surrounding objects and landscapes, as shaped by the interplay of light and the vibrations of the air. They attempted to capture the fleeting moment, the evanescent, the transitory, best reflected in landscapes and sea-scapes, in skies continually changed by moving clouds, in mobile shimmering waters, in volatile mist and haze. They even tackled the most fugitive element of all, smoke, such as can be seen in Monet's *Gare St. Lazare*.

Monet can be considered the Impressionist "par excellence." His stay in foggy England, where he discovered the art of Turner and where he was exposed to the view of a nature always saturated with humidity, helped him appreciate and then illustrate, in the most striking way of all, the importance of light. Particularly eloquent are his "series", such as the *Houses of Parliament* in London, *The Haystacks*, the above-mentioned *Gare St. Lazare* and the notorious *Cathedral of Rouen*: there are over twenty paintings of the same church façade seen from the same angle, but at different times of the day, thus showing the multiple, ever changing reality of the atmosphere. The structure of Monet's buildings itself is reduced to an almost transparent veil or skeleton dissolved by light. In 1899 Monet started painting the famous water-lilies and other flowers in his garden at Giverny in a slightly different style, while using large blobs and trails of color.

Since form and space were considered by Impressionists to be an effect of the intensity of color, they eliminated hard lines and definite contours from their canvasses, as well as the black shadows which had been used hitherto: instead, they applied next to the object casting the reflection its complementary color, thus heightening the intensity of both colors. Juxtaposition also became the technique accepted by the Impressionists. Instead of mixing e.g., green on their palette, they applied dabs of pure yellow next to the blue on the canvas., in order that they "mix in the eyes of the beholder." Grey, brown and black (which is still present in Manet's paintings) were totally banned from their palette.

Some of the other artists associated with Impressionism are Armand Guillaumin (1841-1927); Camille Pissarro (1830-1903), who was at first influenced by Corot, came close to Pointillism and painted mostly in suburban Pontoise, before rendering in his later years the streets of towns themselves; and Alfred Sisley (1839-99), born in France of English parents, who showed a preference for the snow covered scenes of Ile-de-France and the vibrating flood waters he could observe at Louveciennes.

Auguste Renoir (1841-1919), whose advice was to "treat a subject for the hues, not for itself", forsook landscapes and centered on the female figure, while making light penetrate and caress the skin of his attractive, opulent young models. Their radiant faces and sun drenched iridescent naked bodies express Renoir's exaltation and intoxication with life.

Edgar Degas (1934-1917) was also concerned with the human body— mostly in the fugitive expression of a "pose" (such as women in "tubs")— and with contemporary scenes such as horse races. Later in his life he found joy in the depicting of nimble and graceful ballet-dancers. He was visibly influenced by the invention of the camera and frequently placed his main subject away from the center of the canvass, while "cutting off arms and legs", which gave the painting the appearance of a snapshot.

Berthe Morisot (1841-95) became the sister-in-law of Manet whom she drew closer to the Impressionists: after 1874 he started to use, under her influence, brighter and more luminous colors. As mentioned above, Morisot is best known for her sensitive and cheerful depiction of household, motherhood and childhood scenes (her most famous painting is *The Cradle*).

The art of the ever so popular, beloved Impressionists, which freed the artist from the subjection of form and paved the way for abstract painting, is characterized by a poetic quality, as well as by insouciance and spontaneity. The luminosity, mobility and lightness of their scenes, be it river banks, beaches, open-air cafés or dance halls, are filled with fun and love of life: their cheerful palette brought a hitherto unknown sort of beauty and "joie de vivre" into the world of arts.

The "Bourgogne": its history, arts and wines.

Burgundy is yet another attractive, fortunate French province which nature has endowed with all the most precious gifts: an easily accessible location of strategic importance on the crossroads between the valleys of the Seine, the Loire and the Rhône, a fertile soil, and abundance of building materials and an excellent climate, which is responsible for the quality of Burgundian vineyards. These have, since centuries, contributed both to the fame and the wealth of the region.

Burgundy is also rich in art and history. It was a high spot of the civilization of the Gauls: this is where the treasure of Vix was unearthed and where Gallic tribes united (on Mt. Beuvray) under the leadership of Vercingétorix, and waged at Alésia their last battle against the Romans.

This is also where the Burgundians, the least destructive of all Germanic tribes, eventually settled and adopted Christianity. As will be remembered, the Burgundian princess Ste. Clotilde was instrumental in having her husband Clovis, the Frankish chief and first king of France, baptized at Reims.

Burgundy kept its role of lighthouse of Christianity throughout the Middle Ages. The region is strewn with magnificent Romanesque abbeys and churches: Cluny, the largest, most powerful and most influential Abbey of all Christendom; Vézelay, with its imposing tympanum of "Christ in Glory" and its Moorish-inspired cradle-vault (Vézelay was a revered medieval shrine until the day when the earthly remains of St. Mary-Magdalen it boasted of possessing were found in the Provençal town of St Maximin); St. Philibert in Tournus, with its pure, austere, majestic lines; the Cistercian abbeys of Cîteaux and Fontenay, founded by St. Bernard; the cathedral of Autun, which Gislebert adorned with his famous tympanum of the "Last Judgment"; and Auxerre, whose oldest crypt was completed as early as 856 A.D. The Romanesque spread to all the other parts of France from Burgundy, but it is also in Burgundy that we find one of the oldest and most beautiful Gothic churches, St. Etienne in Sens, which served as a model for the Cathedral of Canterbury.

In the 14th and 15th centuries the powerful Ducs de Bourgogne whose territories stretched from the Mâcon region to Flanders and beyond today's Netherlands, made of their province a true foyer of the arts and numerous Burgundian cities bear witness to their patronage. The former capital of Burgundy and eternal capital of wine, Beaune, where a "dégustation" (wine-tasting) beckons the tourist at practically every street corner, offers a wealth of captivating sights: the old ramparts, the medieval City Hall and the Musée du vin, located in the former Palais des Ducs. The Museum owes its existence to the generosity of an American, Charles Codman. It retraces the history of wine dating back to Roman times and houses impressive 11th century wooden wine-presses, which are still in perfect operating condition.

But the most striking edifice in Beaune is its incredible Hôtel-Dieu or "Hospices" which was erected in 1473 and endowed by the founder, Chancellor Rolin, with priceless vineyards, which have provided now for more than 500 years the revenues necessary for the maintenance of the hospital. Whereas the Hôtel-Dieu still functions today in a modern annex, the 15th century building has become a museum. Visitors can admire the huge old kitchen, the apothecary bustling with drugs from yesteryear and the magnificent ward with its neat rows of beds, draped in red curtains for the sake of privacy (the privacy was relative: each bed was shared by two persons, and even by three at times of epidemics). The chestnut ceiling, in the shape of a boat's hull, made the ward insectproof. The awe-inspiring "Last Judgment" polyptich by Flemish master Roger Van der Weyden, which adorns one of the walls, was opened and shown to the patients only on very special occasions.

The Hôtel-Dieu is also the site of the famous wine-auction called "the greatest charity sale in the world", which is held yearly in Beaune on the third Sunday of November, during a three-day "bacchanal" called "Les Trois Glorieuses."

The Dukes eventually moved their capital to Dijon and resided in great pomp in the elegant Palais des Ducs de Bourgogne. It is now a richly endowed museum and houses impressive "gisants" of the Dukes. Other striking tombs and remarkable Flamboyant Gothic sculpture can be seen in the church of Brou, today's Bourg-en-Bresse. Dijon is also the capital of French gastronomy and holds each Fall a very well attended "Foire gastronomique": it features foods from all of France alongside with the typical Burgundian fare, namely, "escargots"; "boeuf bourguignon"; Dijon mustard; cheeses (particularly goat-cheese); "volaille de Bresse" (fowl); and products stemming from "cassis" (black currant), such as the now popular cocktail invented by Dijon's former mayor, Cannon Kir.

But the superb Burgundian food is overshadowed by the still more superb Burgundy wines (see map). While such vineyards as Chablis, Pouilly-Fuissé, Mercurey, Mâcon and Beaujolais are considered excellent throughout the world, the most prestigious "crus" come from the Côte d'Or (i.e. Côte de Nuits + Côte de Beaune). Some of its aristocratic "appellations" are over 1000 years old: Aloxe dates back to 696 A.D.; Fixey to 733; Santenay to 858; Auxey to 859; Chassagne to 886; Savigny to 930; Pommard to 1005; and Meursault to 1094. And how many others are legend and music to the ears of wine lovers! Chambolle-Musigny; Vosne-Romanée; Romanée-Conti; Volnay; Corton-Charlemagne; Clos-Vougeot; and Chambertin, which was saluted by Napoleon and his armies as they marched by; and Montrachet: Balzac knelt down before savoring its unique bouquet.

Today even more than before, Burgundy has to face the competition of other wine-producing regions, notably that of Bordeaux. In order to make their product still better known, a "wine-tasters' brotherhood" from yesteryear was resurrected on the Côte d'Or in the 1930's. The "Confrérie des Chevaliers du Tastevin" proudly resides in the Château du Clos-de-Vougeot (see fig.), where publicity-oriented banquets, called "chapitres", are regularly held in the former cellar of the château for VIPs from a wide cross-section of society.

Taking part in this Rabelaisian meal, accompanied by some 6 to 8 regional wines and spirits in a festive atmosphere, enhanced by the drinking songs of the "Cadets de Bourgogne" and witty anecdotes referring to the salutary qualities of wine, is an exhilarating and unforgettable experience. The Knights, dressed in impressive ermine-bordered velvet garb, use in their initiation or "intronisation" ceremony of new members the text of the last scene of Molière's last comedy, Le Malade Imaginaire.

Burgundy has been called "the land of plenitude and balance", balance between the material and the spiritual (two great saints, Marguerite-Marie Alacoque and Mme de Sévigné's grandmother Jeanne de Chantal, founder of the Order of Visitation were born here). In our own century, it is in Burgundy again that the new monastic community of Taizé (mentioned in Part III) was set up by a young Protestant theologian with the help of Catholic brothers, who not only continue the traditional ideal of poverty, chastity and obedience, but pursue as well one of the most constructive goals of today's Christianity: ecumenism.

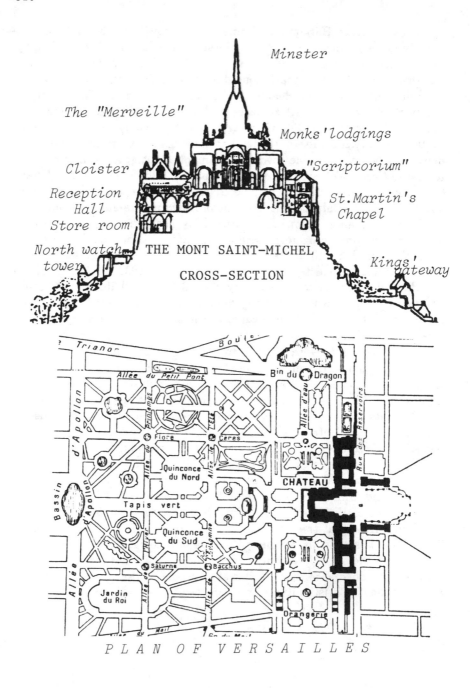

Minster

The "Merveille"

Monks'lodgings

"Scriptorium"

Cloister

Reception
Hall
Store room

St.Martin's
Chapel

North watch
tower

THE MONT SAINT-MICHEL

CROSS-SECTION

Kings'
gateway

PLAN OF VERSAILLES

BRIEF CHRONOLOGY

c. 1000 B.C.	Celts settle in the territory of Gaul
c. 600 B.C.	Phocean Greeks found Massilia (Marseille)
120 B.C.	Romans establish their "Provincia" in Gaul
58-52 B.C.	Roman conquest of Gaul
496	Clovis baptized and crowned at Reims (Merovingian dynasty)
800	Charlemagne crowned Emperor (Carolingian dynasty)
987	Hugues Capet founds Capetian dynasty
1066	Conquest of England by William the Conqueror
1095	Beginning of the Crusades
1270	Death of Louis IX (Saint-Louis) during last Crusade
1214	Victory of Philippe-Auguste over the Plantagenets (at Bouvines)
1337-1453	The Hundred Years' War
1429	Jeanne d'Arc at Chinon and Orléans
1515-1537	Reign of François I
1572	Massacre of St. Bartholomew during Wars of Religion
1598	Henri IV signs the Edict of Nantes
1610-1643	Reign of Louis XIII
1643-1715	Reign of Louis XIV
1789	Beginning of French Revolution
1793	Execution of Louis XVI and Marie-Antoinette
1795-1799	The "Directoire"
1804	Napoleon crowned Emperor
1815	Napoleon's defeat at Waterloo and Restoration of the Capetians
1830	July Revolution and ascent of Louis-Philippe
1852	IInd Empire
1870	IIIrd Republic
1914-1918	World War I
1939-1945	World War II
1945-1958	IVth Republic
1958	De Gaulle and the Vth Republic

INDEX

1. Le Puy: St.Michel d'Aiguilhe

2. *Lascaux grotto*

3. *Orange: Arch of Triumph*

4. *Arles: Arènes and Roman Theatre*

5. Bayeux: The Bayeux Tapestry

6. Caen: Abbaye aux Hommes

7. Les Andelys: Château-Gaillard

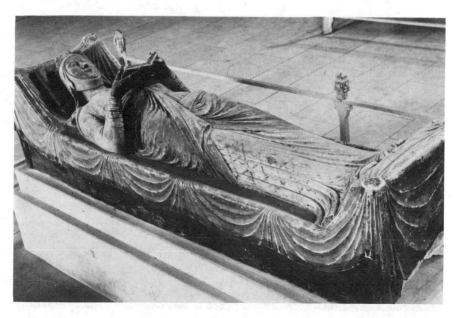

8. Fontevraud: "Gisant" of Aliénor of Aquitaine

10. Vézelay: Tympanum "Christ in Glory"

9. St.Savin-sur-Gartempe

11. Autun: Tympanum "The Last Judgment"

12. Autun: "Eve"

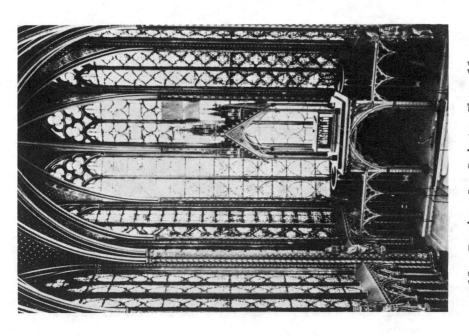

14. Chartres Cathedral

13. Paris: La Sainte-Chapelle

16. Reims: The Annunciation

15. Chartres: West Portal

17. The Mont Saint-Michel

18. Paris: Notre-Dame

19. *Château de Chambord*

20. *Château de Chenonceaux*

21. *Château de Blois*

22. *Château de Fontainebleau*

23 & 24. *St.Denis: "Gisants" of
Henri II and Catherine de Médicis*

25. Poussin : "Selene and Endymion" (Detroit Institute of Arts)

26. Versailles: View from Water Parterre

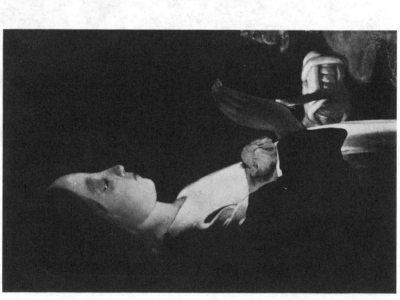

27. G. de La Tour: "The Young Virgin Mary"
(Detroit Institute of Arts)

28. Paris: The Invalides

30. *Paris: Place de la Concorde*

29. *Paris: The Panthéon*

31. *Watteau: "Embarquement pour Cythère" (Louvre)*

32. *Chardin: "Still Life" (The Detroit Institute of Arts)*

33. *Boucher: "Mme de Pompadour" (Alte Pinakothek, Munich)*

34. *Versailles: The Petit Trianon*

35. *Versailles: The "Hameau"*

36. J.L. David: "Le Serment des Horaces" (Louvre)

37. Géricault: "Le Radeau de la Méduse" (Louvre)

39. Gauguin: "Self Portrait"
(The Detroit Institute of Arts)

38. Van Gogh: "Self-Portrait"
(The Detroit Institute of Arts)

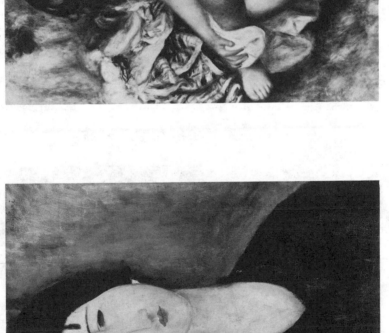

41. Renoir: *"Seated Bather"*

(The Detroit Institute of Arts)

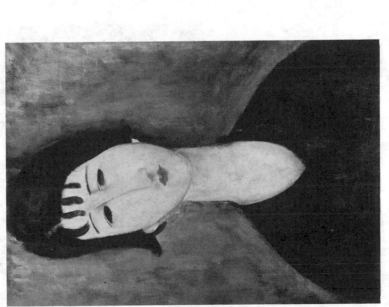

40. Modigliani: *"Portrait of a Woman"*

(The Detroit Institute of Arts)

42. *Vence: Chapelle du Rosaire*

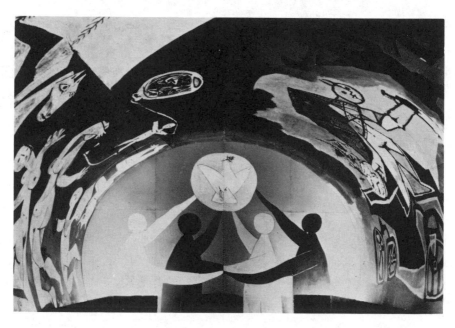

43. *Vallauris: Chapel decorated by Picasso*

44. *Saint-Paul-de-Vence: Fondation Maeght (sculptures by Giacometti)*

45. *Ronchamp: Le Corbusier's church of Notre-Dame-du-Haut*

46. Paris: Louvre. Sculpture by Maillol

47. Paris: Arc de Triomphe

48. *Bourgogne: Château du Clos de Vougeot*

49. *Périgord: "A Truffle!"*